From the Maccabees
to the Mishnah

Library of Early Christianity

Wayne A. Meeks, General Editor

From the Maccabees to the Mishnah

Shaye J. D. Cohen

The Westminster Press
Philadelphia

Book design by Gene Harris

First Edition

Published by The Westminster Press®
Philadelphia, Pennsylvania

PRINTED IN THE UNITED STATES OF AMERICA

9 8 7 6 5 4 3 2 1

Library of Congress Cataloging-in-Publication Data

Cohen, Shaye J. D.
    From the Maccabees to the Mishnah.

    (Library of early Christianity)
    Bibliography: p.
    Includes index.
    1. Judaism—History—Post-exilic period,
568 B.C.–210 A.D.   2. Jews—History—168 B.C.–135 A.D.
I. Title.   II. Series.
BM176.C615   1987   296'.09'014   86-28077
ISBN 0-664-21911-X

Contents

Foreword

Out of the innumerable religious traditions, cults, and movements of the early Roman empire, two alone transformed themselves to outlast that empire—even to our own time. The remarkable thing is that both had their origins in sects of Judaism —hardly the most powerful or conspicuous of Roman religions. Those two are rabbinic Judaism and Christianity. The present book investigates that extraordinarily fertile period of Jewish history—the three and a half centuries "from the Maccabees to the Mishnah"— which gave rise to these two religions that have been so central a part of our own history, and so problematic to each other.

That the Library of Early Christianity should include a book on Jewish history of the Hellenistic and Roman periods is obvious. What may not be so self-evident is that this book, unlike many in similar series in the past, does not treat the history of Judaism as merely ancillary or preparatory to the history of Christianity. The history of Christianity's beginnings is *part* of the history of Judaism in antiquity, and both are part of the history of Greco-Roman culture.

It is no exaggeration, I think, to say that an intellectual revolution has taken place—rather, is still in progress—in our understanding of early Judaism. Such astonishing new discoveries as the Dead Sea Scrolls and the existence of a vast body of Jewish art from antiquity and the deciphering of Jewish mystical texts have been the most dramatic occasions for revising our picture of ancient Judaism. Even more important has been the burgeoning of interdisciplinary methods in studying the sources, both the newly discovered ones and those long familiar, and the employment of multiple methods is the special strength of the present book. It is the achievement of Shaye Cohen to have brought together the results of a wide range of scholarship of fields often separate. In keeping with the design of the series, he has avoided the kind of argument and documentation that is necessary in the scholarly monographs in which work as new as this is ordinarily presented. Nevertheless, the expert as well as the novice will recognize both the erudition that lies behind this book and the freshness of its presentation.

WAYNE A. MEEKS
General Editor

Preface

In order to make this book accessible to students and other nonspecialists, I have kept the bibliographical annotation to a minimum. I provide references for all quoted sources and for most of the obscure texts to which I allude, but I do not as a rule provide references for those sources which are well indexed and readily available in English (notably the works of Philo and Josephus) or which can be tracked down easily through the modern works listed in the suggested readings. I admit that I have been somewhat inconsistent in this matter, and I apologize to any reader who is inconvenienced by my bibliographical shorthand. I cite the Revised Standard Version of the Bible, and the Loeb Classical Library translation of Josephus (by Henry St. J. Thackeray, Ralph Marcus, Allen Wikgren, and Louis H. Feldman, published by Harvard University Press in nine volumes, 1926–65), except that I have occasionally departed from them wherever I felt it necessary. The other translations I have used are listed in the Suggestions for Further Reading under "Sources." Citations from the Tanak are according to the verse numeration of the Hebrew.

The writing of this book was much more difficult and painful than I had anticipated, and I am grateful to various friends for their advice and encouragement. Professor Wayne Meeks read the entire manuscript, made many helpful suggestions, forced me to clarify both my prose and my ideas, and rescued me from errors large and small. Chapter 3 was immeasurably improved by the suggestions and criticisms of Professor George W. E. Nickelsburg, Rabbi Leonard Gordon, and Mr. Bradley Artson. Chapter 6 was similarly improved by the suggestions and criticisms of Professor John J. Collins. Ms. Stefanie Siegmund helped me organize my ideas in chapter 1. The level of accuracy in chapters 2 through 5 was raised substantially by the detailed comments of my teacher Professor

11

Morton Smith. To all of these friends I am deeply grateful, and if I have not incorporated all of their suggestions, it is my own stubbornness which is to blame.

According to rabbinic lore (Babylonian Talmud, *Shabbat* 31a), when a person comes before the heavenly tribunal after his death he is asked, "Did you conduct your trade honestly? Did you set aside time for the study of Torah? Did you raise a family?" My father lived his life in such a way that he could answer all these questions in the affirmative. In business he had a reputation as a man whose word could be trusted. Every morning before going to work and every night before going to sleep, he would sit in his favorite chair and study a Jewish book. I miss him, and I dedicate this book to his memory.

S.J.D.C.

28 August 1986

1

Ancient Judaism:
Chronology and Definitions

The goal of this book is to interpret ancient Judaism: to identify its major ideas, to describe its salient practices, to trace its unifying patterns, and to assess its relationship to Israelite religion and society. The book is arranged thematically rather than chronologically, but in order to make the argument easier to follow, in the first section of this chapter I briefly survey the chronology of ancient Judaism, and in the third section I outline the major themes of each chapter. In the second section I discuss some of the difficulties of periodization and perspective. I conclude with a brief discussion of unity and diversity in ancient Judaism.

Chronology

In 587 B.C.E. many of the citizens of the kingdom of Judah were exiled to Babylonia, thereby inaugurating the *exilic period*. ("B.C.E." and "C.E.," "Before the Common Era" and "of the Common Era," are the religiously neutral equivalents of "B.C.," "Before Christ," and "A.D.," *Anno Domini*, "Year of the Lord.") In 587 Jerusalem and its temple were destroyed and the kingdom was no longer. With the conquest of Babylonia by the Persians in 539 B.C.E., the Judeans (or Jews) were permitted by the conqueror, Cyrus the Great, to return to their homeland. Some of them took advantage of his offer. At least two waves of Babylonian Jews returned to the land of Judea during the 530s and 520s B.C.E. After some complex and bitter feuding with the community of those who never had been exiled, the Jews rebuilt the temple and dedicated it in 516 B.C.E. Jeremiah and Ezekiel were active at the beginning of the exilic period; Second Isaiah and his school (the anonymous authors of Isaiah 40–66), Haggai, and Zechariah (the author of Zechariah 1–8) were active at its end.

The *Persian period* lasted only two hundred years, from 539 B.C.E. (the conquest of Babylonia by Cyrus the Great) to 334 or 333 B.C.E. (the conquest of Persia by Alexander the Great). The most important achievement of the period, aside from the restoration of the temple, was the activity of Ezra (probably 458 B.C.E., although many scholars prefer a date approximately thirty years later) and Nehemiah (445 B.C.E. and 432 B.C.E.). Ezra led another wave of returnees from Babylonia, tried to dissolve the marriages with non-Jews that had been contracted primarily by the priesthood and the aristocracy, and read "the book of the instruction *(Torah)* of Moses" to the people. Nehemiah had a more variegated career, including the fortification and repopulation of the city of Jerusalem, the cancellation of the debts of the poor, and a long list of religious reforms. The generation of Ezra and Nehemiah is the last to be treated by the biblical historians. Malachi was the last of the prophets (actually "Malachi" is probably not a name but a common noun for "my messenger" or, with a slightly different punctuation, "his messenger"; in other words, the book of Malachi is anonymous), and he probably lived just before Ezra and Nehemiah. Ezra and Nehemiah mark the end of "the Bible" and "biblical Israel" (see next section and chapter 6).

The conquest of Persia by Alexander the Great inaugurated *the Hellenistic period.* After Alexander's death his empire was divided by his generals. Thirty years of fighting followed. Finally the dust settled (301 B.C.E.) and Judea was part of the kingdom of Egypt (of the Macedonian Ptolemies). A century later Judea was conquered (200 B.C.E.) by the Macedonian kings of Syria (the Seleucids). In the sphere of cultural history the Hellenistic period endured for centuries, perhaps until the Arab conquests of the seventh century C.E. From the perspective of political history, however, the Hellenistic period was much shorter. For most inhabitants of the Levant, it ended when the rule of the Macedonian kings of Egypt and Syria was replaced by that of Rome in the first century B.C.E. For the Jews, it was even shorter.

Throughout the Persian and Hellenistic periods the Jews maintained a quiescent attitude toward their rulers. There is no indication of any serious uprising by the Jews against the empires that ruled them. This changed dramatically in the 160s B.C.E. In 168–167 B.C.E. Antiochus Epiphanes, the Seleucid king of Syria, profaned the temple and persecuted Judaism. In the temple he erected an altar to Zeus, and everywhere he compelled the Jews to violate the laws of the Torah. Various groups of Jews rebelled against the king, the most prominent of them being the clan of Mattathias the Hasmonean and his son Judah the Maccabee (hence the entire dynasty is often called Maccabean or Hasmonean). In 164 B.C.E. the Maccabees reconquered and purified the temple; the end of Seleucid rule followed twenty years later.

The most striking feature of the Hellenistic period is its spectacular finish, but in their own quiet and poorly attested way the fourth and third centuries B.C.E. emerge as an important transition period in the history of Judaism. These centuries witnessed the growth of the *diaspora*, the "scattering" of the Jews throughout the world; the beginnings of the "canonization" of scripture; the writing of the earliest nonbiblical works that have been preserved; the gradual transformation of prophecy into "apocalyptic"; the emergence of a class of *scribes*, lay people learned in the sacred traditions. Some books of the Bible were written during this period, all of them anonymous, but they are impressive in both number and importance (for example, Jonah and Job). The latest book in the Bible, Daniel, was written at the very end of the Hellenistic period during the dark days of the Antiochian persecution.

The Maccabean period lasted a century, from the victory of 164 B.C.E. to the entrance of the Romans into Jerusalem in 63 B.C.E. During their tenure, the Maccabees gradually increased their power and prestige. They began as rebels against the Seleucid empire, but less than ten years after Judah's death his brother was appointed high priest by a relation of Antiochus Epiphanes! By the 140s and 130s B.C.E. the Seleucids had little choice but to accept the independence of the Maccabean state. The rise of the Maccabees within the Jewish polity was just as phenomenal. They began as insignificant country priests and became high priests and kings, the rulers of an independent state. They pursued an aggressive foreign policy, seeking alliance with Rome against the Seleucids and carving out for themselves a kingdom larger than that of David and Solomon.

Their fall from power was caused by both internal and external enemies. During the reigns of John Hyrcanus (135–104 B.C.E.) and Alexander Jannaeus (103–76 B.C.E.), many Jews opposed Maccabean rule. These opponents were not "Hellenizers" and "lawless" Jews who supported Antiochus' attempt to destroy Judaism, but loyal Jews who had had enough of the Maccabees' autocratic ways. The Seleucids and the Greek city-states of the region never fully accepted Maccabean independence, but the most potent external threat came from a power that first entered the scene as a friend and ally. It was to the advantage of the Romans that the Jews rule themselves, but not too successfully. The Romans wanted an alliance with the Jews, not an alliance between equals but one that would clearly recognize Roman superiority. The Romans quickly realized that the Maccabees were a "nationalist" element that could not be combined easily with their own imperial vision, so the Maccabees were pushed aside and a new dynasty was created.

The new dynasty owed everything to the Romans and therefore supported them wholeheartedly. The founder of the dynasty was Herod the Great (37–4 B.C.E.). He attempted to be the king over all his subjects, not just the Jews. He built pagan cities and temples as well as Jewish cities and the temple of Jerusalem. He also built numerous fortresses, the most famous of which was Masada. To pay for all these projects he imposed heavy taxes, and because he always felt insecure in his rule, he killed numerous members of the aristocracy, whose claims to prestige and status within the Jewish community were stronger than his own. He also killed many of his wives and children, suspecting them (sometimes rightly) of plotting rebellion.

The Roman Jewish symbiosis was at its peak during the reigns of Herod the Great and his grandson Herod Agrippa I (41–44 C.E.). But the Romans were moving away from rule over the Jews through vassal kings to rule through Roman administrators, called *procurators* or *prefects*. These were a motley lot, and for the most part they were not very sensitive to the needs of the populace. Some were brutal (notably Pontius Pilate), others corrupt, most incompetent. As a result of their mistakes, of ethnic strife in the country between Jews and pagans, of social unrest in the Jewish polity, and of severe economic problems, a war broke out against the Romans in 66 C.E., approximately 128 years after the Romans first entered Jerusalem (from 63 B.C.E. to 66 C.E. is 128 years, not 129, because there is no year 0). This is the "great revolt" or the "first revolt."

Taken by surprise, the Romans suffered a few serious defeats at first, but in the summer of 67 C.E. Vespasian marched from Syria into Galilee and began the slow and deliberate reconquest. By the year 68 C.E. the entire country except for Jerusalem and a few isolated strongholds had been pacified. Vespasian was in no rush, however, to storm Jerusalem. The Jews were killing each other in their own power struggles, the siege was causing a famine, and, most important, there was a power vacuum in Rome in the wake of Nero's suicide in June of 68 C.E. Vespasian had everything to gain and nothing to lose by taking his time. He played his cards correctly, with the result that in July of 69 C.E. he had himself proclaimed emperor, and spent the rest of that year securing his power. A new emperor needs a victory to prove his worth, and Vespasian entrusted the war to his son Titus. In the summer of 70 C.E. Jerusalem was retaken and the temple was destroyed. A few "mopping up" operations remained, notably the taking of Masada (73 or 74 C.E.), but for all practical purposes the war was over. The *second temple period* came to an end.

The war of 66–70 was the first revolt against the Romans, but not the last. In 115–117 C.E. the Jews of Egypt, Cyprus, and Cyrenaica (in modern-day Libya) rebelled against the Romans. The Jews of the land of Israel apparently did not participate in this war to any significant extent, and the causes and course of the war are most obscure. (During the same years the Jews of Babylonia, alongside their Parthian rulers, fought the Romans who had invaded their country, but from all indications this was a separate war altogether and need not be considered in this book.) The other major rebellion is that of Bar Kokhba (132–135 C.E.), sometimes called the "second revolt." The causes and course of this war are most obscure as well, but from all indications the wars of 115–117 and 132–135 were serious affairs with serious consequences. The war of 115–117 resulted in the decimation of Egyptian Jewry, which had been the largest and most important Jewish community of the Roman diaspora. The Bar Kokhba war resulted in the paganization of the city of Jerusalem (now rebuilt under the name Aelia Capitolina) and the changing of the country's name from Judea to Palestine.

The latter part of the second temple period, that is, the period from the rise of the Maccabees (160s B.C.E.) to the destruction of the temple (70 C.E.), was another rich and significant chapter in Jewish history. This was the age of sects (Pharisees, Sadducees, Essenes, the Qumran community, Christians, Sicarii, Zealots, and others) and of sectarian literature; of apocalypses and of varied speculations about God's control of human events, the nature of evil, and the secrets of the end time; of the growth of the synagogue, of liturgical prayer and scriptural study; of the "golden age" of diaspora Judaism, especially in Egypt, which produced a rich literature in Greek seeking to package Jewish ideas in Hellenistic wrapping; and of Judaism's intense interaction with its host culture, producing in some quarters a hatred of Judaism, but in others an attraction to it (resulting in "converts" and "God-fearers").

Roman rule over the Jews continued until the Parthian and Arab conquests of the sixth and seventh centuries C.E. (by which time the Roman empire had become Christian and Byzantine), but the centuries after the destruction of the temple often receive the name *the rabbinic period.* The word *rabbi* means "my master" and was originally a deferential form of address (like the French *monsieur*). By the first century C.E. the title was normally used by students when addressing their teacher (John 1:38). In the second century C.E. the meaning of the word began to change. It remained a generic title for "teacher" or anyone in a position of authority, but it also became a technical term designating a member of that society which, from the second century to the sixth, in both Israel and Babylonia, created a voluminous and distinctive literature. The earliest of these works, completed around the year 200 C.E. was the Mishnah. The Mishnah in turn was the subject of two gigantic commentaries (or, more accurately, works that claimed to be commentaries): the *Talmud* of the land of Israel (also called the Palestinian Talmud or the Jerusalem Talmud), completed around the year 400 C.E., and the Talmud of Babylonia (the Babylonian Talmud), completed around the year 500 C.E. (but not edited for another two or three centuries after that). The rabbis also produced a series of commentaries on scripture, and various other works. In this book "the rabbis" and "the rabbinic period" refer to the society and religion of the second to sixth centuries C.E.

Periodization and Perspective

Periodization derived from the political setting of ancient Judaism is relatively objective. That the Persians, the Hellenistic dynasties, the Maccabees, and the Romans successively ruled the Jewish polity in the land of Israel is a "fact" accepted by all historians. In contrast, periodization derived from religious or cultural achievements is not bias-free, at least not when it is applied to ancient Judaism, and therefore is best avoided. The bias may derive from Judaism, Christianity, or any other system of belief that has a stake in the interpretation of ancient Judaism.

At the end of the previous section I gave a relatively objective definition of "rabbinic period," but, as I shall discuss in chapter 7, even my restricted use of the term has an element of subjectivity. The Judaism created by the rabbis of antiquity gradually became the dominant form of Judaism, and thus it remained until the nineteenth century. The rabbis were the "winners" of ancient Jewish history. But in the second to sixth centuries the rabbis were not nearly as dominant as they would become later, and the concept "the rabbinic period" slights the rabbis' opponents (the losers), and falsely implies that after 70 C.E. all Jews accepted the rabbis as their leaders and followed the way of rabbinic Judaism. Nevertheless, in spite of this element of pro-rabbinic bias, the "rabbinic period" remains a useful and justifiable concept because, inasmuch as historians of Judaism rely almost exclusively on literary evidence, it highlights the fact that the major literary evidence for the Judaism of the second to sixth centuries is exclusively rabbinic.

If we accept the claims of the rabbis themselves, the rabbinic period begins much earlier than the second century C.E. The rabbis believe that they are the bearers of a sacred tradition revealed by God to Moses, and the direct heirs of the communal leaders of the Jews throughout the generations. According to this belief (or "myth"), by which the rabbis legitimated themselves and their teachings, the rabbinic period begins with "Moses our rabbi." Only fundamentalist Jews accept the historicity of this perspective, but modern scholars, especially Jewish scholars, have been influenced by it as well. Until recently scholars spoke readily of a normative Judaism, as if rabbinic Judaism (and its antecedents) was always the dominant and authentic expression of Judaism. Many scholars still view the second temple period through rabbinic spectacles, assuming that all the central institutions of society were under rabbinic aegis, and ascribing enormous influence and power to various proto-rabbinic figures. But none of these beliefs can be substantiated by historical evidence. For the believer rabbinic Judaism is normative Judaism, and the rabbis were always at the center of Jewish history. For the historian, however, "the rabbis" and "the rabbinic period" become meaningful entities only after 70 C.E. I shall return to this point in chapters 5 and 7.

Christianity is responsible for an entirely different perspective and periodization. Nineteenth-century scholars, especially in Germany, used the term "late Judaism" (*Spätjudentum*) to designate the religion and society of the Jews after Ezra or after the Maccabees. The term disparaged, and was meant to disparage, the Judaism it designated. The Judaism of the second temple period was "late" because it was approaching the end of its appointed time and was about to relinquish to Christianity whatever value it still retained. "Late Judaism" was a sterile, lifeless organism, waiting in vain for the infusion of spirituality that only Christianity could provide. After the birth of Christianity "late Judaism" lost all importance and could be ignored by scholars and Christians alike. The fact that Judaism continued to flourish and develop for millennia after the period of "late Judaism" did not affect the currency of the term, because the term derived not from historical analysis but from theological belief.

Several modern writers continue to use the term "late Judaism," unaware of its origins and implications, but in recent years many scholars have begun to use the term "early Judaism" as its bias-free replacement. What once was "late" is now deemed "early"! While "early Judaism" lacks the anti-Jewish overtones of "late Judaism," it is chronically vague, and therefore other, more precise expressions are preferable.

Another legacy of Christianity is the term "intertestamental period." Since the "New Testament" is the "end" of the "Old Testament," the centuries that linked the two were dubbed "the intertestamental period." This perspective is not necessarily prejudicial to its subject, but it usually is, because it regards "intertestamental Judaism" as the preparation for the emergence of Christianity. Books with titles like "Judaism in the Age of Jesus" or "The Jewish Background to the New Testament" often have as their purpose, whether explicit or implicit, the demonstration that "intertestamental Judaism" was somehow "fulfilled" or "completed" when it gave birth to Christianity. But ancient Judaism is worthy of study in its own right, not only because it is the matrix of early Christianity. Whether Christianity is indeed the fulfillment of the Old Testament and of intertestamental Judaism is a question that a historian cannot answer.

Many writers, both Jewish and Christian, call the period covered by this book "postbiblical Judaism," in contrast with "biblical Israel," the period that preceded it. The contrast between "Israel" and "Judaism" is important, as I shall discuss in the next section, but the word "biblical" is confusing. By the first century C.E. (see chapter 6), many Jews in antiquity believed that "the Bible" was completed in the time of Ezra during the Persian period (mid-fifth century B.C.E.). If this belief is correct, the distinction between "biblical" and "postbiblical" is simple: something which is "biblical" is pre-Persian, something which is "postbiblical" is post-Persian. The belief, however, is erroneous, because the Bible contains many works that were written after the Persian period, most obviously the book of Daniel. Thus if we apply the label "postbiblical" to the books of Enoch and Ben Sira, because they were written in the third century B.C.E., we are faced with the anomaly that these "postbiblical" works predate the "biblical" book of Daniel. (Of course, we could call Daniel, too, postbiblical, but such a description seems strange since Daniel is in the Bible.) Thus, the believer can use the term "biblical" as a chronological indicator, but the historian cannot.

From Pre-exilic Israel to Second Temple Judaism

Josephus remarks when describing the rebuilding of the second temple that those who returned from Babylonia should be called

"Jews" (or "Judeans," *Ioudaioi* in Greek, literally "those of the tribe of Judah") rather than "Israelites" (*Jewish Antiquities* 11.5.7, §173). Josephus was referring to nothing more significant than a change in name, but that change masks a much more significant shift. The religion, society, and culture of the pre-exilic kingdoms of Judah and Israel differ in many important ways from those of the period after the destruction of the temple in 587 B.C.E. The practices, ideas, and institutions that were elaborated during the second temple period formed and still form the basis of the religion known as "Judaism."

How does Israelite religion differ from Judaism? In many respects, of course, it doesn't. The two are linked by a common belief in the one supreme God who created the world, chose the Israelites/Jews to be his people, and entered into a covenantal relationship with them; by a shared attachment to the holy land of Israel, the holy city of Jerusalem, and the holy temple; and by the same sacred calendar and by many of the same religious observances. Even more important than these commonalities is the fact that the Jews of all times have always seen themselves not merely as the successors to, but also as the continuators of, the legacy of pre-exilic Israel. Christianity claimed (and, to some extent, still claims) to be the true Israel, but this claim was accompanied by an assertion of newness. Christianity is the fruit of a new creation, a new revelation, and a new covenant (a "New Testament"). Premodern Judaism never developed this sense of "newness," and it is this sense of continuity which more than anything else connects second temple Jews to pre-exilic Israel in spite of numerous changes and enormous upheavals.

Pre-exilic Israel was a tribal society living on its ancestral land. Membership in a tribe, and consequently the rights of citizenship (for example, the right to own land), depended exclusively on birth. There was no established process by which a foreigner could be absorbed into the Israelite polity. Second temple Judaism, in contrast, was not a tribal society. When the Jews returned from Babylonia they returned not as tribes but as clans. The entire tribal structure was destroyed. Many Jews did not return to the land of Israel, but remained in Babylonia; later, many Jews left the land of Israel in order to live throughout the Mediterranean basin. As a result of these changes, Judaism gradually defined itself more as a religion than as a nationality. It created the institution of *conversion* which allowed foreigners to be admitted into "citizenship." As a religion Judaism prohibited all marriages between Jews and non-Jews, a prohibition unknown to pre-exilic Israel (see chapter 2).

Pre-exilic Israel worshiped in the temple through the slaughter
and roasting of animals. Most of the actual service was performed
not by lay Israelites but by the priests, since only priests were permitted entrance into the inner precincts of the temple. Prayer was
not a standard part of worship, either in the temple or anywhere else
(although, to be sure, in moments of crisis and joy the Israelites
knew very well how to pray). For as long as the temple remained
standing, Judaism maintained the sacrificial cult, but it also elaborated new liturgies consisting of prayer as well as the recitation and
study of scripture. This mode of worship even influenced the temple
cult, but it acquired for itself a special home in a new institution, the
synagogue.

Second temple Judaism also developed a regimen of private worship unknown to pre-exilic Israel. The word of God was to be the
object of constant study and meditation, not only because this activity would teach the conduct that God expected, but also because the
very act of study was deemed to be an act of worship. In addition
to study, daily prayer became part of the piety practiced by the
religious elite. The commandments of the Torah were elaborated
and expanded, thus affording the individual Jew an opportunity for
demonstrating his or her loyalty to God. The piety of pre-exilic
Israel centered on the group (the people of Israel or the family),
while the piety of second temple Judaism centered on both the
group and the individual. (Throughout this book I shall refer to the
democratization or individualization of religion, but I concede at
the outset that no ancient society, including ancient Judaism, al-
located the individual as much freedom and importance as does
modern Western culture. Relative to modern culture ancient Judaism is not individualistic at all, but relative to pre-exilic Israel it is.)

Pre-exilic Israel and second temple Judaism also differed in their
understanding of *theodicy,* God's administration of justice. Everyone
agreed that God rewards the righteous and punishes the wicked, but
God's accounting methods were the subject of intense scrutiny.
Pre-exilic Israel believed that God administered justice in this
world. The righteous and the wicked were not always the direct
recipients of God's attentions, because God could reward or punish
their offspring in their stead (emphasis on the collective). Second
temple Judaism insisted that God punishes or rewards only those
who deserve it, and that the conduct of one's ancestors is irrelevant
(emphasis on the individual). Since God does not always seem to set
matters right in this world, he must do so in the next. Second temple
Judaism therefore elaborated complex schemes of reward and punishment after death and/or at the end time. Some of these schemes

included the resurrection of the dead. Just as God will reestablish justice for the individual, he shall do so for the nation by destroying the yoke of the nations and restoring the sovereignty of the people of Israel. Jerusalem and the temple will be restored to their former glory and God's anointed one *(messiah)* shall reign securely. All of these *eschatological* doctrines (that is, doctrines concerning the *end time* or ultimate future) are innovations of second temple Judaism.

Even as it elaborated new theories to account for God's mysterious ways in administering the world, some segments of second temple Judaism admitted that the problem was insoluble. They accounted for the triumph of evil by positing the existence of numerous supernatural beings who opposed God's dominion and everything that was good and true. Mirroring this cosmic struggle between the forces of good and the forces of evil is the struggle within each person of good and evil spirits. Some of these schemes are so dualistic that we may debate whether or not they should be called monotheistic (expressing a belief in one God). Even those Jews who would have nothing of these radical dualistic schemes nevertheless believed in angels and spirits of all sorts. The God of second temple Judaism was much more "transcendent" than the God of pre-exilic Israel. God needed intermediaries to run the world, and humanity needed intermediaries to reach God. (All of these theological developments are discussed in chapter 3.)

Pre-exilic Israel was ruled by kings and guided by prophets, second temple Judaism was not. A representative of the Davidic monarchy was the governor of Judea at the beginning of the Persian period, but after him the Davidic monarchy disappears from society, although it exercised a powerful hold on the eschatological imagination. Only in the rabbinic period did alleged descendants of the Davidic line emerge again as communal leaders. Instead of kings, in second temple Judaism the priests wielded temporal power. In Maccabean times they even assumed the title "king," but they were ousted by Herod the Great and his descendants. Nevertheless the office of high priest remained a much more visible post than it had been in pre-exilic Israel.

Prophets no longer enjoyed the prestige and authority that had been theirs in pre-exilic times. In second temple Judaism prophets became apocalyptic seers, mystics, healers, and holy men. A new type of authority figure emerged to replace the classical prophet: this was the *scribe*, whose authority derived not from his pedigree and institutional setting (like the priest), not from his charismatic personality and direct contact with God (like the prophet), but from his erudition in the sacred scriptures and traditions. Various sects as well claimed authority on the basis of their superior erudition. The party against which this superior erudition was brandished usually was the priesthood.

The first temple, at least after the Deuteronomic reform, was the sole institution in which the Israelites could worship God. The second temple too claimed exclusivity, but faced severe competition. Sects arose in the second century B.C.E. and disappeared only after the destruction of the temple in 70 C.E. Most sects seem to have argued that the priests were corrupt and that the temple was polluted, or, at least, unworthy of the exclusiveness and importance it claimed. Each sect presented itself as the true temple and its adherents as the true priests, because only the sect knew how to serve God properly. Other organizations too competed with the temple, but in a more benign fashion. Synagogues and schools were built throughout the land of Israel and the diaspora. After the destruction of the temple these institutions became the focal points of Jewish worship and piety (see chapters 4 and 5).

Second temple Judaism is a "book religion." At its heart lies the Bible, the book which Jews call "Tanak" and Christians call "the Old Testament." Pre-exilic Israel produced the raw materials out of which most of the Bible was constructed, but it was second temple Judaism that created "the Bible," venerated the very parchment on which it was written, and devoted enormous energies to its interpretation. This process is called "canonization." The Jews of the second temple period realized that they lived in a postclassical age. They studied the books of the ancients and did not try to compete with them. They turned instead to new literary genres and new modes of expression. This development is at the heart of the shift from Israelite religion to Judaism (see chapter 6).

Unity and Diversity

Second temple Judaism was a complex phenomenon. Judaism changed dramatically during the Persian, Hellenistic, Maccabean, Roman, and rabbinic periods. Generalizations that may be true for one period may not be true for another. In addition, at any given moment Jews practiced their religion in manifold different ways. The Jewish community of Egypt in the first century C.E. was far from uniform in practice and belief, and we have no reason to assume that any of the Egyptian interpretations of Judaism would necessarily have found favor in the other communities of Greek-speaking Jews throughout the Roman world (for example, in Rome, Asia Minor, North Africa, and parts of the land of Israel). The Judaism of the land of Israel was striated not only by numerous sects but also by numerous teachers and holy men, each with his band of supporters. We have no reason to assume that any of the Palestinian interpretations of Judaism would necessarily have found favor in the other communities of Hebrew- or Aramaic-speaking Jews thoughout the east (for example, in Babylonia and parts of Syria). With such diversity, was there any unity? What links these diverse phenomena together and allows them all to be called *Judaism*?

As I remarked above when discussing the link between pre-exilic Israel and second temple Judaism, the most potent force unifying the two is self-perception or self-definition. The Jews saw (and see) themselves as the heirs and continuators of the people of pre-exilic Israel; the Jews also felt (and still feel) an affinity for their fellow Jews throughout the world, in spite of differences in language, practice, ideology, and political loyalty. Such feelings are normal for minority groups in both ancient and modern times. Because of the Jews' attachment to each other, unsympathetic gentile observers accused (and accuse!) them of hating the rest of humanity (see chapter 2).

This self-perception manifested itself especially in the relations of diaspora Jewry to the land of Israel and the temple. The Maccabees tried hard to win the support of diaspora Jewry, basing their campaign to some extent on loyalty to the mother country. They instructed the Jews of the diaspora through a series of epistles to observe the newly introduced festival of Hanukkah, which celebrated the repurification of the temple in 164 B.C.E. (2 Macc. 1–2). It was during the century of Maccabean rule that First Maccabees was translated from Hebrew to Greek, and that Esther was translated into Greek by a priest from Jerusalem. At this same time the author of the *Letter of Aristeas* described how seventy-two elders went from Jerusalem to Egypt, where they would translate the Torah into Greek. The Maccabees also reinterpreted Exodus 30:11–16 to mean that every Jew was obligated to contribute one half shekel to the temple in Jerusalem every year.[1] Herod the Great continued this policy. He appointed as his high priests Jews from Babylonia and Alexandria, the two largest diaspora communities. When the Jews of Asia Minor needed an advocate to plead their cause before the Romans, Herod sent his chief adviser, who succeeded brilliantly in their behalf.

Even if these overtures were motivated more by a desire for support rather than a sense of kinship, diaspora Jews, especially those of Egypt, responded to them. They contributed large sums of money to the temple, and by Herodian times at the latest streamed in the thousands to Jerusalem in order to witness and participate in the festival rituals of the temple. Philo describes Jerusalem as the "mother-city" of the Jews and went there on pilgrimage at least once.[2] The book of Acts mentions that Jews from virtually every part of the world could be found in Jerusalem (Acts 2:5-11).

The mutual loyalty of Palestinian and diaspora Jews had political implications too. During the second century B.C.E. two Jewish generals of the queen of Egypt refused to lead her army against the Maccabean ruler, because, they said, it was impious for them to fight their co-religionists. In addition, they warned that the Jews of Egypt might rebel against the queen were she to attack their home country. When the last representatives of the Maccabean line were in Rome in the middle of the first century B.C.E. in order to plead their respective cases, the Jews of Rome turned out en masse to support their favorite. During the war of 66-70 C.E. some diaspora Jews supported the revolutionaries and sent them aid. The fact is revealed by a Roman historian of the third century C.E. who wrote that the rebels were assisted by "their co-religionists from across the Euphrates (that is, Babylonia) and, indeed, the entire Roman empire."[3]

Thus, like the bumblebee which continues to fly, unaware that the laws of aerodynamics declare its flight to be impossible, the Jews of antiquity saw themselves as citizens of one nation and one religion, unaware of, or oblivious to, the fact that they were separated from each other by their diverse languages, practices, ideologies, and political loyalties. In this book I do not minimize the varieties of Jewish religious expression, but my goal is to see the unity within the diversity.

2

Jews and Gentiles

The relationship of Jews and Judaism to gentiles and gentile culture is a complex topic that consists of three distinct but interrelated themes: political (to what extent should the Jews submit to foreign domination?), cultural (to what extent should the Jews absorb pagan ideas and practices?), and social (to what extent should Jews mingle and interact with gentiles?). I shall examine each of these separately, beginning with the simplest, the political.

Political: Gentile Domination

From 587 B.C.E., the destruction of the first temple and the exile to Babylonia, until 1948 C.E., the establishment of the modern state of Israel, the Jews of both the diaspora and the land of Israel lived almost exclusively under foreign domination. During extensive portions of the pre-exilic period, the northern kingdom suffered political subjugation at the hands of Aram and Assyria, and the southern kingdom at the hands of Aram, Assyria, Egypt, and Babylonia, but at no point before their actual destruction did either kingdom lose its monarchs or its nominal independence. The dissolution of the northern kingdom in 722 B.C.E. led to the ultimate disappearance of "the ten tribes" (although the Samaritans would later claim, perhaps correctly, to be the descendants of these tribes). The dissolution of the southern kingdom, however, did not lead to the disappearance of the Judeans. They returned to their land, rebuilt their temple, and tried to continue as before—but without a king and without political independence.

This political situation raised religious questions: Why did God allow the Jews to be subjugated by gentiles? Why didn't God protect his people? Why do the gentiles but not the Jews deserve temporal power? The answers to these questions will be treated in the next chapter. Here our theme is the response of the Jews to the political questions raised by the fact of subjection to foreign rule: How should the Jews relate to the state? Should they support it, oppose it, or adopt a neutral stance? Should their support or opposition be active or passive?

The answer was provided by Jeremiah. This prophet had warned the inhabitants of Jerusalem that their rebellion against the king of Babylonia was also a rebellion against God. The prophet counseled surrender. Nebuchadnezzar was performing God's will in his assault on the holy city, and the Jews were foolish to believe that they could flout God's will. The Jews were condemned to failure because of their sins; Nebuchadnezzar was merely God's agent for their punishment (Jer. 25). In this conception Jeremiah transferred to his own day the prophetic interpretation of the fall of Samaria enunciated by Isaiah generations before (Isa. 10).

But Jeremiah also added a different interpretation, a new conception not articulated by previous prophets. The fall of Jerusalem and the triumph of Babylonia are the consequence not of sin and punishment but of immutable fate. God, who controls the destiny of nations and empires, has for undisclosed reasons decided that Babylon shall rise and that Judah and other states shall fall (Jer. 27:2–8). The dominion granted the Babylonians was only temporary; after a predetermined amount of time, whether the three generations of Jeremiah 27 or the "seventy years" of Jeremiah 25:12 and 29:10, the Babylonian empire will fall and/or the Jews will return from exile in triumph and glory. The last two prophecies of the book are visions of doom directed against Babylonia (Jer. 50 and 51). In the interim the Jews were powerless to change the divine decree. Let them support their conquerors and pray for the welfare of the countries in which they lived (Jer. 29:5–7).

How much of this was enunciated by Jeremiah during the dark days of the 590s and 580s B.C.E., and how much was added by later disciples and editors, is not easy to determine, but, whatever their origin, these ideas had an enormous impact on subsequent Jewish thought and practice. When the author of Daniel sought to understand the meaning of the desecration of the temple by Antiochus Epiphanes in 167 B.C.E., he turned to the prophecies of Jeremiah, especially the prophecy concerning the period of "seventy years" (Dan. 9:2). When the author of the *Apocalypse of Baruch,* Josephus, and the rabbis sought to understand the meaning of the destruction of the second temple by the Romans, they too turned to Jeremiah. Jeremianic influence is particularly noticeable in the apocalypses. These texts, beginning with Daniel, regularly combine the two basic elements of the political theology of Jeremiah: the gentiles rule the Jews in order to punish them for their sins; the gentiles will continue to rule the Jews until the immutable sequence of empires has run its course and the predetermined day of their destruction has arrived.

The prophecies of Jeremiah also provide the ideological context for the political behavior of the Jews in antiquity (and, indeed, of medieval and modern times as well). When Cyrus the Great of Persia conquered Babylonia in 539 B.C.E. and issued his edict permitting the Jews to return home and rebuild their temple (Ezra 1:1–4), many Jews chose to remain. They had adjusted to life in Babylonia and were prepared to remain there until God would redeem them. The Jews who returned, or who were preparing to return, to the land of Israel were reassured by an anonymous prophet that an emancipation proclamation issued by a gentile king was precisely the redemption forecast by Jeremiah (Isa. 45:1–13; see too Ezra 1:1). Of all the nations exiled from their lands by the Assyrians and the Babylonians, only the Jews returned to their homeland in order to rebuild their ancestral temple. For these Jews the redemption promised by Jeremiah was to consist of repatriation and the renewal of the temple cult; perhaps many of them also hoped for a restoration of the kingship and political independence, but they were to be disappointed. The Jews who stayed behind in Babylonia, like all the Jews of the diaspora communities that would flourish during the subsequent centuries, were willing to forgo even their temple and their land. For both communities, then, complete redemption would have to await the promised day of the Lord.

In the meantime they supported the state. For over a thousand years the Jews of antiquity lived under the rule of the Persians, the Hellenistic kingdoms of Egypt and Syria, the Romans and and their Christian continuators, and the Parthians. They seldom rebelled, even when provoked. The best illustration of this attitude is the history of the Jews during the reign of Caligula (37–41 C.E.). In Alexandria a mob let loose by the Roman governor destroyed Jewish homes and property, and threatened the political existence of the Jews of the city. Rather than rebel against the state, however, the Jews sent a delegation to the emperor requesting him to listen to their grievances. While these events were taking place, the governor of Syria, acting upon Caligula's instructions, was attempting to erect a statue of the emperor in the temple in Jerusalem. Faced with the possibility that the temple might be desecrated, the Jews of Judea threatened to have themselves massacred en masse by the soldiers. The stated goal of these Jews was not the elimination but the amelioration of Roman rule. Ancient Jewish history provides numerous other instances of appeals to the imperial power for the adjudication of some dispute or the bequest of some favor. The early Christians adopted the same stance toward the state (Rom. 13:1–7).

During the period surveyed by this book only four exceptions break the overall pattern: the revolt of the Maccabees against Antiochus Epiphanes (167–164 B.C.E.); the two major rebellions of the Jews of Israel against the Romans, the first in 66–73 (or 74) C.E., the second in 132–135 C.E.; and the rebellion of the Jews of Egypt, Cyrene, and Cyprus against Roman rule in 115–117 C.E. I shall examine each of these separately.

The Maccabean Rebellion

The Maccabean rebellion began as a struggle for religious liberty. Either King Antiochus, or a group of Jews acting under his authority, desecrated the temple by erecting in the sacred precincts a statue and/or an altar of a foreign god, and attempted to compel the Jews to abandon their traditional religious practices (circumcision, Sabbath, etc.). The goal of the king and his supporters was to remove all the peculiar features of Judaism that made it different from the other religions of the world. The religious persecution that accompanied this forced "Hellenization" (on this term see below) provoked Judah the Maccabee and his followers to rebel against the state. This was the Jews' first departure from the Jeremianic political tradition, and it was prompted by the state's first departure from a policy of religious toleration. In antiquity religious persecutions were something of a rarity. The polytheistic and polyethnic empires of both Mesopotamia and the Mediterranean basin tolerated religious and cultic diversity. As long as the peace was maintained and the taxes were paid, the state did not care much about the religious life of its citizens. What provoked the persecution by Epiphanes remains an enigma in spite of intense study by many scholars, but a persecution there was, and the war it provoked is history's first recorded struggle for religious liberty.

At some point during the struggle the goals of Judah and his party changed. He was no longer fighting for religious liberty but for political independence. He and his brothers after him sought to make Judea free and independent, under the rule of a new dynasty, that of the Maccabees themselves. Even after they regained the temple and put an end to the persecution (164 B.C.E.), they did not cease their fight. Some Jews supported them in the first phase of the war, but abandoned them during the second and third phases. They were prepared to fight against their rulers for the sake of religious freedom, but they were not prepared to support the dynastic pretensions of the Maccabees and to create an independent state (1 Macc. 2:42 and 7:13). Indeed, the state and dynasty that the Maccabees created never succeeded in garnering the total support of all the Jews.

Social factors played an important role in this war as well. Mattathias, the patriarch of the clan, and his son Judah the Maccabee, were country priests who drew the bulk of their support from the countryside and fought against the well-to-do priests of Jerusalem. The Maccabees expelled or killed many of the "old guard" and advanced "new men" like themselves to become the new aristocracy.

The Rebellion Against the Romans (66–74 C.E.)

The war of 66–74 is similar in many ways to the rebellion of the Maccabees, but also very different. The revolutionaries who fomented this war and saw it to its catastrophic conclusion consisted of diverse groups, each with its own leaders, history, and ideology. Some hailed from the countryside, others from the city of Jerusalem. Some were priests, others lay. Some were wealthy, others poor. Some had socialist or utopian goals, and spent most of their energy in attacking the rich and the hereditary aristocracy. Others, notably some of the priests, fought to maintain and expand their traditional prerogatives and power. Others were motivated by an intense hatred of the Romans and a desire to rid the holy land of foreign contagion. Many of the revolutionaries believed that the Messiah would soon come to redeem Israel and that all the Jews had to do was to get the ball rolling; God and the angelic hosts would do the rest. We may assume that the messianic theories which motivated the revolutionaries were as numerous and diverse as the revolutionaries themselves. The Zealots and the Sicarii are the best known of these groups, but there were many others (see chapter 5 below).

One of the major reasons the Jews lost the war is that they were unable to mount a united front against the Romans. They spent much of their time killing each other rather than fighting the enemy. Thus both the Maccabean revolution and the war of 66–74 were motivated in part by social factors, but the "war party" of the rebellion against Epiphanes was far more united than the "war party" of the rebellion against Nero.

The two wars also had very different beginnings and conclusions. The war of 66–74 was sparked not by a profanation of the temple and a religious persecution, but by the administrative incompetence of the Roman procurators, by the fighting between Jews and pagans in the cities of Palestine and Syria, and by the action of some Jewish hotheads who suspended the temple sacrifice on behalf of the emperor. The two wars also had very different outcomes. The rebellion of the Maccabees prevented Judaism from becoming just another local variation of Syrian Hellenism, and thereby saved it from extinction. The war of 66–74 removed the institutional foundations of Judaism, brought tremendous destruction upon the land of Israel and its inhabitants, and endangered the status of the Jews throughout the Roman empire; it threatened the very survival of Judaism.

In the eyes of the revolutionaries Roman rule was as oppressive and intolerable as that of Epiphanes, but many Jews disagreed with this assessment and participated in the war only in its initial chaotic stages, if at all. For every peasant willing to give up everything in order to fight the Romans, there was a peasant who did not want to suffer the inevitable disasters inflicted by war. These Jews felt that the Romans had done nothing to justify a departure from the Jeremianic political tradition. Fighting against the Romans was foolish at best and sinful at worst. God will redeem Israel by sending the messiah, but Israel can do nothing to hasten the appointed time. This point of view was advanced by Flavius Josephus in his *The Jewish War*, our major source for the history of the war and its antecedents. The same perspective is ascribed by rabbinic literature to Rabban Yohanan ben Zakkai, who is alleged to have left Jerusalem during the siege and to have hailed Vespasian as a man destined to destroy the temple and to become emperor.[1] At his meeting with the soon-to-be-emperor, the rabbi quoted from Isaiah (10:34): "And the Lebanon [= the Temple constructed from the cedars of Lebanon] shall fall by a majestic one [= Vespasian]." The rabbi neglected to inform the Roman that the next verse of the prophecy begins with the messianic prediction "There shall come forth a shoot from the stump of Jesse." Had Vespasian known the Bible of the Jews he might not have received the rabbi so kindly.

The Wars of 115–117 C.E. and 132–135 C.E.

The other two exceptions to the Jeremianic political tradition can be treated briefly, not because they are less important than the wars just discussed, but because their documentation is so poor. In 115–117 C.E. the Jews of Alexandria, the Egyptian countryside, Cyprus, and Cyrenaica (part of modern-day Libya) fought the Romans. Archaeological evidence proves that this was a major uprising that

caused much destruction for both Jew and gentile. The Jewish community of Alexandria, one of the largest and most important of the
ancient world, was dealt a serious blow. The causes of this war are
most obscure. Apparently its root cause was the political tension
between Jews and gentiles in the cities of the Greek east, a tension
that had flared up many times in the first century c.e. Messianic
speculations also played an important part.

Equally important and only slightly less obscure is the war of
132–135. The war of 115–117 was the revolt of parts of the Greek
diaspora; there is no reliable evidence that the Jews of the land of
Israel participated. By contrast the war of 132–135 was the revolt
of the land of Israel, or, to be more accurate, the district of Judea.
Its leader was Bar Kosiba, better known as Bar Kokhba ("Son of a
Star"), the name given to him by those who accepted his messianic
status. On his coins he styled himself "Simon the Prince *(Nasi)* of
Israel." One ancient historian says that this war was provoked by
Hadrian's decision to rebuild Jerusalem as a pagan city. The coinage
of the new city, named *Aelia Capitolina* in honor of Hadrian (whose
family name was Aelius) and Jupiter (the god of the capitol), shows
that the city was indeed established before the outbreak of the
rebellion, but whether the construction *caused* the rebellion is a
point that cannot be confirmed. Another ancient historian claims
that the war was provoked by a prohibition of circumcision. Castra-
tion and other mutilation of the male genitalia had been long prohibited by the Romans, but Hadrian extended the prohibition to
include circumcision, a step which the Jews found intolerable. Rabbinic literature confirms that during and after the war the Romans
forbade circumcision as well as other Jewish practices (including the
recitation of the *Shema,* the public study of the Torah, and the
observance of the Sabbath), but whether this persecution was a
cause or a consequence of the war is an important point which,
again, we cannot determine precisely. In any case, both historians
agree that this war was provoked by a Roman action against the
Jews.[2] In the rabbinic imagination Hadrian was another Epiphanes,
another gentile ruler who sought to destroy Judaism, but for us
Hadrian's motives, as well as those of Epiphanes, remain obscure.

The war of Bar Kokhba was the product of internal factors as well.
Modern scholars have highlighted the social and economic stress
engendered by the war of 66–74 c.e. In the wake of that war the
Romans confiscated a great deal of land, leasing or giving it to their
supporters and soldiers. This process created a large number of
landless peasants in Judea, and it is this group which seems to have
provided Bar Kokhba the bulk of his support. Another important

factor is Bar Kokhba's messianism. Little is known about this either, but the timing of the war is very suggestive. Seventy years after the destruction of the first temple the second temple was built in fulfill-ment of Jeremiah's prophecy. The Jews had no doubt that the prophecy would be fulfilled again, but sixty years had already gone and nothing had happened. By the 130s C.E. the Jews must have been very restive as they contemplated the rapid approach of the septuagintal year. Bar Kokhba was seen by some of his followers as the anointed redeemer who would inaugurate the end by destroying the Romans and rebuilding the temple. In the wake of his defeat we may imagine the Jews of the second century C.E., no less than Daniel in the second century B.C.E., contemplating with renewed intensity the opaque words of the prophet from Anathoth.

Conclusion

I end this survey where I began, with Jeremiah. In spite of these four exceptions, the basic political stance of the Jews of both the land of Israel and the diaspora was not rebellion but accommoda-tion. The Jews must support the state until God sees fit to redeem them. This was the counsel of Jeremiah in the sixth century B.C.E., of Josephus in the first century C.E., and of the rabbis of the second through the twentieth centuries C.E. This advice was accepted by the masses of the Jews throughout antiquity. The only principled rejec-tion of it was by the Sicarii and assorted other grouos in the first century. Their actions contributed mightily to the war of 66–74, but as we have seen, that war was caused by many different factors and was joined by many different groups. The revolt of the Maccabees and the rebellion of Bar Kokhba were caused, at least in part, by the hostile actions of the ruling power. Even Jeremiah might have ap-proved.

Cultural: Judaism and Hellenism

From biblical until modern times Jews have seen themselves, and have been seen by others, as a distinct group. The world consists of Jews and gentiles ("the nations"). God chose the Jews from among all the nations and made them his special people. They alone possess his Torah and perform his will. God placed the sun, moon, and stars in the heavens for the nations to worship; but the Israelites are permitted to worship only the true God alone (Deut. 4). Be-tween the "us" of Judaism and the "them" of paganism was a boundary that separated the holy from the profane. The precise contours of this boundary were never very clear, but one of the characteristic themes of Jewish thought throughout the ages is this sense of contrast between the "us" and the "them," between Jew and gentile, between the ideas of Judaism and the ideas of the gentile world (whether paganism, Christianity, or Islam).

The Greeks drew a similar distinction between "Hellenes," the bearers of enlightened culture, and "barbarians," the members of foreign nations, but the demarcation between Jew and gentile was much stricter than that between Hellene and barbarian. A barbarian could become a Hellene by adopting the Greek language and culture, but a gentile could become a Jew only by "converting," that is, by denying the pagan gods and affirming exclusive loyalty to the god of the Jews. A pagan who wished to become a Jew did not merely add Judaism to his paganism or apply Jewish terminology to his pagan practices; he replaced his pagan beliefs and practices with Jewish ones. Polytheism was tolerant, monotheism was not. But for all its vaunted intolerance Judaism was an active participant in the cultural and social life of antiquity.

"Hellenism," "Hellenization," and "Hellenistic Judaism"

Modern scholars use the term "Hellenism" in two different ways. In one usage "Hellenism" means the culture, society, and way of life brought to the peoples of the east by Alexander the Great and his successors. The culture was "Hellenistic" (the adjective spun from the noun "Hellenism") because its language was Greek, its literary classics were Greek, its ideas were Greek, its gods were Greek, its social elite was Greek (and Macedonian), and its most distinctive form of social organization (the *polis*) was Greek. Hellenism was the way of life brought by the conqueror and was a great challenge to the Jews and to all the other inhabitants of the East. In this conception "Hellenism," the worship of the Greek gods and the practice of Greek ways, is an antonym to "Judaism," the worship of the God of Israel and the practice of Jewish ways. This conception and usage were inspired by the accounts of the Antiochan persecution and the Maccabean revolt contained in First and Second Maccabees. Indeed, in separate passages Second Maccabees uses the terms "Judaism" (2:21) and its antonym "Hellenism" (4:13).

This conception of "Hellenism" gave rise in turn to the conception of "Hellenistic Judaism" as an antonym for "Palestinian Judaism." According to this view "Hellenistic" Jews are the Jews who lived in the diaspora, spoke Greek and wrote literature in Greek, and adulterated their religion with ideas and practices imported from the "Hellenistic" world. In contrast, the Jews of Palestine lived in the mother country, spoke Hebrew and Aramaic and wrote literature in those languages, and struggled to observe their religion in all its rigor and to keep it pure from foreign contagion. This conception was inspired by the figure of Paul of Tarsus, who seemed to represent the urbane and cosmopolitan (that is, not law-observant) Jew of the diaspora in contrast with the "orthodox" and legalistic Jew of Palestine, and by passages like Acts 6:1 which spoke of tension between the "Hebrews" and the "Hellenists" in the early church.

Many scholars have argued that this conception does not do full justice to the complexities of either "Hellenism" or "Hellenistic Judaism." Whatever it was that Alexander the Great tried to achieve, and whatever the purity of the "Hellenism" which he brought with him from Macedon, within a very short time after his death all the cultures of the East began to contribute to the new creation we call Hellenism. Hellenistic culture was not merely a debased version of the culture of classical Athens. Its substrate was Greek and its language of expression was Greek, but it absorbed ideas and practices from all the cultures with which it came into contact, thereby assuming many and diverse forms. The natives were Hellenized, and the Greeks were "Orientalized."

In the Egyptian countryside the peasants expressed their traditional hopes and prayers in Greek, even as the Ptolemies adopted the royal ideology of the ancient Pharaohs in order to bolster their command over their subjects. Some of the new *poleis* were bastions of high culture and "Hellenism," but more often than not the Hellenism which reached the man in the street or the peasant on his farm was a mixture of traditional with novel elements: the ancestral gods were given Greek names, traditional ideas were dressed in Greek garb, etc. The cultures of the East were too powerful and too attractive to lose their grip on their adherents. Through intermarriage with local women and through veneration of the local gods, the Greeks often lost much of their Greekness. When used as a descriptive epithet for the culture of the world from Alexander the Great to the first century B.C.E. or C.E., Hellenism ought to mean not "Greek culture" but the fusion of various cultures. In this conception "Judaism" and "Hellenism" are *not* antonyms, since, by definition, Judaism was part of Hellenism and Hellenism was part of Judaism.

This approach attempts to get beyond the rhetoric of the Jews of antiquity. If various Jews of antiquity saw Judaism and Hellenism as antithetical, that hardly means that these entities *were* antithetical.

Several church fathers expressed a similar hostility toward Hellenism, even after the triumph of the church over paganism. Jerome was warned in a vision that he was spending too much time on Cicero and not enough on sacred scripture.[3] Statements like these advance the claim that Christianity is the exclusive source of truth and has no need for classical culture. But we would err badly if we deduced from these texts that Jerome and the other fathers who make similar pronouncements viewed classical culture as antithetical to Christianity. Similarly, we cannot deduce from Maccabean and rabbinic ideology and rhetoric the real relationship of Judaism to Hellenism. Nor can we generalize from that very unusual Jew, Paul.

This conception of "Hellenism" leads to a redefinition of "Hellenistic Judaism." All the Judaisms of the Hellenistic period, of both the diaspora and the land of Israel, were Hellenized, that is, were integral parts of the culture of the ancient world. Some varieties of Judaism were more Hellenized than others, but none was an island unto itself. It is a mistake to imagine that the land of Palestine preserved a "pure" form of Judaism and that the diaspora was the home of adulterated or diluted forms of Judaism. The term "Hellenistic Judaism" makes sense, then, only as a chronological indicator for the period from Alexander the Great to the Maccabees or perhaps to the Roman conquests of the first century B.C.E. As a descriptive term for a certain type of Judaism, however, it is meaningless, because all the Judaisms of the Hellenistic period were "Hellenistic."

Since the second approach is much more convincing than the first, I shall avoid the term "Hellenistic Judaism" for the rest of this book. I shall, when necessary, distinguish the Judaism of the diaspora from that of Palestine, and the Judaism of Greek-speaking Jews from that of Hebrew- and Aramaic-speaking Jews, but the term "Hellenistic Judaism" is too vague to be helpful.

Judaism and Hellenistic Culture

The basic problem that confronted all the Jews of antiquity was to determine a working relationship with Hellenistic culture. How to preserve Jewish identity while simultaneously partaking of the riches of Hellenistic culture? How to balance the conflicting claims of universalism and particularism, the desire to be part of the larger world and the desire to be separate and distinct? Where was the line that separated the licit foreign element which enriched and fructified, from the illicit foreign element which threatened and destroyed? This was a perpetual dilemma, not only for the Jews in their homeland but especially for the Jews in the diaspora.

The problem was not new. Even in pre-exilic times the Israelites had to determine the extent to which they could draw on the riches of the cultures among which they lived. King Solomon built the temple of God with the aid of Phoenician architects and on the standard plan of Syrian temples. The psalmist modeled some of his poems on Canaanite hymns to Baal and Egyptian hymns to Aton. The author of Proverbs drew upon the wisdom of Amenemope. When the Israelites, however, began to worship Baal alongside their own God and to incorporate Canaanite practices into their religion, the prophets objected vociferously.

Complicating all these issues was the political setting. The lack of political autonomy increased the need for the erection of clear boundaries that would safeguard the group's identity. In pre-exilic times Ahaz the king of Judah replaced the altar in the temple with an altar constructed like one he saw in Damascus (2 Kings 16: 10–18), thereby indicating his fealty to his master the king of Assyria. Political subjugation brought in its wake enormous pressure to conform to the ways of the conqueror, even if the conqueror did not actually initiate a "persecution."

In the second temple period the integration of the Jews in the Hellenistic world manifested itself in three different areas: material culture; language; and philosophy and way of life. I shall consider each of these separately.

Material Culture

The pottery, clothing, art, architecture, and the myriad other details that constituted the realia of Jewish life were all standard Hellenistic types or variations on them. That this was the case in the Greco-Roman diaspora should occasion no surprise, but it was also the case in Palestine. Cities were built on the Greek pattern. The elders no longer sat at the gate as in pre-exilic times, but in the *agora* or central plaza of the city, an architectural feature unknown to the Hebrew Bible. All of Herod the Great's building projects, including the reconstruction of the temple in Jerusalem, were in the Hellenistic style of the Near East, and this fact is not to be attributed to the idiosyncrasy of one mad ruler. Josephus remarks that the buildings of one Galilean village closely resembled those of Tyre, Sidon, and Berytus (Beirut). All the coins issued by the Jews, from the Maccabees to the Herodian kings to the revolutionaries of 66–70 C.E., were minted on the Tyrian standard, which was widespread throughout the Hellenistic East.

Language

The essence of Hellenization, of course, is the Greek language. In the diaspora the triumph of the Greek language was complete. Hebrew was virtually unknown to Egyptian Jewry. Even Philo, certainly the most learned and literate Jew produced by the Jewish community of Alexandria, was no Hebraist; in all likelihood his knowledge of Hebrew did not extend beyond select words and phrases of the Torah. Elsewhere in the diaspora the situation was the same. Virtually all the inscriptions engraved by diaspora Jewry, from Egypt to Rome to Asia Minor, were in Greek. In Rome a few were in Latin, and a few epitaphs append the Hebrew word *shalom*, but again there is no sign that the Jews of these places spoke or knew any Semitic language. The earliest literary work produced by diaspora Jewry was a translation of the Torah into Greek, known as the *Septuagint* (third century B.C.E.). By the second century B.C.E. the Jews of Egypt were writing scholarly essays, philosophical tracts, and poetry based on this Greek translation. As far as we know, Greek was the exclusive language of literary expression for diaspora Jewry.

In the land of Israel the situation is much more complicated, because Greek had to compete with Hebrew and Aramaic, but even here many Jews spoke and wrote Greek. The Maccabees arranged for the translation of First Maccabees from Hebrew into Greek (it is this translation which survives, the Hebrew original having completely disappeared). A Jew from Jerusalem translated the book of Esther into Greek. The Wisdom of Ben Sira, a work written in Hebrew by a Palestinian sage around 200 B.C.E., was translated into Greek by the author's grandson. By the first century C.E., if not before, Palestinian authors like Josephus and his archrival Justus of Tiberias were writing original compositions in Greek. Greek documents have been found at Qumran and constitute a large part of a private family archive that was discovered in the Judean desert and dates from the first quarter of the second century C.E. (the "Babata" archive). Bar Kokhba wrote some of his letters in Greek. In the burial caves at Beth Shearim, which were in use during the third and fourth centuries C.E., most of the epitaphs are in Greek, although most of the inscriptions of contemporary synagogues are in Hebrew and Aramaic.

Even in rabbinic circles the Greek language had an enormous impact. This is evidenced not only by the thousands of Greek (and Latin) words in the rabbinic lexicon and by the fact that in a synagogue of Caesarea in rabbinic times the *Shema* was recited in Greek, but also by the fact that some rabbinic Jews needed a Greek translation of the Bible which was more faithful to the Hebrew text than was the Septuagint. According to both Christian and rabbinic legend a convert to Judaism named Aquila translated the Bible anew into Greek under rabbinic aegis, his goal being a faithful word-for-word translation. Whether there is any truth to this legend is hard to establish, but the important point is that the translation attributed to Aquila is a revision of the Septuagint in the direction of the emerging newly standardized Hebrew text. Qumran fragments show that revisions in this direction were being done already in the first century c.e., demonstrating the existence in Palestine of a group of Jews who needed a Greek translation of the Bible, but a translation which would be closer to the Hebrew original than that produced by diaspora Jewry.

The Greek language, then, had an enormous impact in Palestine in both second temple and rabbinic times. As far as we know, however, Hebrew remained the primary language of literary expression. The Qumran scrolls demonstrate that Hebrew was the original language of most of the works written in Palestine between the period of the Maccabees and the destruction of the temple in 70 c.e. The same pattern continued into rabbinic times. The Mishnah and ancillary works were all written in Hebrew. To what extent Hebrew was a spoken language in Palestine in second temple and rabbinic times remains a disputed question. It is likely that many of the people used Aramaic.

As a result of the influence of the Arameans, knowledge of the Aramaic language became widespread among the political elite of Judea even in pre-exilic times (2 Kings 18:26). By the fourth or third century b.c.e. it became a literary language for the Jews (Dan. 2–7, Tobit, *Enoch*) and would so remain until the Middle Ages. By the first century b.c.e. it was used for the translation and paraphrase of scripture. In rabbinic times, from the third century c.e. onward in both Palestine and Babylonia, Aramaic was the language of both scholars and boors, and was used for Bible translations and legal discussions, synagogue homilies and prayers, popular storytelling and magical incantations.

The survival and later efflorescence of Hebrew and Aramaic are sometimes taken as proof that the Jews of Palestine both before and after 70 C.E. resisted the blandishments of Hellenism. There is some truth to this generalization, but we must avoid both simplification and exaggeration. Language certainly is a critical part of human identity, but the fact that some Jews continued their use of a Semitic language hardly proves that they sought to separate themselves from the culture of the world around them. The Jews were not the only people of the Near East to preserve their ancestral language. The centuries that witnessed the height of rabbinic creativity also witnessed the birth of Armenian, Coptic, and Syriac literatures, all of which were heavily imbued with Greek ideas. The Greek language, then, is neither a necessary nor a sufficient criterion for Hellenization.

Philosophy and Way of Life

All the Jews of antiquity were "Hellenized" to some degree. All shared in the material culture of the larger world and all were exposed to the Greek language. But usually the term "Hellenization" involves more than just pots, pans, and language. It involves the way of thought and way of life. To what extent did the Jews of antiquity adopt and adapt the ideas and practices of the world around them? How did they reconcile the truths of their tradition with the truth of contemporary culture?

Some Jews in both Israel and the diaspora sought to obliterate all distinctions between themselves and the gentiles. These Jews are usually called "apostates" (rebels). Their reasons were diverse. Some, hoping to make a career in the civil service, felt that their Judaism was an obstacle in their path. The most spectacular example of this type is Tiberius Julius Alexander, the nephew of Philo, who abandoned his Judaism for the sake of a government career. He succeeded brilliantly; he was in turn procurator of Judea, prefect of Alexandria, and a member of Titus' general staff during the siege of Jerusalem. Some apostates were motivated by the desire to partake fully of the delights of Hellenistic civilization. Particularly onerous in their eyes were the laws that prevented social and sexual intercourse between Jew and gentile. They wanted to "belong." Others were "uprooted intellectuals" who could accept the truths of Greek philosophy but had difficulty accepting the truths of Judaism. In a polytheistic world they could not believe in monotheism, in a society that revered philosophy they could not accept revelation, and in a universal culture they could not remain distinct. These three categories of apostasy are not mutually exclusive. Sometimes it is hard to determine precisely which motives were operative in any given case; indeed, sometimes it is hard to determine whether the term "apostate" is appropriate at all.

During the reign of Antiochus Epiphanes a group of Jews known to modern scholarship as "the extreme Hellenizers" tried to remove the distinctive characteristics of Judaism and to make it indistinguishable from other forms of Semitic-Hellenistic polytheism. Their program was to "go and make a covenant with the Gentiles round about us, for since we separated from them many evils have come upon us" (1 Macc. 1:11). Whether they were motivated primarily by social, economic, political, religious, or economic desires is difficult to determine. The adherents of the Maccabean interpretation of these events had no doubt, however, that these Jews were sinners and rebels. But it is likely that these Jews, who included many priests, high priests, and aristocrats, were attempting not to destroy Judaism but to reform it. Two centuries later in Alexandria Philo describes a group of "extreme allegorists" who argued that the laws of the Torah, including the laws of circumcision and forbidden foods, were meant to be observed not literally but allegorically (an interpretation that would find its way into some elements of early Christianity). These Jews obviously believed that they were remaining loyal to the Torah all the while they were not observing its laws in the normally accepted fashion, but Philo castigates them. Like the "extreme Hellenizers," they too were attempting to remove the distinctive characteristics of Judaism.

The number of apostates in Jewish antiquity, if we exclude the Jewish Christians and the Christian Jews, was never very large. Both in the diaspora and in Israel, even in rabbinic times, there were always some Jews who were prepared to obliterate the distinction between Jew and gentile, and between Judaism and Hellenistic culture. Universalist trends had always existed in Judaism, even in pre-exilic times, especially in intellectual circles. The "Wisdom Literature" of the Bible (Proverbs, Job, Ecclesiastes) completely ignores the distinctive elements of Israelite cult, history, and theology; freely draws upon the wisdom literature of the ancient East, especially Egypt; and emphasizes the common morality and ethics applicable to all peoples. Thought of this type had an enormous influence on later Jewish writers, including Philo and the rabbinic author of *Chapters of the Fathers* (who omits nearly all distinctively Jewish practices). Other universalist trends in ancient Judaism will be discussed below. But the universalism of these apostates was different from the universalism of the Wisdom school and the other Jewish philosophers, because the apostates actualized their universalism and surrendered their Jewish identity. For the vast majority of Jews this was not an acceptable response to the challenges of the Hellenistic world.

For most Jews the ideal solution was to create a synthesis between Judaism and Hellenism. The rabbis expressed this beautifully in a comment inspired by Genesis 9:27, "May the beauty of Japheth (= the Greeks) dwell in the tents of Shem (= the Jews)."[4] Since the definition of Hellenism is complex and elusive, as I discussed above, the statement that the Jews were influenced by Hellenistic culture or that they "borrowed" this or that idea from Hellenism does not necessarily imply that they consciously and purposefully imported material from abroad. For some Jews, especially in the diaspora, the adaptation of Judaism to contemporary culture was a conscious process. For others it was not. Sometimes it is hard to determine whether a phenomenon that appears in both Judaism and other forms of Hellenistic culture is to be attributed to the "influence" of the one upon the other or to parallel development. As a participant group in Hellenistic culture, the Jews gave and received. What the Jews gave I shall discuss in the next section. Here I shall discuss what the Jews received, as well as developments in Judaism that are paralleled by developments elsewhere in Hellenistic culture.

Many scholars have noted that the religions and philosophies of the Hellenistic period share a concern for the individual whereas the religions and philosophies of classical Greece centered more upon the *polis*, the collective. The same development can be seen in the Judaism of the Hellenistic period (see chapter 3). The concern for the fate of the individual in both this world and the next, the elaboration of a system of requirements for the individual to follow (prayer, Torah study, performance of the commandments, etc.), and the creation of new social structures in which the individual figures prominently (school, synagogue, and sect)—all these developments attest to the new ethos in Judaism, an ethos closely paralleled by, and perhaps derived from, Hellenistic culture.

Much of the Jewish literature of the Hellenistic period follows Greek literary forms and/or the canons of Greek taste (see chapter 6). This fact is not particularly surprising for works written in Greek in the diaspora, but it is no less true for many of the works written in Hebrew or Aramaic in the land of Israel. The book of *Judith*, originally written in Hebrew, is a typical Greek novella or romance, complete with a heroine in distress, narrow escapes, and a happy ending. The *Genesis Apocryphon*, an elaboration in Aramaic of the stories of Genesis, employs Hellenistic literary techniques to dress up its narrative (warning dreams, the pathos of the hero). One member of the Maccabean circle in Jerusalem wrote an epic poem in Greek, apparently paraphrasing the Bible.[5] The commentary form, which is first attested in the Qumran scrolls and later was to play such an important role in rabbinic culture, also is of Hellenistic origin. All of these works are fiercely loyal to Jewish tradition, but all of them are expressions of Greek literary taste. The beauty of Japheth did indeed reside in the tents of Shem.

I turn now from the *form* of the literature to its *content*. No area of Hellenistic culture influenced the Jews as much as philosophy. The God of the Hebrew Bible is very different from the supreme God of Plato or Aristotle. The former is a anthropomorphic being capable of anger, joy, and other emotions, who created the world and continues to direct human affairs. The God of the philosophers, however, was a much less human and much more abstract figure, incapable of emotion, and far removed from the daily concerns of humanity (see chapter 3). Many Jews tried to combine these two conceptions, or, more precisely, to reinterpret the God of the Bible in the light of the ideas of the philosophers, especially Plato. In his numerous essays on the Torah, Philo tried to demonstrate that the God of Judaism was very like the God of Plato, and that the stories of Genesis were not mere amusing diversions but hid profound philosophical truths. This approach to scripture was developed even further by Origen, Ambrose, and other fathers of the church, but its first great exponent was Philo and its origins reach back to Alexandrian Jewry of the third century B.C.E.

The impact of "philosophy" upon Judaism went much deeper than the exegetical essays of Philo. Much of the Jewish thinking on the questions of fate, free will, immortality, and divine providence was influenced by, or at least was expressed in, the terminology of Greek philosophy. Many authors, even those of a decidedly non-philosophic character (like Josephus), present Judaism as a "philosophy," a system of practice and thought that cultivated pagans could appreciate and admire. These writers emphasize those aspects of Judaism which we call "ethics" and "morality," arguing either implicitly or explicitly that the ideal way of life recommended by Greek legislators and thinkers had been put into practice by only one people, the Jews.

The interaction with the Hellenistic world was not limited to the realm of ideas. In the public sphere Jewish life not only in the diaspora but also in the land of Israel was radically transformed by the building of cities and by the creation of new urban elites. Adopting a page from Greek political theory Judah the Maccabee had the people declare by acclamation that Hanukkah was to be celebrated annually in commemoration of the great victory over Epiphanes. A generation later Simon the Maccabee had himself declared the high priest through acclamation. In Greek political theory the power to declare festivals, appoint priests, etc., was vested in the people (the *demos*), but such an idea was completely foreign to Judaism. The Maccabees, the alleged opponents of foreign ways, adopted a Hellenistic practice for their own ends. By Roman times the chief judicial body of the land was known by a Greek name *(synedrion,* or, in Hebrew pronunciation, *sanhedrin)* and perhaps was modeled on a Greek or Roman institution.

Private life too was enriched by Hellenistic social forms. Schools, clubs, and associations were common features in the social and civic life of the Hellenistic world, including the social and civic life of the Jews (see chapter 4). The impact of the new ways is evident too in some of the most basic social forms. According to the custom in force in pre-exilic times, a custom that was almost universal in the Semitic East, a groom "buys" his bride from his prospective father-in-law by tendering a "bride-price." Already in the third century B.C.E. the Jews began to follow the Greek practice (shared by the Romans) according to which a groom receives money or goods (a dowry) from his father-in-law in advance of the marriage. The shift from bride-price to dowry may well be connected with other major developments (for example, the shift from polygamy to monogamy) that may have been occasioned by the entrance of the Jews into Hellenistic society.

Conclusion

"To Hellenize or not to Hellenize" was not a question the Jews of antiquity had to answer. They were given no choice. The questions that confronted them were "how?" and "how far?" How should Judaism adapt itself to meet the new conditions of the age? How far could Judaism go in absorbing foreign ways and ideas before it was untrue to itself and lost its identity? These were the questions which the Jews of antiquity had to answer, and they answered them in numerous and diverse ways. Some were prepared to become "apostates" by abandoning all those beliefs and practices which made Judaism distinctive. Others in response adopted an anti-Hellenistic stance, but their rhetoric cannot mask their willingness to follow Hellenistic ways as long as those ways did not threaten Judaism. Even if the majority of Jews agreed that the golden mean was best, the diversity of their responses indicates that the precise definition of this golden mean remained elusive.

Social: Jews and Gentiles

The Jews of both the diaspora and the land of Israel had an uneasy relationship with their environment. For the most part they were willing to support the state and to partake of the cultural bounty of the Hellenistic world, but they were unwilling to surrender their identity. They wished to "belong" but at the same time to remain distinct. Support for the state was not to be confused with the abnegation of nationalist dreams. Hellenization was not to be confused with assimilation. This tension is also evident in the social relations between Jews and gentiles.

Anti-Judaism and "Anti-Semitism"

In order to maintain their distinctiveness and identity most Jews of the ancient world sought to separate themselves from their gentile neighbors. In the cities of the East they formed their own autonomous ethnic communities, each with its own officers, institutions, and regulations (see chapter 4). Some cities, notably Alexandria and Rome, had neighborhoods inhabited mostly by Jews. (These were not "ghettos" but "ethnic neighborhoods.") Following the lead of Ezra, the Jews of the second temple period grew more and more intolerant of marriages with foreigners. Even Philo admired the zeal of Phineas, who killed an Israelite chieftain for consorting publicly with a Midianite woman (Num. 25). The Jews also buried their dead separately, thus maintaining separation from gentiles in death as in life. They refused to participate in public ceremonies that involved worship either of the pagan gods or of the emperor; in other words, they refused to participate in practically all the communal events of ancient society. The pagan empires tolerated this behavior; Julius Caesar even exempted the Jews from appearing in court on the Sabbath and from serving in the army. In the polyethnic Hellenistic and Roman empires, national distinctiveness and loyalty to ancestral customs were not unusual, but the Jews carried their separateness to unusual lengths. In particular, the refusal of the Jews to participate in any religious ceremony, including emperor worship, was unparalleled, because the Jews alone of all the peoples of antiquity were monotheists who believed in a jealous God.

But their exclusiveness and separation did not prevent the Jews from seeking civic equality with their gentile neighbors. During the first century of our era severe disturbances broke out in Alexandria, Caesarea (in Israel), Antioch (in Syria), and several cities of western Asia Minor (modern Turkey). The details behind these events are obscure, but most scholars agree that the Jewish communities of these places antagonized certain elements of the local population by demanding both tolerance and equality. They asked that the city continue to recognize their autonomous communal organization while also extending them the rights of citizenship. (These rights included a certain degree of political power, various tax advantages, and increased prestige.) The city refused. "If the Jews wish to be Alexandrians, let them worship the gods of the Alexandrians" was the reply, and the battle was joined. In Alexandria the troubles first erupted in 38 C.E. There was a virtual war between the Jews and the pagan mob of the city. Synagogues were desecrated, Jewish shops and homes were pillaged, and many Jews were killed. The situation did not quiet down until 41 C.E., when the emperor Claudius declared that the Jews should not seek more than their due. But the tension between the Jews and Alexandrians continued to fester and broke out anew (not only in Alexandria but in cities throughout Palestine and Syria) in 66 C.E. on the eve of the great rebellion. In Alexandria and Cyrene it reached its climax in the war of 115–117 C.E.

In order to support their position the opponents of the Jews, especially in Alexandria, resorted to anti-Jewish propaganda. Their leader, Apion, wrote a book which attacked the Jews on three fronts. First, he contended that the history of the Jews demonstrates that they are an ignoble lot with an ignoble history. In particular, Apion said, the exodus from Egypt was really an expulsion, since the Israelites were lepers, and the Pharaoh threw them out so that they would not infect the people and shrines of Egypt. Second, the Jews are not, never were, and have no right to be Alexandrian citizens. Third, the Jewish religion is not a religion at all but, at best, an agglomeration of silly superstitions, and, at worst, a conspiracy aimed at Greeks and at all those who share Greek values. In particular, Apion said, when Antiochus Epiphanes entered the temple in Jerusalem he discovered that the Jews annually hold a festival at which they slaughter a Greek youth, especially fattened for the occasion, and eat his corpse while swearing fearsome oaths of hostility toward all Greeks. (A slightly different version of this accusation, known as the "blood libel," was later raised by the Romans against the Christians and, in the twelfth century, by Christians against Jews.)

How is this ferocious outburst against the Jews to be explained? To dismiss it as "anti-Semitism" will not work, because "anti-Semitism" did not exist in antiquity. This term was coined in the middle of the nineteenth century by a German writer who wished to bestow "scientific" respectability upon the hatred of Jews by arguing that Jews and Germans belonged to different species of humanity ("races"). But the ancients did not have anything resembling a racial theory. They observed that Ethiopians were dark skinned and that Germans were pale skinned. They further observed that different nations had different moral characteristics, both good and bad (Egyptians are superstitious, Arabs are thieves, Greeks are fast-talking tricksters, and so on), but neither the Greeks nor the Romans ever explained these differences by appeal to what we would call a racial theory. They argued instead that climate, soil, and water determine both the physical and moral characteristics of nations. Therefore the notion of "anti-Semitism" is inappropriate to antiquity, even if many of the motifs and arguments of the anti-Jewish literature of antiquity are familiar from their subsequent reuse in the "anti-Semitism" of the medieval and modern worlds.

Furthermore, the social and economic tensions that produced the virulent anti-Semitism of nineteenth- and twentieth-century Europe did not exist in antiquity. There were no "nation-states" in antiquity in which the Jews were an unassimilable foreign element. The Jews of antiquity had a variegated economic life in both the diaspora and the land of Israel. They were farmers, laborers, artisans, soldiers, etc. Most of them, like the vast majority of the people of antiquity, were very poor. Not a single ancient text says or implies that the Jews are hated or feared because of their economic power. Money-lending was still centuries in the future, and the rise of the Jewish middle classes did not begin until the nineteenth century.

Finally, an unmistakable component of modern anti-Semitism is its theological justification developed by Christianity. But the pagans of antiquity had no reason to believe that the Jews were cursed by the gods or were in league with the devil. When they accused the Jews of *atheism,* they were objecting to the fact that the Jews refused to worship the pagan gods. Although they may have despised Judaism, the Greeks and Romans respected its exclusiveness as an ancestral usage that the Jews themselves were not free to change. The Christians too were accused of *atheism,* and since they could not defend their refusal by appeal to ancestral custom, they were persecuted. But when the Christians accused the Jews of being "Christ-killers" and of denying the Trinity, they meant something much more serious. In their eyes the Jews were cursed by God, doomed to hell, and denied salvation in the hereafter, concepts that are foreign to the perception of Judaism by pagans.

In sum, "anti-Semitism" did not exist in antiquity, but "anti-

Judaism" did. "Anti-Judaism" was the consequence of political strife between the Jews and their neighbors in both Palestine and the diaspora. The revolt of the Maccabees against the Seleucid empire marks the entrance of the Jews into the rough-and-tumble world of the politics of the Hellenistic world. Before that point, most of the references to Jews in pagan literature are favorable. In the fourth and third centuries B.C.E. many pagans thought that the Jews were a race of "philosophers," like the Brahmans of India. After the rise of the Maccabees the literary tradition becomes ambivalent. Positive evaluations persist, especially of Judaism's avoidance of images in worship, but negative voices predominate. In order to justify his attack on the temple Antiochus Epiphanes had his "propaganda bureau" attempt to prove that the Jewish temple was not a real temple and that the Jewish religion was not a real religion. Many of the anti-Jewish stories first circulated by the Seleucid government were reused centuries later by Apion to justify his opposition to the Jews of Alexandria and by Tacitus (a Roman historian of the early second century C.E.) to justify the destruction of the temple in 70 C.E. Although the persecution of Judaism by Epiphanes, the attack on Alexandrian Jewry by the pagan mob, and the destruction of the temple by Titus were each caused by local factors and not by some deep-rooted anti-Judaism, nevertheless, the literary propaganda spawned by these conflicts helped shape the "anti-Semitic" image of the Jew of later generations.

Philo-Judaism

We shall err badly, however, if we imagine that all social relations between Jews and gentiles were characterized by "clannishness" on the part of the Jews and anti-Judaism on the part of the gentiles. The period from the middle of the second century B.C.E. to the first part of the second century C.E. (approximately from the Maccabees to Bar Kokhba), which witnessed the growth of political and literary hostility toward the Jews, also witnessed the development of admiration and veneration for many Jewish rituals and ideas. It was the age of philo-Judaism as well as anti-Judaism, of conversion to Judaism as well as hatred of Judaism. Although the Jews sought to keep themselves separate and distinct, they also were eager to accept and retain gentile converts. Indeed, some of the anti-Jewish literature of this period is motivated (in addition to the political motives just discussed) by a desire to discourage conversion to Judaism. The literature that evinces a dislike of Judaism paradoxically confirms Judaism's powerful attraction.

Conversion to Judaism

The Hebrew Bible is not familiar either with the prohibition of intermarriage or with the conversion of gentiles to Judaism. Deuteronomy 7:1–4 prohibits the marriage of Israelites with the seven Canaanite nations; other nations, apparently (except perhaps those listed in Deut. 23:2–9), were not included in the prohibition. Leviticus is not familiar with any such prohibition, even for Canaanites. Upon his return from Babylonia in 458 B.C.E. Ezra tried to compel the priests and nobles of Jerusalem to divorce their foreign wives, whose abominable ways resembled those of the Canaanites (Ezra 9:1), but it is not until the Maccabean period that a general prohibition is attested.

The explanation for this development is not the sudden irruption of intolerance and "particularism" into the Jewish psyche, but the new social setting of the community. In pre-exilic times, when the Israelites were a nation living on their own land with their own king, they had nothing to fear from an occasional intermarriage with foreigners. The Canaanites, who still lived in substantial numbers on the land, were the sole group that was prohibited (according to Deuteronomy), because it was the sole group that posed a threat to Israelite identity. (Of course, according to Judg. 3:5–6 many Israelites married Canaanites anyway.) The primary ingredient in Israelite identity was *nationality,* that is, birth (*natio* in Latin). Even if many Israelites condemned intermarriage as something improper (Judg. 14:3), it was never outlawed, and the children of intermarriages were never expelled from the community.

In pre-exilic times "conversion" to Judaism did not yet exist because birth is immutable. An Ammonite or an Aramean could no more become an Israelite in pre-exilic times than an American can become a citizen of Liechtenstein in our own. Mere residency in the land does not confer citizenship, and a social system which defines a citizen solely as the child of a citizen has no legal mechanism by which to assimilate a foreigner. Biblical law frequently refers to "resident aliens" (*gerim* in Hebrew) who are grouped with the widow, the orphan, and the Levite. All of these are landless and powerless, and all are the potential victims of abuse. (An American analogy to the *ger* is the Chicano farm worker; a European analogy is the Turkish laborer in Germany.) The Bible nowhere states how a *ger* might ameliorate his status and become equal to the native born, because there was no legal institution by which a foreigner could be absorbed by a tribal society living on its ancestral land. Resident aliens in the cities of pre-Hellenistic Greece fared no better.

The exile of 587 B.C.E., however, brought in its wake the destruction of the old order. The tribal structure was gone; the Jews who returned from Babylon to Judea were organized as clans, not tribes. Their ritual classification was "Priest, Levite, and Israelite," the classification that has endured in Judaism to this day. Land ownership was no longer tied to membership in a tribe. Many Jews, of course, did not return at all, but remained in Babylonia. Within a few centuries the diaspora in the East was complemented by an extensive diaspora in the West. Political autonomy was lost. In this new setting the old conception of Israelite nationhood no longer made sense. The Jews began to redefine themselves as a *religion,* and it was Judaism, not the religion of pre-exilic Israel, that prohibited intermarriage but permitted conversion.

The transition is clearly under way by the period of Ezra and is more or less complete by the period of the Maccabees. Ezra attempted to expel from the Jerusalem community approximately one hundred thirteen foreign women and the children whom they had borne to their Jewish husbands. Several texts of the Maccabean period (notably *Jubilees* 30) speak of intermarriage as a capital crime. One Roman historian writing about the year 100 C.E. remarks that the Jews refrain from intercourse with foreign women.[6] Although we may be sure that many Jews, especially in the diaspora, did intermarry, most Jews did not. As Philo explained, basing his remarks on Deuteronomy 7:3–4, intermarriage leads to impiety and disloyalty to God. Intermarriage was a threat to the religious community.

But these centuries saw the creation of an institutionalized method for the admixture of gentiles. Ezra was still unfamiliar with the notion of "conversion," but some of his contemporaries were discussing the idea. One prophet assured the "foreigners who join themselves to the Lord, to minister to him, to love the name of the Lord, and to be his servants" that they would not be excluded from the rebuilt temple but would be gathered to God's people (Isa. 56:6–8). Several prophets predicted that in the end of days foreigners would join in the worship of the true God in Jerusalem, either as servants of the Israelites or as independent worshipers. One prophet declared that the resident aliens "will join them [the Israelites] and will cleave to the house of Jacob" (Isa. 14:1); another even predicted that some gentiles would become priests and Levites (Isa. 66:21)!

In the Maccabean period these visions of the end began to influence the behavior of the Jews and gentiles in this world. The book of Judith, a romance written, or at least redacted, during the second century B.C.E., describes the conversion of an Ammonite general to Judaism: "And when Achior saw all that the God of Israel had done [to protect his people], he believed firmly in God, and was circumcised, and joined the house of Israel, remaining so to this day" (Judith 14:10). Here are all the essential elements of conversion to Judaism: belief in God, circumcision, and joining the house of Israel. I shall discuss each of these elements separately.

Belief in God (and denial of other gods). In the Bible various foreigners, impressed by the might of the God of Israel, bless God or otherwise acknowledge his suzerainty. Even generals and kings of foreign nations revere the Lord, but these are not cases of "conversion." None of these gentiles "joins the house of Israel." None swears exclusive loyalty to the God of Israel. "Conversion" means a "turning around," a spiritual reorientation, a denial of the past and a pledge for the future. The convert to Judaism denies his foreign gods and accepts the God of Israel as the only true God (and, according to the rabbis, acknowledges the truth and binding authority of the Torah). None of the biblical figures (except, perhaps, for Naaman in 2 Kings 5) promises exclusive loyalty to God; rather, they polytheistically add the God of Israel to their list of gods. This is not true conversion.

Circumcision and baptism. The central ritual for conversion was circumcision. This practice, quite common in the ancient Orient (Jer. 9:24–25), figures prominently in only a few sections of the Bible, notably Genesis 17 (the institution of circumcision, including the requirement that all acquired slaves must be circumcised), Genesis 34 (the rape of Dinah and the massacre of Schechem), Exodus 4:24–26 (the incident of Moses, Zipporah, and the angel), and Exodus 12:43–49 and Joshua 5:2–11 (the celebration of the Passover sacrifice). All of these passages assign some unusual importance to circumcision, but the Bible as a whole generally ignores it and nowhere regards it as the essential mark of Jewish identity or as the sine qua non for membership in the Jewish polity. It attained this status only in Maccabean times. Some of the extreme Hellenizers of the Maccabean period, in their zeal to remove Jewish distinctiveness, tried to hide their circumcision (other Jews tried to do the same in the time of the Bar Kokhba war). For the Maccabees circumcision was such an essential component of Jewish identity that upon conquering various sections of the holy land they compelled the inhabitants to follow Jewish customs, a demand that meant first and foremost circumcision. The Greek version of the book of Esther, completed about 114 B.C.E. by a resident of Jerusalem, understands the phrase "and many from the peoples of the country declared themselves Jews" (Esth. 8:17) to mean that the gentiles "were circumcised." By the end of the first century B.C.E. circumcision was widely known to the Greeks and Romans as a typically (though not exclusively) Jewish practice. For Paul circumcision represents subjugation to the demands of the Torah.

Were there any other rituals that signaled the entry of a gentile into the people of Israel? According to rabbinic law, transmitted in the name of authorities who lived in the second century C.E., a convert must also be immersed in water (in Christian terminology, be "baptized") and must offer a sacrifice at the temple. The same rabbinic authorities insist that the convert's inability to bring a sacrifice after the destruction of the temple in 70 C.E. does not impair his or her Jewishness, however. The convert merely incurs an obligation that will have to be satisfied in the messianic future. According to rabbinic law, then, in the second temple period the ritual requirements for conversion were three: circumcision, immersion, and sacrifice. The first of these applied only to men, the latter two applied to both men and women.

The major problem raised by this rabbinic tradition is that no text from the second temple period knows of immersion and sacrifice as rituals of conversion. The baptism that figures so prominently in certain portions of the New Testament obviously bears some relationship to the immersion for converts, but the precise nature of that relationship has been debated endlessly by scholars. The fact that gentile converts to Christianity were baptized is the strongest argument for the view that gentile converts to Judaism must have been baptized already in the first century. A pagan writer living about the year 100 C.E. also is aware that Jews baptize their converts (or does the writer have Christian Jews in mind?).[7] All in all, it seems most likely that baptism/immersion was part of the conversion process in at least some Jewish circles in Palestine by the first century of our era. Whether the baptism was initiatory, purificatory, or some combination of the two, remains unclear.

Not all Jews of the first century recognized baptism/immersion as a ritual of conversion, and we have no evidence that any Jew of the first century considered a sacrifice at the temple to be the culmination of the conversion ceremony. If, then, neither baptism/immersion nor sacrifice was generally a part of the conversion process, what ritual served to demarcate the change of status of a female convert? Was there a rite of passage by which a woman born a gentile became a Jew? Apparently not. In pre-exilic times, when "conversion" did not exist for either man or woman, a foreign woman was assimilated into the community through marriage with an Israelite husband. Solomon may have sinned by marrying foreign wives but no one suggested that they should be divorced or that his children were not members of the people of Israel. In fact, Solomon's successor was his son Rehoboam, the offspring of an Ammonite woman. In the first century of our era Josephus still adheres to the same system: intermarriage is prohibited, but if a Jewish man marries a non-Jewish woman she joins his house and bears him legitimate children. Marriage with a Jew was the de facto equivalent of conversion for a woman. Nonmarital conversion for a woman, in those communities where baptism/immersion was not yet practiced, meant apparently the simple fact that a woman observed Jewish practices. Rabbinic texts of the second and third centuries are the earliest references to conversion rituals for women.

Joining the house of Israel. The third element in Achior's conversion to Judaism was his acceptance into the community. He "joined the house of Israel, remaining so until this day" (Judith 14:10). Acceptance by the Jewish community is essential if conversion is to be something other than a theological abstraction, but the social mechanisms that effected this acceptance in antiquity are obscure. Presumably the convert became a "member" of the synagogue or the community. If the sources tell us nothing about this process, at least they tell us something about the attitudes of native-born Jews toward converts and conversion.

Attitudes toward converts. In the second temple period there are few traces of either opposition to conversion or disdain for converts. One text from Qumran asserts that converts will be barred from the temple to be built in Jerusalem in the messianic future. (A parallel rabbinic law excludes the convert from the entire city of Jerusalem.) The opponents of Herod the Great called him a "half-Jew" because he was a descendant of the Idumeans, who had been forcibly converted to Judaism by the Maccabees. Does this sneer prove disdain for all converts and their descendants or is it merely a statement of opposition to Herod? Probably the latter. The Idumeans looked upon themselves as Jews and participated (along with the descendants of other converts) in the great war against the Romans. Philo has generous praise for converts, because they abandon their former people and way of life in order to join a new people and follow a new way. Many Jews regarded converts so highly that they actively propagated Judaism among the gentiles in order to increase the number of the faithful, a phenomenon which I shall discuss below.

Rabbinic texts are full of sentiments in favor of converts. The convert is equal to the native-born Jew "in all respects," the rabbis say. Many homilies begin with phrases like "Beloved are converts in the eyes of God." However, other rabbinic texts assert that the convert can never be fully equal to the native born because, like Ralph Rackstraw of *H.M.S. Pinafore*, he lacks birth. A gentile can convert to Judaism by accepting the God and Torah of the Jews, but he can never become an "Israelite." One Mishnah declares (*Bikkurim* 1:4) that a convert in his prayers ought not to say "Our God and God of *our* fathers," because the God of the Jews was not the God of his fathers. He ought instead to say "Our God and God of *their* fathers." This law was ultimately rejected, but it reflects a deeply held view about converts. Some rabbis were not comfortable with the entire idea of conversion. Others pointed to cases of recidivism or irreligiosity. In the Middle Ages this negative attitude came to prevail. In ancient times, however, the rabbinic views were much more balanced, with the positive outnumbering the negative. A gentile who fully and faithfully converted to Judaism encountered only minimal disabilities in rabbinic society.

"God-Fearers"

Conversion to Judaism entails three elements: belief in God (and denial of pagan gods), circumcision (and immersion/baptism), and integration into the Jewish community. Many gentiles, both men and women, converted to Judaism during the last centuries B.C.E. and the first two centuries C.E. Even more numerous, however, were those gentiles who accepted certain aspects of Judaism but did not convert to it. In polytheistic fashion they added the God of Israel to their pantheon and did not deny the pagan gods. Throughout the Roman empire various practices of Judaism found favor with large segments of the populace. In Rome many gentiles observed the Sabbath, the fasts, and the food laws; in Alexandria many gentiles observed the Jewish holidays; in Asia Minor many gentiles attended synagogue on the Sabbath. Although these gentiles observed any number of Jewish practices and venerated in one form or another the God of the Jews, they did not see themselves as Jews and were not seen by others as Jews. One Jewish practice they studiously avoided was circumcision. They resemble the pagans of the pre-exilic period who feared the Lord but who never changed their identity. In pre-exilic times conversion was not yet an option; in late second temple times it was an option, but these gentiles did not wish to exercise it. The book of Acts calls these people "those who fear" *(phoboumenoi)* or "those who venerate" *(sebomenoi)* the Lord (Acts 13:16, 26; 16:14; 17:4, 17; 18:7). Modern scholars call them "sympathizers" or "semi-proselytes," but these terms lack ancient attestation and are best avoided.

Those who see Judaism and Hellenism as discrete entities are perplexed by the phenomenon of the "God-fearers." Some have even questioned their existence. After all, how can a gentile become a "little bit Jewish"? And why would he or she want to? The explanation is to be sought in the other conception of Hellenism discussed above. Many Greeks and Romans adopted the gods (for example, Isis, Cybele, Mithras, Jupiter Dolichenus) and practices of various "barbarian" nations, without "converting" or losing their identity. Similarly, thinking that the God of the Jews was like the god of other nations, they added him to their pantheon. They observed the Sabbath much as they would the sacred days of other peoples. They frequented the synagogues of the Jews much as they would the temples of other foreign gods. The motives for this behavior were many and diverse, and need not be investigated here; this is the domain of the historians of the Roman empire.

Rather than look upon "God-fearers" as gentiles interested in Judaism, perhaps we should see in the phenomenon the contribution of Judaism to the cultural mix we call "Hellenistic." Pagan culture provides various analogies to Jewish ideas and practices (for example, many philosophers rejected polytheism and the cult of images; Stoic ethics closely resemble rabbinic ethics; in the first centuries of our era burial replaced cremation as the most common means of disposing of the dead), but none of these is the product of Jewish influence. But through the "God-fearers" Judaism had a clear and distinctive impact on its environment. Observance of the Sabbath and holidays, attendance at synagogue, and the veneration of God, were parts of Hellenistic culture.

The phenomenon of "God-fearers" implies another important point as well. Ancient Judaism was visible and open to outsiders. Gentiles were able to enter synagogues and witness the Jewish observances. Josephus insists that Judaism has no mysteries, no secrets that it keeps hidden from curious observers (*Against Apion* 2.8, §107). This claim is not entirely true, but it is essentially correct. Some Jews even engaged in "missionary" work. The Pharisees travel about the land and the sea in order to make even one *proselyte* (the Greek word for convert to Judaism; Matt. 23:15). Josephus narrates that in the middle of the first century C.E. the royal house of the kingdom of Adiabene became Jewish under the tutelage of itinerant Jewish merchants. Several writers from the city of Rome refer to the eagerness of the Jews to win gentiles to their side. There is no evidence for an *organized* Jewish mission to the gentiles, but individuals seem to have engaged in this activity on their own.

Some scholars have suggested that much of the Jewish literature written in Greek had as its goal the propagation of Judaism among the gentiles, since the literature often emphasizes those elements of Judaism which would make it attractive to outsiders. Of course, those elements which make Judaism attractive to outsiders are precisely those which also strengthen its hold on insiders, and it is impossible to tell whether the literature was written in order to attract gentiles to Judaism or to encourage Jews to stay within the fold. In any case, during the first century C.E. at least some Jews were trying to attract converts and "God-fearers."

Even after the destruction of the temple in 70 C.E., the decimation of Alexandrian Jewry in 115–117 C.E., and the Bar Kokhba disaster of 132–135 C.E., Judaism remained attractive to outsiders. Gentiles were still eager to buy the spiritual wares of the Jews. Perhaps because of the growth of Christianity pagan philosophers began for the first time to treat Judaism seriously as a philosophical system, and some of them liked what they found. "What is Plato if not Moses speaking Attic Greek?" was the remarkable observation of one Neo-Platonist.[8] Judaism contributed its God and its angels to the religious syncretism of the second to fifth centuries. But pagans were not the only "God-fearers" during these centuries. Many Christians, generally called "Judaizers" by modern scholarship, were drawn to Jewish practices. For some of these Christians Judaism was attractive *because* of Christianity. Through Christianity they learned the Jewish scriptures and became familiar with Jewish observances. Many Christian groups, for example, insisted that Easter must coincide with the Jewish Passover and that it be celebrated with rites similar to those of the Jewish Passover. Other Christians, however, were really pagan "God-fearers" in disguise. In Antioch in the late fourth century John Chrysostom was shocked that many Christians were doing what pagan "God-fearers" had been doing in other parts of the empire three centuries previously: they were attending synagogues and observing the Jewish festivals.

In addition to these "God-fearers" of various sorts, converts too testify to the fact that Judaism's power of attraction had not dimmed. Rabbinic literature mentions a dozen or so converts in Palestine and many more than that in Babylonia. The church fathers and pagan writers mention several others. Hadrian's edict against circumcision, one of the causes (or consequences) of the Bar Kokhba war, was rescinded by the following emperor but only for native-born Jews. It was now a violation of law for a gentile to be circumcised. At the end of the same century the Roman emperor outlawed conversion altogether, a prohibition that would be repeated by the Christian emperors of the fourth century (and later). This legislative activity implies that conversions were continuing. Perhaps fewer gentiles than before were converting to Judaism or becoming "God-fearers," but Judaism clearly had not lost its allure.

What did change after 70 c.e. was that Jews, or at least the rabbis, were no longer eager to sell their spiritual wares to the gentiles. The motives of the mission to the gentiles are obscure, but whatever they may have been—whether to hasten the messianic deliverance, whether to save souls, whether to garner political support—the rabbis were not interested. They were not active messianists. In their eyes the souls of gentiles did not need to be saved, because all righteous gentiles who observe certain basic norms of (what we would call) religion and ethics were guaranteed a share in the world to come. (Not all rabbis subscribed to this ecumenical view, but even those who did not felt no moral obligation to convert the heathen.) Perhaps (and this is the common explanation) the rabbis saw the growing power of Christianity and decided not to try to compete with it. Outside of rabbinic circles perhaps some Jews still actively attempted to interest gentiles, especially Christians, in Judaism, but the evidence for such activity is minimal.

Conclusion

Throughout the second temple and rabbinic periods the Jews stood in an uneasy relationship with their environment. They learned early on to live under the political dominion of gentile powers and to find a theological justification for this fact, but they always dreamed of their own kingdom. Several times in antiquity the Jews tried to make their dream into reality, but only once with any degree of success. The Maccabees successfully turned a war for religious freedom into a war for political independence, but their rule was of limited duration and mixed success. In the cultural sphere the challenge was much clearer. Hellenistic culture was by its very nature a "melting pot" of ideas and peoples, and some Jews wished to obliterate all the distinctions between themselves and the gentiles among whom they lived. Most Jews, however, tried to find a way to combine the ideas, beliefs, and values of the dominant culture with their own. It was never very easy to define the line that separates the illicit influence which threatens to dilute and destroy Judaism from the licit influence which enriches Judaism and makes it modern. This was the subject of ongoing debate. In the social sphere, the Jews kept themselves apart, prohibiting all marriages with outsiders but allowing gentiles to convert to Judaism. Mirroring this ambiguity was the response of the gentile world. Many gentiles converted to Judaism or became "God-fearers," but others, because of political tensions between the Jews and other elements in their communities, expressed a pointed anti-Judaism.

The challenges mounted by the gentile world in the political, cultural, and social spheres were sufficiently distinct so as to permit varied responses to each. A Jew might, say, be quite accommodating in the political sphere, wholeheartedly supporting the ruling power, but quite unyielding in the cultural or social sphere. Ezra, for example, enjoyed the protection of the Persian king and supported the Persian state in return, but opposed intermarriage. The Maccabees, by contrast, rebelled against the state but did not divorce themselves from Hellenistic culture. Some Jews, the extremists, were consistent. The "extreme Hellenizers" who supported Epiphanes wanted to merge Judaism more fully into the Hellenistic world in all three spheres. The revolutionaries of 66–70 c.e. had as their goals the creation of an independent state, the purification of the land of Israel from all foreign contagion, and the separation of Israel from the gentiles. Most Jews, however, were not so consistent. Their goal was not adherence to principle but the perpetuation of Judaism.

3

The Jewish "Religion": Practices and Beliefs

Introduction: Defining "Religion"

In the eyes of the pagans of antiquity the essence of religion was neither faith nor dogma, but action. Humanity was enjoined by the gods to perform certain acts and to refrain from certain acts, and these commandments and prohibitions (especially the prohibitions) constituted the essence of *religio*. When Greek conquerors wished to benefit their subjects, they guaranteed them the right to observe "the ancestral laws" or "the ancestral constitution"; they had no need to mention "the ancestral beliefs" or "the ancestral faith." This fact does not mean that the ancients had no deeply felt beliefs about the gods, but the paganism of antiquity produced few literary works that delineate either its dogmas or its "theology." If a contemplative person in antiquity sought systematic answers to questions about the nature of the gods and their involvement in human affairs, he would have studied philosophy, not "religion." Many philosophers maintained radical notions about the gods. In the fifth century B.C.E. some sophists argued that the gods did not really exist but were invented by humans in order to promote fear in the masses and thereby maintain social order. This position gained currency among segments of the aristocracy in Hellenistic and Roman times, but the adherents of such views generally were not persecuted or harassed as long as they did not violate religious taboos and as long as they participated in the religious rituals of the state. Radical belief did not make them "heretics" or "irreligious."

These generalizations must be stated at the outset because the pervasive influence of Christianity on our thinking makes us equate "religion" with theology or "faith." This equation is true, perhaps, for Christianity, but is false not only for the paganism but also for the Judaism of antiquity. Both Jews and gentiles recognized that the

Jews denied the gods of the nations and claimed that their God alone was the true Lord of the universe, but for both Jews and gentiles the boundary line between Judaism and paganism was determined more by Jewish observances than by Jewish theology. Josephus defines an apostate as a Jew who "hates the customs of the Jews" or "does not abide by the ancestral customs." He defines a convert to Judaism as a gentile who through circumcision "adopts the ancestral customs of the Jews." These definitions omit the theological tenets of Judaism. When describing conversion to Judaism, Philo at least mentions the fact that the proselyte denies the gods of the gentiles and believes in the one true God, but that is all. For Philo too the essence of conversion is the adoption of the way of life of the Jews.[1] When gentile observers described "Judaism," they generally meant the peculiar practices and distinctive way of life of the Jews, not their theology or philosophy.

Practices, not theology, also determined the boundary lines within the Jewish community. The debates between sectarians and the nascent Christian "orthodoxy" of antiquity centered on theological matters (notably the nature and function of the second person of the Trinity), but the debates among Jewish sects centered for the most part on matters of law (see chapter 5). The Jews of Qumran criticized not the theology of their co-religionists but their way of life, especially their calendar, their purity rules, and their administration of the temple. Many works of the second temple period are devoted to theological or philosophical themes, but none of these works is creedal or dogmatic in character. The library of books assembled by the Essenes of Qumran contains a bewildering variety of theological ideas and eschatological scenarios. Sometimes a single text juxtaposes several different eschatological or messianic theories. Not a single tractate of either the Mishnah or the Talmud is devoted to a "theological" topic. The rabbis have many things to say about God, sin, atonement, the creation of the world, the election of Israel, the covenant, the messiah, the reward of the righteous, the punishment of the wicked, and the resurrection of the dead, but their theological speculations on these topics are presented only in scattered utterances and do not receive that detailed and sustained analysis that characterizes the rabbinic discussions of legal opinions.

Christianity and Islam are creedal religions. The church council of Nicaea (325 C.E.) defined Christian faith thus: "We believe in one God, the Father, almighty, maker of all things visible and invisible; and in one Lord Jesus Christ, the Son of God, begotten from the Father . . . God from God, light from light . . . ; and in the Holy

Spirit."[2] From its inception Islam has expressed its central tenet with the phrase "There is no God but Allah, and Mohammed is his prophet." Each of these statements is a *creed,* a fixed formula which summarizes a religion's essential articles of belief (its *dogmas*) and which is sanctioned by ecclesiastical authority. Creeds serve as an admission test for converts and as a loyalty oath for the faithful. In the Middle Ages, in response to the challenge presented by Christianity and Islam, Maimonides and several other Jewish philosophers formulated creeds for Judaism as well. Those Jews who subscribed to his thirteen principles of belief were, Maimonides said, loyal Jews; those who rejected any one of them were sinners and heretics, hardly deserving the name Jew at all. Defining Judaism in this way is completely foreign to antiquity. Ancient Judaism had no creeds. The Jews of antiquity devoted much energy to theological speculation, and achieved almost unanimous agreement on certain theological principles, but Judaism was not defined as a theology.

A final point. Modern scholars use different methods when describing a religion. Some treat a religion's system of thought, and seek to define the "essence" of a religion or to contrast one religion with another. Others center upon a religion's development and social setting. The former approach emphasizes the ideal, the latter the real; the former yields the theory of a religion, the latter its actual implementation. In this chapter I draw on each of these approaches, the former to give a unified picture of the whole, and the latter to illustrate its development and complexity.

Practices

The practices of Judaism are so numerous and varied that they cannot all be surveyed here. In this section I concentrate on four areas: the worship of God (through sacrifice, prayer, and the study of scripture); the ritual observances; ritual, ethics, and the "yoke" of the law; and "legalism."

The Worship of God

In both the first and the second temple God was worshiped through sacrifices, that is, the slaughter, roasting, and eating of animals. Offerings of grain, fruit, bread, and incense played only an ancillary role. The most important sacrifice was the *Tamid* ("continual offering") which was burnt on the altar every morning and afternoon (Num. 28:1–8). The Tamid was God's daily "food" (Num. 28:2), and the priests did their utmost, even at times of great danger, not to let the offerings lapse. The profanation of the temple by Epiphanes and the destruction of the temple by Titus caused the cessation of the Tamid, a tragic event (Dan. 11:31 and Josephus, *Jewish War* 6.2.1, §94–102). The Tamid, like the special sacrifices offered on the Sabbath and the festivals, was purchased with public monies and was burnt on the altar in the name of the entire nation. Other types of sacrifices, notably the "whole-burnt offering" (usually known by its Greek designation, "holocaust"), the "peace offering," and the "sin offering," were purchased and brought to the temple by individuals, either to seek atonement or to express gratitude to God. (The Passover offering was of a different sort altogether: it was a family or group feast at or near the central shrine.) Since only the priests were allowed to enter the inner precincts of the temple and approach the altar, they alone did the slaughtering and the roasting (and much of the eating). They ministered before the Lord on behalf of the people.

The regulations governing the sacrificial cult are set forth in great detail in Leviticus, Numbers, and the last chapters of the book of Ezekiel. Nowhere, however, does the Hebrew Bible prescribe or regulate the worship of God through prayer. "Prayer" in the technical sense means a request or petition presented to a deity, but I use the term here to include any speech addressed to God that establishes communion between God and man. (Thus prayer includes words of praise and thanksgiving, and, as we shall see, the study of scripture.) The rabbinic term is "the service of God in the heart."[3] Both prayer and sacrifice were "spiritual" experiences, but the former consisted of speech and the latter of the slaughter of animals. The contrast between them goes further. Sacrifices can be offered only at the temple in Jerusalem (Deut. 12), only by the priests, only at set times, and only in certain ways. Prayer can be offered anywhere by anyone at any time and in any way. The contrast between sacrifice and prayer is the contrast between elitism and populism, an idea that I shall develop below, and the contrast between fixed form and free form. But these contrasts did not prevent the two modes of worship from blending together. The process was twofold: prayer gradually entered the temple cult, and the fixity and regularity that characterized the sacrificial system gradually came to characterize prayer as well. I shall briefly survey this twofold process and then summarize the constitutive elements of communal prayer in the last century of the second temple period.

Prayer in the Temple Cult

The Hebrew Bible is filled with prayers to God. In times of distress and happiness Israelite heroes, prophets, kings, and, occasionally, the entire people turned to God in prayer. These prayers are
both public and private, both prose and poetry, both original and
traditional, but they are not obligatory rituals (that is, they are not
"statutory"). They are the spontaneous, even if highly studied,
expressions of reverence for God. Sometimes, especially in cases
of emergency, the Israelites would pray at the temple, but these
prayers were not part of the temple cult. King Solomon prayed that
the temple might serve as a house of prayer for both Israelites and
foreigners, but all the prayers that Solomon mentions are the spontaneous expressions of need or joy (1 Kings 8). Neither Leviticus
nor Numbers nor Deuteronomy nor Ezekiel mentions prayer as an
integral part of the sacrificial cult. The atonement sacrifice for both
the individual (Lev. 5:5 and Num. 5:7) and the community (Lev.
16:21) was accompanied by a confession, and the presentation of
the first fruits at the sanctuary was accompanied by the recitation of
a summary of Israel's sacred history (Deut. 26:1–11), but these are
the only exceptions. The act of sacrifice was silent; neither the priest
nor the worshiper was required to say anything. The cult of the
second temple too was silent. A writer of the second century B.C.E.
admires the remarkable silence that prevailed in the temple as the
priests scurried about performing their sacred tasks (*Aristeas* 92–95).
Neither the Qumran scrolls nor Philo nor Josephus (except, perhaps, *Against Apion* 2.196–197) nor any other work of the second
temple period records that prayer either was or was supposed to be
part of the temple cult. Scholars debate the reliability of the claim
of the Chronicler that the songs of the Levites were an integral part
of the cult even in the time of King David (1 Chron. 25), but no
matter when it was instituted the song of the Levites always remained in the background. The central element of the cult was the
sacred ballet of the priests, not the musical accompaniment of the
Levites.

The best evidence that prayer was part of the ritual of both the
first and the second temple, if not for the priests, then for the laity,
is the book of Psalms. Virtually all the biblical Psalms, even those
that lament personal or national catastrophes or that hail a king at
his coronation, are hymns of praise to God. They range in date from
the period of the monarchy, if not earlier (some of them are Israelite
versions of Canaanite or Egyptian hymns), to that of the Maccabees.
But the fact that they were written down and assembled as a collec-

tion implies—most scholars agree—that they were meant to be re-cited liturgically, and it is most likely that the recitation took place at the temple. Having come to the temple, either with or without a sacrifice, the worshiper would recite either a psalm of joy and thanksgiving or a psalm of woe and lament, whichever was appropri-ate for his situation.

The canonical Psalter represents only a portion of the hymns that were composed and/or recited during the second temple period. A Psalms scroll from Qumran contains several hymns that were not incorporated in the biblical collection. Another Qumran scroll is a collection of hymns *(Hodayot)* which differ in content from those of the canonical Psalter but resemble them greatly in phraseology and form. The pseudepigraphic work *The Psalms of Solomon* is yet another collection of poems heavily indebted to the canonical Psalms. These texts show that the psalmic tradition was still living in late second temple times. Further, numerous works of the period contain hymns and prayers that may well reflect some of the real prayers used by the community in daily life. In sum: three bodies of evidence (the book of Psalms; the hymns written in later second temple times in the style of the canonical Psalms; and the prayers scattered through-out the literature of the second temple period) imply that the recita-tion of prayers was a prominent feature of Jewish piety. It is probable too that these were the prayers or, at least, the sort of prayers which were recited at the temple. That many Jews did pray regularly at the temple is clear from Luke 1:10 ("And the whole multitude of the people were praying outside [the temple] at the hour of incense") and Acts 3:1 ("Now Peter and John were going up to the temple at the hour of prayer, the ninth hour").

None of these texts implies that prayer was part of the temple cult; Jews prayed *at* the temple, not *in* the temple. According to the Mishnah, however, prayer was a statutory part of the daily Tamid sacrifice in two ways. First, the priests, immediately after bringing the sacrifice and before offering the incense, would pray on behalf of the nation and recite scriptural verses (the *Shema*). I shall return to this Mishnaic passage *(Tamid* 5:1) in my discussion of communal worship. Second, the Mishnah claims that "the prophets of old" divided the laity into twenty-four divisions (called "stations") to parallel the twenty-four divisions (called "watches") of the priest-hood. Each week a different division of priests officiated in the temple, and each week a different division of Israelites gathered in the temple and in the villages in order to recite scriptural verses (and, apparently, prayers) while the priests were offering the Tamid. The point of this practice was to make explicit the connection between the people, as represented by their lay delegates, and the sacrifices offered on their behalf by their priestly representatives. The historicity of these two claims is hard to assess, but their basic truth is plausible enough. The institution of daily prayer in the temple cult seems to have been an innovation of the Maccabean or Herodian period (it certainly was not the work of "the prophets of old"!). Prayer, then, did attain a modest role in the temple cult, and the temple was a "house of prayer" (Isa. 56:7).

Prayer and Sacrifice

Perhaps visitors to Jerusalem and the inhabitants of the holy city prayed at the temple, but for other Jews, whether of the land of Israel or of the diaspora, this was not practical. Perhaps on occasion they would go on pilgrimage to the temple in order to pray and sacrifice, but these occasions must have been few and far between, especially for diaspora Jews. Since they were prohibited by Deuteronomy from building temples and offering sacrifices in their own localities, how were they to worship God? Prayer was the obvious answer. Unlike sacrifice prayers could be offered to God anywhere. Individuals could pray in their houses. Daniel 6:11 narrates that its hero, then living in Babylon, "went to his house where he had windows in his upper chamber open toward Jerusalem; and he got down upon his knees three times a day and prayed and gave thanks before his God." The community could pray in the town square, on street corners (Matt. 6:5), or in any place of assembly. By the third century B.C.E. diaspora Jews began to build special "prayer-houses" which they called *proseuchai*. Instead of "prayer-houses" the Jews of the land of Israel built "meeting-houses" which they called *synagōgai*. Whether they prayed regularly in their "meeting-houses," which are not attested before the first century C.E., is not entirely clear. Although prayer figures prominently in the literature of the second temple period, very few texts mention synagogues or locate prayer within them (cf. Matt. 6:5). I shall return to this question in my discussion of the history of the synagogue (chapter 4).

Both in and out of the temple and the synagogue the Jews prayed to God. Prayer was accessible to all and a much more personal experience than sacrifice. In the tradition of the prophets who declared that God wants goodness instead of (or in addition to) the sacrifices, five passages in the Psalms state that prayer is superior (40:7–10; 69:31–32; 51:19) or equal (119:108; 141:2) to the sacrificial cult. The same theme is echoed in various works of the second temple period. The Psalm passages (whose precise dating is uncertain, although all seem to be of the Hellenistic period) are not polemics against the sacrificial cult but pleas to God to recognize the validity of worship that did not include sacrifices. The temple was the site of God's name, the holiest place on earth, and the center of Israelite religion, but its cult was exclusively sacrificial. Pilgrims were instructed not to appear there "empty-handed" (Deut. 16: 16–17). Those who did appear there, for whatever reason, with empty hands apologized to God by asserting that prayer and contrition are the real sacrifices which God desires. The Psalm passages show that prayer, even prayer at the temple, was easily understood to be an equivalent or a substitute for the sacrifices. Sectarian circles, like Qumran and certain segments of Christianity, had a much more hostile stance toward the temple and its rituals, as I shall discuss later (chapter 5).

Perhaps because prayer was seen as a counterpart or equivalent to sacrifice, it gradually absorbed some of the fixity and regularity that characterized the sacrificial cult. The background to this process is the dilemma encountered in many religions: How to stimulate piety and encourage creativity while maintaining order and preventing chaos? Communal prayer requires order and direction, but the close regulation of the texts and times of prayer might stifle the spontaneity that is required if prayer is to be a spiritual experience. Christian monasticism of the fourth and fifth centuries was divided on this issue. Egyptian monasticism reduced the public liturgy to its barest essentials in order to allow the monks to implement Paul's injunction to "pray without ceasing" (1 Thess. 5:17), while Syrian monasticism developed the public liturgy at great length. Jesus felt that short prayer in private was better than long prayer in public (Matt. 6:5–8).

The rabbis keenly felt the same dilemma. Their conclusion was a compromise between their desire for order and their desire for spontaneity. They declared that every Jew must pray twice daily (morning and afternoon), since prayer corresponded to the Tamid sacrifices and was no less obligatory than the Tamid itself. These prayers could be recited privately, but the rabbis felt that they would be more acceptable to God if they were recited in a communal setting. (A third prayer, which was not paralleled by the sacrificial cult, was recommended but not required.) The regularity of the sacrificial system was transferred to prayer. The rabbis also determined the content of the central prayers, fixing their themes and structure. However, in order to encourage individual creativity, the rabbis allowed the worshiper (or prayer leader) to choose the precise language by which to express these themes. As long as certain crucial phrases and formulae were incorporated, the rabbis were content. (It was not until the early Middle Ages that the rabbis standardized the language of virtually all the prayers. The Christian Eucharist underwent a similar development. In the second century the Eucharist had set themes and formulae but a fixed text did not begin to emerge until the third century.) Although the rabbis did not say so, the regulation of the content and structure of the prayers was another step in assimilating prayer to sacrifice. Worship of God had to have a fixed form. Some rabbis were upset and warned that the overregulation of the liturgy would render the prayers perfunctory and devoid of meaning, just as the prophets had centuries earlier criticized the sacrificial cult, but they were the clear minority.

To what extent these rabbinic developments reflect the ideas of the second temple period is very uncertain. Ezra made sure that his penitential prayer coincided with time of the afternoon incense (or Tamid; Ezra 9:4–5), and the same practice is attested in texts of the Maccabean period (Judith 9:1; cf. Dan. 9:21) and the first century c.e. (Luke 1:10 and Acts 3:1). The offering of the Tamid was a time for prayer. Some pious individuals added an evening prayer (Dan. 6:11; cf. Ps. 55:18) to the two that parallel the Tamid. But none of these texts implies that prayer was as obligatory as the sacrifices or that any attempt was made to regulate the communal liturgy. The coordination of prayer with sacrifices reflects the idea that the times ordained by God for sacrifices were propitious for prayer as well. Before the rabbis regulated the content and frequency of the prayers, the editors who canonized the book of Psalms and the various authors of the numerous prayers of the second temple period were already determining and developing liturgical genres, themes, and formulae. But none of these prerabbinic writers mentions the rabbinic idea that every Jew is obligated to pray to God twice a day at specific times, and that his prayers must follow a certain pattern. In second temple times sacrificial worship had fixed form and fixed content. Prayer did not.

In sum, the nature of the statutory prayer in second temple times is unclear. At times of joy and sorrow and on special days of the calendar (Sabbaths and festivals) people prayed to God, and the extant literature gives us an idea of the kinds of prayers they recited. Many Jews prayed every day as well, but we know neither the extent of this practice, nor the content of their prayers, nor the degree to which this worship was regarded as obligatory. The only clear evidence for the existence of statutory prayer is provided by rabbinic tradition.

The Elements of Communal Prayer

The rabbinic statutory prayers derive from two sources: the daily prayers which, according to the Mishnah cited above, the priests offered after slaughtering the Tamid and before burning the incense; and the communal prayers of the proto-rabbinic circles of Palestine in the first century C.E. The identity and popularity of these circles are the subjects of scholarly debate (see chapter 5). If they were the Pharisees, and if the Pharisees were the spiritual leaders of second temple Judaism, their liturgy, together with that of the temple, fairly represents the communal prayer of the majority of the population. If, however, the sphere of influence of the Pharisees (or whoever constituted the proto-rabbinic circles) was more limited, their liturgy cannot claim to represent the "norm." Whether or not they represent the liturgy of the population as a whole, the earliest rabbinic prayers merit attention here because their roots reach back into the second temple period. I shall survey the major elements of the statutory liturgy as outlined in the Mishnah (*Tamid* 5:1): (a) the recitation of the Ten Commandments and the *Shema;* (b) praise of God; and (c) petitions to God. Finally I shall describe (d) the public study of scripture.

a. *The recitation of scripture.* The centerpiece of the priestly prayer in the temple was the recitation of the Ten Commandments (Ex. 20:2–14 or Deut. 5:6–18) and the *Shema.* The *Shema* consists of three paragraphs (Deut. 6:4–9; 11:13–21; and Num. 15:37–41) and draws its name from the opening Hebrew word of the first of them: "Hear *(Shema),* O Israel: The Lord our God, the Lord is one." Although neither the Ten Commandments nor the *Shema* is a "prayer" (each is a series of commands and exhortations from God), they were incorporated in the liturgy because they represent some of the core ideas and commandments of Judaism. The importance of the Ten Commandments and the *Shema* is confirmed by their inclusion in many of the phylacteries found at Qumran (see below) and by their appearance together on a lone papyrus written in Egypt in the third or second century B.C.E. In fact, one teacher in the first century C.E. stated that the first two verses of the *Shema* constitute the "greatest commandment" (Mark 12:29–30). Josephus remarks that Jews recite the *Shema* twice daily "in order to thank God for his bounteous gifts" (*Jewish Antiquities* 4.7.13, §212). In the rabbinic synagogue the Ten Commandments were removed from the liturgy, because heretics argued that only those ten were revealed by God. The *Shema*, however, remained (and remains) one of the essential parts of the service. The theological import of the *Shema* is discussed at some length below.

b. *Praise of God.* The most common element in Jewish prayer is praise. In the temple the recitation of the Ten Commandments and the *Shema* was preceded and followed by benedictions (or blessings, in Hebrew *berakhot;* sing. *berakha*). Praise of the deity is universal, but benedictions are a quintessentially Jewish mode of worship which was adopted by Christianity (see the *Benedictus*, Luke 1:68–79; cf. 2 Cor. 1:3; Eph. 1:3; 1 Peter 1:3) and Islam. The worshiper proclaims *barukh attah adonai*, "Blessed (or, perhaps more accurately: praised) are you, O Lord." Various figures in the Hebrew Bible, beginning with Jethro (Ex. 18:10), proclaim that the God of Israel is blessed, and two texts written in the early part of the second temple period employ the phrase, as the rabbis would later do, in the second person (1 Chron. 29:10 and Ps. 119:12). The familiarity of this formula cannot mask its peculiarity, however, for how can humanity bless God or pronounce God blessed? The answer to this question is not clear. In spite of the obscurity of its theological premise, the benediction pattern was popular in the hymns *(Hodayot)* of Qumran and triumphed over all others in the rabbinic prayer book. Although the *berakha* is a formula of praise, it is used by the rabbis not only to praise God or declare his attributes (for example, "Blessed are you, O Lord, the holy God") but also to thank God (for example, "Blessed are you, O Lord, king of the universe, who brings forth bread from the earth," a benediction which thanks God for food) and to petition him (for example, "Blessed are you, O Lord, the redeemer of Israel," which concludes a request for the redemption of Israel). According to the Mishnah, then, the Ten Commandments and the *Shema* were accompanied by "benedictions." It is most unfortunate that the Mishnah does not present their text. The rabbinic prayer book still uses benedictions to introduce and conclude the *Shema*.

Praise of God was not restricted to benedictions. The Psalter and the literature of the second temple period are filled with psalms and hymns of many types. A special kind of hymn is the *Qedushah* (Sanctification; literally, "Holiness"), the antiphonal recitation of Isaiah 6:3. According to Isaiah, when the angels behold God seated on his heavenly throne they sing before him "Holy, holy, holy is the Lord of Hosts." By inserting the *Qedushah* into their own prayers, the Jews tried to imitate the angels, perhaps even to join them. While the earliest direct evidence for the liturgical usage of Isaiah 6:3 stems from the second century C.E., indirect evidence is provided by a passage in the book of *Enoch* (*1 Enoch* 39:12) and by several Qumran scrolls. The Jews of Qumran describe the hymns recited by the angels on various days of the year; armed with this knowledge, the members of the group themselves praised the Lord at the proper times and in the proper fashion by joining their voices to those of the angelic chorus. Probably under mystic influence, the *Qedushah* became very popular in rabbinic times and was incorporated in the prayers in several places. Under the Latin title *Sanctus* it also entered the Christian liturgy.

c. *Petitions:* The main petitionary prayer of the rabbis of the second century is the *Shemoneh 'esreh,* a series of petitions called the "Eighteen Benedictions."[4] The first three benedictions form an introduction, the last three a conclusion, while the intervening ones form the body of the prayer. Here, for example, are the first three petitions from this central section (I present the text from the standard prayer book):

> You graciously give humanity knowledge and teach mortals understanding. Grant us knowledge, understanding and insight. Blessed are you, O Lord, gracious giver of knowledge.
>
> Return us, our Father, to your Torah; draw us near, our King, to your worship; cause us to return to you in perfect repentance. Blessed are you, O Lord, who are pleased with repentance.
>
> Forgive us, our Father, for we have sinned; pardon us, our King, for we have transgressed; for you are one who pardons and forgives. Blessed are you, O Lord, who are gracious and ever forgiving.

First humanity prays for knowledge of God; the knowledge of God leads to a cognizance of sin and the desire for repentance; the desire for repentance in turn leads to the plea for forgiveness. These opening petitions for knowledge, repentance, and forgiveness, like all the other petitions of the Eighteen Benedictions, are couched in the first person plural (the petitioner says "us," not "me"), and conclude with the formula "Blessed are you, O Lord."

The history of this prayer is immensely complicated, but its basic contours were established no later than the second century C.E. and its nucleus certainly derives from the latter part of second temple times. It bears obvious similarities to the "Lord's Prayer" (Matt. 6:9–13 and Luke 11:2–4). After reciting the Ten Commandments and the *Shema*, the priests in the temple prayed that the sacrifices should find favor before God, and this petition became part of the

Eighteen Benedictions. (After the destruction of the temple the petition was changed from a prayer for the acceptability of the sacrificial cult to a prayer for its restoration.) One scholar has argued that the petitions for health, prosperity, and peace, from the central portion of the Eighteen Benedictions, constituted the "Civic prayer of Jerusalem," which was offered by the people in good Hellenistic fashion on behalf of the security and welfare of the capital city. The Hebrew text of Ben Sira, who flourished about 200 B.C.E., incorporates a hymn that seems to be an early version of many of the benedictions (Ben Sira 51:12a; the hymn is omitted by the Greek and Syriac versions). In rabbinic times the prayer was still in flux. Rabban Gamaliel (about 90 or 100 C.E.) edited a benediction asking God to frustrate the heretics (see chapter 7). The actual wording of the petitions was not established for centuries. By the time the process was over the Eighteen Benedictions actually contained nineteen benedictions!

d. *Scriptural study:* Priestly prayer in the temple featured the *recitation* of the Ten Commandments and the *Shema;* communal prayer outside the temple also included the *study* of scripture, notably the Torah. This practice is based on the idea that God can be worshiped through the study of his revealed word.

In the first two paragraphs of the *Shema* (and elsewhere) God commands the Israelites to study the law constantly so that they will know how to find favor in his eyes. Study of the Torah is here conceived as a means to an end, since its purpose is to teach which actions are to be avoided and which to be pursued. Gradually, however, Torah study became an end in itself. The author of Psalm 119 can imagine no greater joy than meditating on the words of the Lord. "Oh, how I love your instruction *(Torah)*! It is my meditation all the day. . . . With open mouth I pant, because I long for your commandments" (Ps. 119:97 and 131). Ben Sira (39:1) extols the one who "devotes himself to the study of the law of the Most High" and "[seeks out] the wisdom of the ancients." This is a new type of piety whose origins are not clear. Perhaps it derives from the tradition that enjoins the constant study and pursuit of "Wisdom," here equated with Torah. Perhaps it emerged under Hellenistic influence, reflecting the Socratic view that the soul is ennobled and made virtuous through the acquisition of knowledge. In any case, this idea had a profound influence on the Judaism of the second temple and rabbinic periods. Its ultimate expression is the ideal of the sage who meditates on the words of the Lord day and night, even those words which have no practical application. It is the basis of all rabbinic piety.

The idea was implemented in the communal liturgy. Josephus and Philo boast that all Jews are learned in the law because Moses, unlike other legislators, ordained the regular study of his statutes. According to rabbinic tradition, too, the public reading of a section of the Torah every Sabbath was a custom introduced by Moses. The basis of these claims is the Deuteronomic ordinance that the Torah be read publicly at the central shrine (Deut. 31:10–13), but while Deuteronomy has the Torah read every seven years, by the end of the second temple period sections of the Torah were read publicly in synagogues every week. In rabbinic times the sequential reading of the Torah was practiced in two different ways. In Babylonia the Torah was divided into 54 sections and the entire Torah was read through every year. In the land of Israel the Torah was subdivided into more numerous sections and the cycle of readings was completed every three or three and a half years. The cycle of readings in first-century Palestine (if indeed there was a cycle) is unknown to us.

At public services the Torah was not only read, it was also *explained* and *interpreted.* The model for this activity was Ezra (Neh. 8:8). The highlight of the Sabbath gatherings of the Therapeutae and the Essenes was (according to Philo) a sermon on the allegorical meaning of the Law. Jesus taught in the synagogues of Galilee; Paul, in the synagogues of Asia Minor. In first-century Jerusalem, one Theodotus erected a synagogue "for the reading of the law and the teaching of the commandments." For the benefit of those who did not know sufficient Hebrew the text was translated into the vernacular, Aramaic in Babylonia and parts of Palestine, Greek in the Greco-Roman diaspora and parts of Palestine. Several different ancient Greek and Aramaic translations are extant (see chapter 6). In addition to, or instead of, the translation, synagogue services featured the sermon, the explication of the meaning of the sacred texts. The combination of communal prayer and scriptural study made synagogue services unique in the ancient world.

Ritual Observances

The Torah contains many regulations that govern the daily behavior of the Israelite. An Israelite must put fringes on his clothing, put a railing around the roof of his home, abstain from certain foods, refrain from working on the seventh day of the week, and so on. The purpose of all these rituals was to ensure that the Israelite would always be mindful of God and obedient to his will. In order to better achieve this objective the Jews of the second temple period developed new rituals, broadened the application of many of the laws of the Torah, and in general intensified the life of service to God. Daily prayer and regular Torah study are two of the most important innovations. The injunction of the *Shema* that the Israelites were to place the words of God upon their heart, hand, forehead, and doorpost (Deut. 6:6–9), clearly a metaphorical demand for constant meditation upon God's commandments, was, by the second century B.C.E., interpreted literally and gave rise to the custom of wearing *tefillin,* or phylacteries (Matt. 23:5), and affixing *mezuzot* to the doorposts. Each of these is a specially shaped capsule that contains a copy of the *Shema* and other excerpts from the Torah, and each is a physical and ritualized expression of the desire to maintain constant awareness of God's presence. Many phylacteries were found at Qumran. The laws governing the Sabbath, diet, and purity were greatly expanded. New prohibitions were added to those provided by the Torah, new rituals were invented, and new meanings were attached to the observance of the rituals and prohibitions. For the pagans of the Greco-Roman world the most characteristic features of Judaism were, aside from circumcision, the observance of the Sabbath and the abstention from certain foods (notably pork). The stringent observance and idiosyncratic interpretation of the purity laws assumed a particularly important place in the definition of "sectarian" groups (see chapter 5).

The goal of these innovations was threefold: (a) to ensure that every moment of a Jew's life was spent in service to God; (b) to bring the Jew into contact with the sacred; and (c) to democratize religion. The first goal is shared by the piety of the Torah and the piety of the second temple period, but the second is a development and the third is a radical transformation of the legacy of the Torah.

The Holiness code enjoins upon the Israelites to "be holy, because I the Lord your God am holy" (Lev. 19:1). In the Torah there is only one place of holiness, the central shrine, where the divine presence dwells. According to the Torah God also dwells among the people in the "camp," but this conception is adduced in legal contexts only to justify the prohibition of certain acts lest they pollute the camp and cause God to withdraw his presence (for example, Num. 5:1–4 and Deut. 23:10–15). Prophetic inspiration was supposed to be restricted to the central shrine, not the "camp" (Num. 11:24–29). Like the Israelites of the pre-exilic period, the Jews of the second temple period did not try to determine whether the divine presence was to be found in the temple, among the people of Israel, or, indeed, throughout the world. These conceptions were mutually contradictory but simultaneously true (see the second part of this chapter). But one of the hallmarks of Judaism, in contrast to Israelite religion, is the transferral of sanctity from the temple to areas outside of it, from the priests to the laity, and from the temple cult to actions of daily life. Many sectarian groups argued that the purity laws applied outside the temple as well as inside it, and that the food on the table was to be considered as holy as meat on the altar. Many groups emphasized the importance of washings and immersions ("baptisms"). And for the broader reaches of the population the worship of God through prayer and Torah study brought a measure of sanctity and communion with God that the Torah never envisioned.

As long as the temple, the sacrificial cult, and the priesthood remained the central, if not the only, religious institutions, Judaism remained a religion that allowed the individual little role. The development of the synagogue meant that the temple, for all its uniqueness, was no longer the only place where people could communicate with God. The development of prayer and Torah study meant that the sacrificial cult was no longer the only means for reaching God. The emergence of scribes and other sages meant that the priests no longer had a monopoly on religious truth. The synagogue is a lay institution, prayer and Torah study are activities open to all, and the scribe is but a learned layperson. These developments, and various theological innovations to be discussed in the second part of this chapter, show that during the second temple period Judaism was democratized. It was much more concerned with the piety and fate of the individual Jew than the religion of pre-exilic Israel had been with the individual Israelite.

Even if the democratization of religion and the sanctification of life outside the temple reached their apogee in the piety of various sectarian groups in second temple times and of the rabbis after 70 c.e., they fairly characterize nonsectarian and nonrabbinic Judaism as well, in both the land of Israel and the diaspora. The earliest attestation of phylacteries and *mezuzot* is the *Letter of Aristeas,* a product of Alexandrian Judaism, written in Greek, and adhering to allegorical exegesis. That the life of a loyal Jew is a constant spiritual quest marked by the contemplation of scripture and the observance of the commandments is as true for Philo as for the rabbis. In sum: Judaism became a religious system that sanctified the life of each individual through the constant observance of the commandments of God. This system was incumbent not only on the religious elites but upon all (male) Jews equally.

Ritual, Ethics, and the "Yoke" of the Law

The legal portions of the Hebrew Bible are not familiar with the distinction between ritual and ethics, or the distinction between those rules which are peculiarly Israelite (or Jewish) and those which are followed by all civilized peoples. The prohibitions of idolatry and the worship of other gods are no less part of the Ten Commandments than are the prohibitions of murder and theft. The Holiness Code (Lev. 19) imagines that the quest for holiness includes the proper observance of the Sabbath and the sacrificial cult as well as helping the poor and loving one's neighbor as oneself. When they paraphrase the laws of the Torah, Philo, Josephus, and the *Temple Scroll* (from Qumran) depart from the order of the original, but none of them distinguishes "ritual" from "ethics" or implies that the one is more important than the other.

The wisdom literature of the Hebrew Bible has a different perspective. It is universalist in outlook and cosmopolitan in spirit, so that Job, Proverbs, and Ecclesiastes ignore all the Israelite rituals and focus instead on virtues that were respected by all peoples (see especially the code of a gentleman, Job 29–31). In this tradition a Greek poem written by a Jew in the first century B.C.E. (?) emphasizes the universal aspects of Jewish piety (ethics, proper sexual conduct, morality, etc.) and ignores all the "ritual" laws (Sabbath, food laws, etc.).[5] Most of the wisdom literature of the later second temple period muted the universalism of the genre by "Judaizing" it. Ben Sira (24) argued that true wisdom was to be sought only in Israel and only in the law of Moses. But even Ben Sira devoted most of his work to values shared universally. Similarly, the *Testaments of the Twelve Patriarchs* (probably second century B.C.E., although many scholars have argued that large portions of it are of Christian origin) preaches loyalty to the Torah but, influenced by the wisdom tradition, singles out for special mention only those virtues which have universal appeal (honesty, integrity, generosity, industry, temperance, etc.). Tobit often went to Jerusalem for the feasts and carefully observed the food laws (Tobit 1:5–12), but in his deathbed instructions to his son (4:5–21) he ignores all the ritual laws. He emphasizes the importance of charity and the evil of immorality, but fails to mention all the commandments which he had observed throughout his life. This emphasis on ethics and universal virtues is the legacy of the wisdom tradition.

This wisdom tradition probably forms the background to the several attempts that were made to identify the "most important" commandments. Jesus answered that the most important commandments were the love of God and the love of one's neighbor (Matt. 22:34–40). A very similar position was attributed by rabbinic tradition to Hillel, a proto-rabbinic figure of the late first century B.C.E. The church council described in Acts 15 decreed that gentile converts to Christianity need obey only three (or four) of the commandments: to abstain from meat sacrificed to idols, from illicit sexual relations, (from strangled things,) and from blood. This ruling is strikingly similar (if we omit "strangled things" and interpret "blood" to mean "bloodshed" rather than "the eating of blood") to the rabbinic law, formulated apparently during the Bar Kokhba period, which ordered a Jew to accept martyrdom if asked to violate the prohibitions of murder, idolatry, or fornication (Babylonian Talmud *Sanhedrin* 74a).

Here then is evidence that some Jews were trying to identify the core of Judaism, the indispensable kernel, what would have been called in the nineteenth century "the essence of Judaism." Some scholars, especially Christian scholars of the late nineteenth and early twentieth centuries, used this evidence to prove that some Jews found "the yoke of the law" hard to bear (cf. Acts 15:10), and that Paul (and Jesus?) was not the only Jew in the first century who wished to lighten it. The Christian critique of "the law" was interpreted as the fulfillment of the prophetic critique of the law. The prophets argued that God desired righteousness and ethics, not sacrifices; their heirs in the first century of our era were arguing the same thing: God desires righteousness and ethics (and faith), not the ritual laws.

This is not the place for a discussion either of the prophets' polemic against the sacrificial cult or of the sources of Paul's polemic against circumcision and the law. However, the unlikelihood of this "Christian" interpretation of the wisdom tradition and of the attempts to identify the most important commandments, has been noted by many scholars, both Jewish and Christian. (In recent scholarship this earlier interpretation has been abandoned entirely.) Ben Sira (34:18–35:11) affirms the validity of the sacrificial cult even while he criticizes the insincerity and corruption of its practitioners. Following the wisdom tradition the Mishnaic tractate *Chapters* [or: *Ethics*] *of the Fathers* virtually ignores all the ritual laws, and it is most unlikely that the editor of the tractate was arguing that the ritual laws (including the Sabbath, food laws, festivals, etc.) were less important than spirituality and ethics. The Jewish law, then, contained more than just ritual. Some teachers emphasized the "ethical" element more than others did, but all believed that the command to love one's neighbor was as much a part of the Torah as the command to love God through the observance of the rituals.

"Legalism"

Another issue entirely, however, is the degree of success with which the ideology of democratization and sanctification penetrated the broad reaches of Jewish society. As usual, our sources are inadequate for an accurate portrayal of Judaism as actually lived by the Jews of antiquity. Some Jews undoubtedly did regard the ritual observances as burdensome. Of these some became apostates, others simply ignored some or all of the commandments, while others protested that the Torah did not really demand the literal observance of the ritual laws (see the discussion of apostasy and assimilation above in chapter 2). Many Jews, perhaps the majority of the population, lacked the time and education to implement the noble ideals of the religious elite. They were more interested in ensuring good health and good harvests than in communion with God or constant meditation on the words of the Torah. These Jews might employ "magic," and might resort to religious virtuosi who were not part of the recognized elite. Jesus spent much of his time healing the sick and performing miracles. In fact, many Jews in the first centuries of our era had a deserved reputation in the magical arts. Even in rabbinic times, as I shall discuss in chapter 7, many Jews had no patience for the rabbinic way of life. They respected the rabbis as "holy men" and miracle workers, but were not dedicated to the rabbis' way of Torah.

And then there were Jews who integrated the new piety into their lives through the observance of the myriad rituals and observances, but did not seek to sanctify their lives thereby. They ignored the meaning and purpose of the entire regimen, the sanctification of life and the direction of one's thoughts to God and to God's revealed truth. These are the Jews whose "legalism," that is, reliance upon the mere external observance of the rituals to ensure them favor in God's eyes, has loomed so large in Christian polemics against Judaism. Such people are to be found in all religious communities (including Christian, as the sermons of the church fathers abundantly attest) in all ages, and we may assume that such Jews existed in ancient times, even if we disbelieve the jaundiced portrayal of the Pharisees in the Gospels. Jesus was not the only preacher to attack the hypocrisy and ostentatiousness of the self-righteous (cf. *Psalms of Solomon* 4, a text often attributed to a Pharisaic teacher!). Whether Jewish piety lends itself more readily than the Christian to a focus on external observances rather than inner spirituality is a question that a historian cannot answer. The Jewish ideal was the democratization of religion and the sanctification of life, and this ideal deserves a sympathetic hearing even from those who do not practice it.

Beliefs

Although ancient Judaism eschewed dogmas and creeds, its liturgy contains the closest approximation to a "normative" or "official" theology. As I discussed above, the temple prayer of the priests featured the recitation of the three paragraphs of the *Shema*. The first paragraph (Deut. 6:4–9) commands the Israelites to love God and meditate on his words constantly. The theme of this paragraph is the recognition of the suzerainty of God, what the Mishnah calls "the acceptance of the yoke of the kingdom of heaven." In the second paragraph (Deut. 11:13–21) the Israelites are warned that they will suffer drought and famine if they sin, but will enjoy prosperity if they observe God's word. The theme of this paragraph is the recognition of God's justice, what the Mishnah calls "the acceptance of the yoke of the commandments" (Mishnah *Berakhot* 2:2). The third paragraph (Num. 15:37–41) details the obligation of placing special fringes on one's clothing. The theme of this paragraph might appear to be the same as that of the first, the obligation to meditate constantly on God's commandments, but the Mishnah emphasizes instead the last verse of the paragraph ("I am the Lord your God, who brought you out of the land of Egypt, to be your God") and gives as its theme the exodus from Egypt, in other words, redemption (Mishnah *Berakhot* 1:5).

Thus, according to the Mishnah, the three themes of the *Shema* are the Kingship of God, Reward and Punishment, and Redemption. It is impossible to know whether the Mishnah's interpretation accurately reflects either the original meaning of the three scriptural paragraphs or the original intent of the people who first arranged them to constitute a unified prayer. However, the *Shema*, by virtue of its central place in the liturgy, serves well as a convenient outline of Jewish beliefs, much as the Ten Commandments served Philo and some medieval Jewish philosophers as a convenient summary of the laws of the Torah.

Kingship of God

The first line of the *Shema* declares that God is "one." In the pre-exilic period the Israelites had diverse views of God's oneness.

Some passages of the Hebrew Bible ascribe to God absolute uniqueness, for example, "The Lord is God in heaven above and on the
earth beneath; there is no other" (Deut. 4:39), while other passages
(especially in poetry) ascribe to God only a relative superiority, for
example, "Who is like you, O Lord, among the gods?" (Ex. 15:11).
Concerning the extent of God's power there is a similar inner biblical tension. Some passages seem to say that the power and attention
of the God of Israel are directed solely toward the people of Israel,
while others state explicitly that the God of Israel is the God of the
entire world and of all peoples. Contrast, for example, "Will you
[the Ammonites and Moabites] not possess what Chemosh your god
gives you to possess? And all that the Lord our God has dispos-
sessed before us, we will possess" (Judg. 11:24, part of a letter of
Jephthah to the king of the Ammonites) with "It is I who by my great
power and my outstretched arm have made the earth, with the men
and the animals that are on the earth, and I give it to whomever
seems right to me" (Jer. 27:5, explaining that Nebuchadnezzar is
destined to rule a large empire).

The Hebrew Bible also has a vitriolic and extensive polemic
against Israelite worship of any god other than the God of Israel,
a polemic that regularly equates "idol worship" with "the worship
of foreign gods," but the historical narratives show that many
Israelites of both the northern and southern kingdoms actively worshiped Baal and other gods alongside the God of Israel. The usual
scholarly explanation of these facts is to posit a development between the early faith of Israel and the later beliefs introduced by the
prophets. At first the Israelites believed that their God was merely
the God of their nation, mightier than the other gods but not mate-
rially different from them. The prophets, however, taught that the
God of Israel was the Lord of the entire universe who controls the
destiny of all peoples, and that the Israelites must worship this one
God alone.

By the sixth century B.C.E. the prophetic view was clearly triumphant. At the very beginning of the second temple period Second
Isaiah hailed the God of Israel as the creator of the world and
mocked the gods of wood and stone as things of nought. God's
universal power was also highlighted in the epithet that was widely
used in the Persian period, "the God of the Heavens" (for example,
Jonah 1:9 and Ezra 1:2). That God is the omnipotent, omniscient
creator of the universe, exalted above all his creatures, ruling in
majestic splendor, and ultimately beyond human ken, is a common
motif in the literature of the second temple and rabbinic periods.
Like the monarchs of Persia and the Hellenistic empires who ruled

over the Jews, God too was the all-powerful Lord of an enormous empire. Whether the product of internal development or external influence, this conception of God brought with it many ambiguities and tensions. Theology does not demand consistency, and the Jews of the second temple period were able to affirm the truth of conflicting doctrines about God. I shall examine briefly the four major tensions in the new conception of God. They are universalism versus particularism; monotheism versus polytheism; immanence versus transcendence; the God of the philosophers versus the God of the Bible.

Universalism vs. Particularism

God is both the Lord of all, the supreme deity, and also the national God of Israel, who chose Israel from among all the nations and revealed his Torah to it alone. The tension between these conceptions is as evident in the Hebrew Bible (compare Gen. 1–11 with Gen. 12ff.) as in the literature of the second temple and rabbinic periods. Just as some texts emphasize universal ethical norms while others emphasize the Jewish ritual laws (see above), similarly some texts, especially apocalypses attributed to figures who lived before God's selection of Abraham (for example, Enoch), emphasize God's universal dominion and deemphasize or omit the covenant with Israel, while others do the reverse. Some texts, written in the face of disaster (for example, 4 Ezra, a response to the destruction of Jerusalem in 70 C.E.), lament that God, the Lord of the universe, has bestowed power upon the gentiles, but that God, the Lord of Israel, has not protected his people (see below). Christianity resolved the tension between these conceptions by affirming the universality of God and denying all doctrines that bound God to a particular nation or land. For most Jews, however, this was not a viable option. In its rabbinic interpretation the *Shema* proclaims the existence of the one God who is king of the universe as well as king of the Jews.

Monotheism vs. Polytheism

By Hellenistic times the phrase *Heis Theos*, "God is One!" (or: "There is one God!") became a Jewish slogan, but monotheism is an ambiguous concept. Clearly it means the belief in one supreme God, but that belief may or may not involve a denial of the existence of other supernatural beings. The Jewish monotheism of antiquity did not exclude belief in many and diverse supernatural beings aside from God. Precisely because the deity had grown so in power and prestige, a need was felt during second temple times to populate the intermediate world with beings of all sorts, notably angels.

The Hebrew Bible occasionally refers to angels, the supernatural messengers that God uses on an ad hoc basis for special purposes (for example, Gen. 22:15 and Ex. 23:20). During the second temple period the role of angels increased dramatically in Jewish theology. A mighty potentate requires numerous attendants, and God's heavenly palace was equipped with angels far more numerous and far more differentiated in function and title than were envisioned in Isaiah 6 and Ezekiel 1. The palace was located in the seventh (or eighth) heaven, each heaven being guarded by myriads of angels. Each of the nations in God's cosmic empire had its own angelic supervisor called a "prince"; Michael was the prince of Israel who stood up for his people in times of distress (Dan. 10:13, 21; 12:1). At the end of time God would be aided by his angelic hosts in the final battle against the forces of darkness and evil. Thus the angels fulfilled various tasks: they guarded the heavenly palace, sang hymns of praise to their creator, and served in the army of the God of Hosts; they functioned as God's intermediaries in his communication with humans, notably as the sources for the revelations experienced by apocalyptic visionaries; and they also functioned as humanity's intermediaries in its communication with God, by bringing people's prayers before God and interceding with him on their behalf.

For Philo and other Greek-speaking Jews the *Logos*, God's "speech" or "reason" (often mistranslated "Word"), more than the angels, served to mediate between God and the world. Logos has a wide variety of meanings, but the most common one is that manifestation of God which comes into contact with the material world and which is perceptible by humans. God himself is far removed from this world, so that it is only through his "speech" that we know him and through his "speech" that he created the universe which we perceive with our senses. Philo is not clear whether the Logos is merely an "aspect" (or attribute) of God, or whether it is a "being" in its own right (cf. John 1:1). Whereas angels, says Philo, are man's intermediaries with God, the Logos is God's intermediary with man.

The Logos of Philo resembles the figure of Wisdom in Proverbs 8. (Philo explicitly connects the two.) Wisdom declares (8:22), "The Lord created [or: acquired] me at the beginning of his work," and describes how she was at God's side during the creation of the world (8:30): "Then I was beside him, like a master workman [the meaning of the Hebrew is obscure]; and I was daily his delight, rejoicing before him always." Like the Logos, Wisdom assists God during the act of creation (or should we say that God's Wisdom was manifested in the creation?). Because of its obscurities and ambiguities, the passage does not make clear whether Wisdom is merely an attribute of God or whether she is a being endowed with some measure of autonomy and independence. Philo identified Wisdom with the Logos. John and other Christians identified Wisdom with the Logos and the Logos with Christ. The rabbis of the third and fourth centuries identified Wisdom with Torah (cf. Ben Sira 24) and argued that God created the world by consulting the Torah. Many of the Gnostic creation myths feature the figure of *Sophia* (Greek for Wisdom) as one of the chief supernatural beings through whom the world was created. Thus the personified figure of Wisdom was another power that intermediated between God and the world, especially at the creation.

In addition to the angels, the Logos, and Wisdom, who were either morally good or morally neutral, the intermediate world also consisted of wicked angels and malevolent spirits (or demons). In the Hebrew Bible the verb *stn* ("to oppose," "to accuse," or "to trouble") and its derivative nouns refer either to humans (for example, 1 Kings 11:14, 23, 25) or to angels (for example, Num. 22:22, 32) who cause someone mischief. In the early second temple period the term "the accuser" *(ha satan)* began to refer to a member of the heavenly court who, while still subservient to God, was able to exercise some initiative on his own (Job 1–2; Zech. 3:1–2). "Satan" was not yet a proper name (many translations of 1 Chron. 21:1 read "Satan," but a more likely rendering of the word is "a troublemaker"). The third and second centuries B.C.E., however, witnessed the emergence of Satan as a clearly defined being. Sometimes called Mastema or Belial or various other names, he was the supernatural leader of the forces of evil. He was an enemy both of God and of the righteous, and was blamed for most of the maladies that befall humanity. Protection from these malevolent forces could be obtained through prayer and piety, or through amulets and spells (cf. Tobit). It was widely believed that illnesses were the symptom of possession by one of these hostile powers, and so medical care often took the form of exorcisms, the "abjuring" or "casting away" of the demonic force.

The impulse to believe that myriads of angels serve the Lord both in this world and in the world above was apparently the belief in God's cosmic majesty. The more exalted God became, the more he required retainers to sing his glory and intermediaries to communicate with the world. The impulse to believe that myriads of demons and spirits delight in attacking humanity was apparently the desire to explain the origins of evil in the universe. If God is good and if the world that God created is good (Gen. 1), whence evil? I shall return to this point in my discussion of theodicy (see below).

One God, then, but many supernatural beings and powers. Is this not a thinly disguised polytheism masquerading as monotheism? For the rabbis of the Talmud, at least, the distinction is reasonably clear. God created the universe, including all its supernatural beings (Genesis 1 neglected to mention that the angels were created by God, but the gap was filled by rabbinic lore, as it had been by *Jubilees* 2:2), and only God is endowed with the will and ability to act independently. Angels only perform the will of their creator. The rabbis were prepared to deduce from the enigmatic plural of Genesis 1:26 ("Let *us* make man in our image") that the angels assisted God in the creation of Adam, but their monotheism was compromised not by the belief in the existence of supernatural powers but by the attribution of independence to them. Consequently, it was forbidden to pray to any being other than God, since such imprecation would imply that a being other than God was an independent power. Monotheism demanded *monolatry*, the worship of only one God from among many supernatural beings. So far the rabbinic theory. In practice the rabbis were less certain that the demons lacked the ability to act independently, but while defense against demons was permissible, the use of demons was not. (Following Deut. 18:9–14 the rabbis did not doubt either the existence of spirits or the efficacy of witchcraft.) Any prayer directed to any supernatural being other than God, whether that being was allied with God or opposed to him, violated monotheism. It was, at best, the heresy of belief in two heavenly powers. At worst it was paganism.

This was the system worked out by the rabbis of the third and fourth centuries. Many of their Jewish contemporaries, however, ignored the distinctions that the rabbis wrought so finely. They addressed prayers to angels, hailing their power and beseeching them to grant their requests. The rabbis themselves had a great deal of trouble distinguishing the licit use of angels and demons from the illicit.

The rabbinic system mirrors the theology of some strands of second temple Judaism. The monotheism ascribed by Josephus to Abraham closely resembles the rabbinic view: Abraham "was the first to boldly declare that God, the creator of the universe, is one, and that, if any other being contributed anything to man's welfare, each did so by his command and not in virtue of its own inherent power" (*Jewish Antiquities* 1.7.1, §155). The cult of the temple, like the cult of the rabbinic synagogue, recognized God alone and ignored all other supernatural beings. But in other circles angels and, especially, demons were given some measure of independent power. Even if Satan and his hosts were created by God (cf. Col. 1:16), they act as enemies of God and as the opponents of his will. The angelic "archons" who control this world and try to prevent human happiness and salvation also are not easily reconciled with a monotheistic worldview. Demonology and magic flourished. Philo too, in a few passages, seems to describe the Logos and God's "powers" not merely as extensions of God but as if they were independent beings. Many literary works of the period emphasize that Judaism is superior to paganism because belief in the One is superior to belief in the many, but the contrast was not always as neat and simple as this anti-pagan rhetoric suggests. And even within pagan circles, many philosophers would agree with the rabbinic analysis of the relationship between the chief God and his subordinates. These philosophers denied the Jewish doctrines of creation, revelation, and the election of Israel, but their monotheism was very close to that of the Jews.

Jewish monotheism in antiquity is not easily defined. The very conception that highlighted God's uniqueness and emphasized his sovereignty, in paradoxical fashion almost necessitated the belief in angels and other intermediary forces. Pre-modern Judaism never fully resolved this tension. In the Middle Ages Maimonides defined monotheism to be the belief in only one supernatural being. Demons and spirits are mere figments of the imagination; angels, the Logos, and the divine powers are mere "attributes" of God which have no existence whatever independent of the deity. But this radical monotheism of Maimonides was rare even in the Middle Ages, and is unattested in antiquity. Christianity resolved this tension by arguing that the Monad was plural, that the One consisted of Three, one of whom was the chief intermediary between God and the world. This was an option which most Jews were not prepared to accept.

Immanence vs. Transcendence

Does God dwell "in" the world or far above it? The answer, of course, is both. At the dedication of the first temple Solomon declared, "But will God indeed dwell on the earth? Behold, heaven and the highest heaven cannot contain you; how much less this house which I have built!" (1 Kings 8:27). Indeed many biblical passages say that the occupant of the temple was not God but God's "Name" (Deut. 12) or "Glory" (1 Kings 8:11). The developments described in the previous paragraphs testify to the growth of God's transcendence. The further God was removed from the world, the more the "fullness" in between (called the *plērōma* in Greek) had to be populated with divine beings. But God's transcendence did not, in any way, negate his nearness to those who believed in him. To many pagans of the Hellenistic period the gods seemed distant and uncaring. In 291 B.C.E., the Athenians sang to their ruler, "The other gods either are far away or do not have ears or do not exist or do not pay attention to us at all; you, however, we see before us, made of neither wood nor stone, but a real god. To you we pray." Such was the flattery which the Athenians heaped upon their mortal ruler.[6] The Jews would have agreed with the Athenians that the worship of the gods was silly and useless (for example, Ps. 115:4–8 and 1 Kings 18:27), but for the Jews the nearness of God was as real as the nearness of the general Demetrius Poliorcetes was for the Athenians. Although the God of the Jews was the king of the universe, he also was near enough to hearken to the prayers of humanity.

This paradox is highlighted in a remark of a rabbi of the fourth century.[7] "Pagan gods seem to be near [because their images are so near] but in reality are far away [because they do not hearken to prayer]; but the Holy One, blessed is he, seems distant [because of his transcendence] but there is none closer than he [because he hearkens to prayer]." Whatever feelings the Jews had about God's elusiveness and ineffectiveness were caused not by his transcendence or remoteness but by the incomprehensibility of his actions. Why does a moral God allow evil to flourish? To this question I shall return below.

The God of the Philosophers vs. the God of the Bible

The God of the Hebrew Bible is for the most part an anthropomorphic and anthropopathic being, that is, a God who has the form and emotions of humans. He (it is a he) walks and talks, has arms and legs, becomes angry, happy, or sad, changes his mind, speaks to humans and is addressed by them, and closely supervises the affairs of the world. The God of the philosophers is a different sort of being altogether: abstract (the Prime Mover, the First Cause, the Mind or Soul of the Universe, etc.), immutable, and relatively unconcerned with the affairs of humanity. The tension between these rival conceptions of the Deity is evident in the work of Philo, who is able to find a philosophically respectable God in the Torah only through allegorical exegesis (see chapter 6). Philo is particularly careful to sanitize the anthropomorphic and anthropopathic passages. In the land of Israel the pressure to interpret the Bible in this fashion was less intense, but even here many of the Targumim, the Aramaic translations of scripture, reduce or eliminate the scriptural anthropomorphisms.

Perhaps some Jews were concerned about the very unphilosophical image of God in the Hebrew scriptures, but most Jews were not. Apocalyptic visionaries and mystics persisted in seeing God sitting on his throne surrounded by his angelic attendants. The rabbis had no difficulty in believing in a God who loves and is loved and with whom one can argue. The masses needed (and need!) a God who is accessible and understandable. In the fourth century most of the monks in Egypt understood the anthropomorphisms of scripture literally. After all, God declares, "Let us make man in our image" (Gen. 1:26), proof that the image of man is the image of God. After hearing a pastoral letter from the bishop of Alexandria and a sermon from his abbot which insisted that the scriptural anthropomorphisms were to be understood allegorically because God has no shape, one elderly monk arose to pray but could not. "Woe is me! They have taken my God away from me!" he wailed.[8] Popular piety does not need or want an immutable and shapeless Prime Mover; it wants a God who reveals himself to people, listens to prayer, and can be grasped in human terms. This is the God of the *Shema*, the Bible, and the liturgy. This is the God of practically all the Hebrew and Aramaic, and some of the Greek, Jewish literature of antiquity. It is not, however, the God of the philosophers.

Reward and Punishment

A major issue throughout this period is the justice of God, known since Leibniz as *theodicy*. God is the king over his people and over the universe, and it is the responsibility of a king to maintain justice in his domain. Indeed, Absalom succeeded in deposing King David because the son administered justice more effectively than the father (2 Sam. 15:1–6). The basic thesis of almost every book in the Hebrew Bible is that God controls human affairs (or, at least, the affairs of the Israelites), rewarding the righteous and punishing the wicked. Although God's control is evident in many ways, most spectacularly through the display of miracles, the Bible itself is aware that the ways of God are sometimes unclear, since his ways are not the ways of humanity.

The second paragraph of the *Shema* explains that the Israelites are rewarded for their righteousness by rain and prosperity, and are punished for their wickedness by drought and famine. Rain was not God's only weapon. Success in battle against foreign enemies, good health, and an abundance of all good things were proffered to those who followed God's commandments, and their opposites to those who did not. This was justice maintained on a national level; I shall return to this theme in the section below on redemption. Here I shall discuss the reward and punishment of the individual.

In the pre-exilic period the individual was seen more as a member of the whole than as a separate entity. This perspective is evident in many passages, most clearly in God's explanation of his ways to Moses (Ex. 34:6–7; cf. Num. 14:18):

> The Lord, the Lord, a God merciful and gracious, slow to anger, and abounding in steadfast love and faithfulness, keeping steadfast love for thousands, forgiving iniquity and transgression and sin, but who will by no means clear the guilty, visiting the iniquity of the fathers upon the children and the children's children, to the third and the fourth generation.

In these verses the visitation of the sins of the fathers upon the children (intergenerational or "diachronic" responsibility) is considered an aspect of God's *mercy,* not anger. Although God "forgives iniquity" (a better translation would be "tolerates iniquity"), he insists that the guilty party be punished, but through his mercy he allows the punishment to be spread over a span of three or four generations. From the point of view of the fathers this is real mercy. From the point of view of the children this might seem to be unjust, but the Israelites (at first) did not think so, because they readily accepted the fact that an individual was part of a clan and a nation, and that one's fate was indissolubly linked to that of one's ancestors, descendants, and contemporaries. Later in the pre-exilic period, opinions changed and the visitation of the sins of the fathers upon the children was reckoned an aspect of divine *anger.* One concession was now made to the right of the individual: accumulated guilt devolved upon the third and fourth generation only if the children wickedly persisted in the sinful ways of the fathers (Ex. 20:5).

The destruction of the temple in 587 B.C.E. and the exile to Babylonia delivered this system a mortal blow. While it seemed clear enough that God was using Nebuchadnezzar and the Babylonians as his "rod of anger" against Israel, why did God allow his temple to be destroyed? Did the punishment fit the crime? No one denied that the Israelites sinned, but the punishment was so great and the suffering so enormous that God appeared to some to be a malevolent deity who inflicts suffering on the innocent (Lam. 3: 1–19). Some Israelites were content with the notion that they were suffering in part for the guilt accumulated by prior generations (Lam. 5:7), but many complained that this was the work of an unjust God. "The fathers have eaten sour grapes, and the children's teeth are set on edge" was a widely quoted proverb of the time (Jer. 31:29 and Ezek. 18). A few Israelites even attributed their misfortunes to their failure to maintain their worship of the Queen of Heaven (Jer. 44:15–19)—in other words, they were being punished by a deity, but the deity was not God! Clearly a new understanding of theodicy was needed.

In his response to the Israelites who complained that they were suffering for their ancestors' sins, Ezekiel responded that each person is judged by God individually. "The soul that sins shall die. The son shall not suffer for the iniquity of the father, nor the father suffer for the iniquity of the son" (Ezek. 18:20). This notion was a major departure from the system that God himself revealed to Moses in Exodus 34. Another novel doctrine introduced by Ezekiel in the same chapter was the efficacy of repentance for the individual. A sinner who repents is no longer a sinner in the eyes of God, and a righteous person who goes astray is no longer righteous. Each is rewarded according to his or her new state. These ideas, in conjunction with the doctrine of retribution in the hereafter, were enormously influential.

Immortality and Resurrection

Ezekiel claims that every person receives his or her just deserts from God. The author of Chronicles, a work of the Persian or early Hellenistic period, implemented this theory in his revision of the book of Kings. The Deuteronomic historian was satisfied with the doctrine of corporate responsibility, but the Chronicler was not. Wherever Kings explains a catastrophe on the basis of guilt incurred by someone other than the one experiencing the catastrophe (for example, God destroyed the temple on account of the sins of King Manasseh, who reigned a century before the destruction), Chronicles changes the narrative to show that no one suffers for a crime committed by someone else. Such a cheery view of the world, however, does not accord with experience. Often the righteous suffer and the wicked prosper. This was the question raised forcefully by the book of Job, a work of unknown date but often ascribed by scholars to the Persian or Hellenistic period. Job rejects the idea that sins of the fathers are visited on the children, and that reward and punishment are meted out in an afterlife. Why, then, does he, a righteous man, suffer? The book suggests that suffering is not always punitive and therefore not always a sign of wickedness. Sometimes God wishes to test the righteous or to purify them of their minor imperfections, ideas that would have an enormous impact on both Jewish and Christian piety (from the later second temple period see, for example, Tobit, the *Psalms of Solomon,* and *2 Baruch*). Ultimately, however, the book concludes that God's ways are unknowable and that humanity must not presume to understand what is beyond its ken.

Job's answer, then, is that there is no answer. The third and second centuries B.C.E. witnessed the birth of intense speculation about the origins of evil, on the one hand, and the mysteries of theodicy on the other. In this period we hear for the first time of fallen angels, one of whom becomes the cosmic leader of the forces of evil, and of the corruption introduced on earth by these beings. Many of these legends were attached to Genesis 6:1–5, the fragmentary account of the miscegenation of the "sons of God" (or however the phrase *benei elohim* ought to be translated) with the fair daughters of men. Even in the book of Job, Satan was beginning to emerge as a clearly defined figure (Job 1), and it was not long before he (or his equivalent) became the leader of the forces of evil who delight in causing troubles for humans and leading them astray (see above).

These ideas developed rapidly. At Qumran they formed the heart of a dualistic system that divided the entire world into two camps, the sons of light and the sons of darkness. The sons of light—that is, the members of the sect—will aid the angel of light in the final struggle against the forces of evil led by the angel of darkness. This cosmic struggle is mirrored by the struggle within each person of the Spirit of Truth with the Spirit of Perversity (see below). Various passages in the Pauline writings echo similar sentiments, although not in such extreme form. In the second century of our era many Christian "gnostics" developed a radical dualism which explained that the world was created either by the leader of the forces of evil or through a series of mistakes and accidents. These gnostic systems explained why evil seems to triumph in the world, but their explanation was gained at the expense of monotheism. In fact, it is difficult to reconcile any of these views with monotheism, as I discussed above. This fact is not particularly surprising since many of these ideas entered Judaism from Platonism and Zoroastrianism, in both of which they are parts of dualistic theological structures. Many of the gnostic systems are both non-monotheistic and anti-Jewish in that they identify the evil Creator with the God of the Jews (who is also the God of the Hebrew Bible). Nevertheless, most scholars now agree that these non-monotheistic, anti-Jewish ideas have their ultimate origins, at least in part, in the Jewish speculations of the second temple period.

In the third and second centuries B.C.E. we also hear for the first time of immortality and resurrection as the rewards that await the righteous, and of eternal punishments that await the wicked. In the pre-exilic portions of the Bible, *sheol* is the ultimate destination for the disembodied souls of everyone, righteous and wicked alike. In Sheol, much like the Greek Hades, there is no judgment and no reward. A few poetical passages imply that God can bring back from Sheol those who have been consigned there (1 Sam. 2:6), or that the dead might live again (Isa. 26:19; Ezek. 37:1–14), but these are metaphorical expressions of God's prowess, not crucial elements in a system of theodicy. Neither Job nor Ben Sira (about 200 B.C.E.) knows anything of reward and punishment in the hereafter. Ecclesiastes, almost certainly a product of the Hellenistic period, asks (3:21), "Who knows whether the spirit of man goes upward and the spirit of the beast goes down to the earth?" Since neither the righteous nor the wicked receives his or her due in either life or death, what is the incentive to be righteous? Where is God's justice? These are the taunts that the righteous hear in the book of *Enoch*, in Wisdom of Solomon, and in many other works, including rabbinic literature. Since the present was inexplicable, the answer had to be the future. Death does *not* mark the end; the righteous—and perhaps the wicked too—*do* receive their due in the hereafter.

The new doctrine appears in inchoate form in a section of the book of *Enoch*, which derives from the third century B.C.E. (*1 Enoch* 22 and 27). A clearer account is provided by Daniel 12:2–3, a description of the events of the end time:

> And many of those who sleep in the dust of the earth shall awake, some to everlasting life, and some to shame and everlasting contempt. And those who are wise shall shine like the brightness of the firmament; and those who turn many to righteousness, like the stars for ever and ever.

Daniel seems to imply that only some ("many") of the dead will be resurrected, presumably only those who did not receive their due in their lifetimes. The elect will shine forever like the stars of heaven, a notion that scholars call "astral immortality." Later texts supply many of the details Daniel omits. In some the resurrection is reserved for everyone, in some for the righteous alone, while in others (as in Daniel) for some of the righteous and some of the wicked. In many texts the resurrection is accompanied by a judgment scene, although whether the judgment was to take place immediately after death or only in the end time was never very clear. In some texts the resurrection is bodily, while in others it is only spiritual. How the resurrection was to be coordinated with the arrival of the messiah (a concept that Daniel 12 omits) was also the subject of intense speculation.

Although the roots of the doctrine of resurrection are much older than the book of Daniel, the major impulse to its acceptance by the Jews was the crisis of the mid-second century. For the first time in recorded history, a nation fought a battle for religious liberty. For the first time in Jewish history, men, women, and children were killed because they refused to violate the demands of the Torah. Just as the desecration of the temple and the persecution of Judaism provided the impulse for visions of national redemption (see below), the death of the righteous martyrs provided the impulse for the belief in immortality and resurrection. Like Daniel in the lions' pit and Daniel's friends in the fiery furnace, the martyrs were tortured but emerged "alive." Through their deaths they attained immortal life. This idea recurs frequently in the earliest extant Jewish martyrology, 2 Maccabees 6–7, a product of Greek-speaking Judaism, which describes the death of an old man and of seven brothers at the hands of Antiochus Epiphanes. That martyrs would be resurrected to life eternal was a doctrine which played an enormous role in the development of Christianity.

A close ally of the doctrine of bodily resurrection is the doctrine of the immortality of the soul. Because of its affinities with the speculations of Greek philosophy, this doctrine was popular with Greek-speaking Jews, notably Philo (although 2 Maccabees explicitly refers to bodily resurrection). When Josephus describes the three Jewish sects, he presents them as "philosophies" arguing about the immortality of the soul.

This discussion of life after death began with Ezekiel's argument that each person receives his or her due from God in this world. Since reality, then as now, did not confirm such optimism, the Jews of the second temple period elaborated the doctrine of reward and punishment in the hereafter. Ezekiel rejected the doctrine of familial responsibility (the visitation of the sins of the fathers upon the children), but that doctrine at least explained why the righteous and the wicked were not rewarded in their lifetime. The doctrine of reward and punishment in the hereafter was a much more elegant solution.

Repentance and Free Will

Human courts do not accept repentance. A criminal must pay a penalty for his or her crime. A human judge might be swayed by the contrition of the accused to lighten the penalty, but the act of contrition obliterates neither the crime nor the punishment. Not so the divine judge. A wicked person who repents of his or her misdeeds can escape the consequences of the sin. This was Ezekiel's argument, but the extent to which repentance could remove sin, or, what is perhaps more significant, sinfulness, was a question that aroused much speculation in the second temple and rabbinic periods.

Ezekiel's theodicy is predicated on the fact that people have free will. People decide whether to be righteous or wicked, whether to change their ways or not, and are rewarded accordingly. In the same tradition Ben Sira argues that a sinner cannot evade responsibility for his deeds. "Do not say, 'Because of the Lord I left the right way. . . . It was he who led me astray' " (Ben Sira 15:11–12). "Do not say, 'I shall be hidden from the Lord, and who from on high will remember me? Among so many people I shall not be known, for what is my soul in the boundless creation?' " (Ben Sira 16:17). The first sinner's error is the argument that humans do not have free will, that everything is determined in advance by God (or Fate). The second sinner's error is the argument that God does not pay attention to humanity's actions, because humanity is so insignificant and God is so powerful. These arguments are false, says Ben Sira; the truth is that each person is responsible for his or her own deeds, and receives appropriate treatment from God.

Ben Sira, therefore, like Ezekiel, counseled repentance. Numerous works of the last centuries of the second temple period feature the efficacy and importance of repentance. Perhaps the most beautiful expression of this piety is the Prayer of Manasseh, which reads in part:

> You, O Lord, according to your gentle grace, promised forgiveness to those who repent of their sins, and in your manifold mercies appointed repentance for sinners as the way to salvation. You, therefore, O Lord, God of the righteous, did not appoint grace for the righteous . . . but you appointed grace for me, I who am a sinner. . . . And now, behold, I am bending the knees of my heart before you and I am beseeching your kindness. I have sinned, O Lord, I have sinned . . . ; forgive me, O Lord, forgive me!

John the Baptist, Jesus, and, we may assume, other popular preachers of the first century also encouraged the Jews to repent of their sins. Rabbinic piety lays great store in the efficacy of repentance for the removal of sin and the restoration of favorable relations between God and the individual Jew. Medieval casuists, both Jewish and Christian, debated the finer points of this system: Is repentance efficacious for all sins? How does one repent? How much repentance is enough? And so on.

Not only does humanity have free will according to this system, God does as well. When a prophet speaks in the name of the Lord, he is not uttering an inescapable fate that will inevitably overtake his audience. This is the task of Greek oracles and modern-day weather forecasters. When the Israelite prophets announced doom to the Israelites, their goal was to stir the people to repentance, in the hope that the doom could be averted. Prophets are watchmen who, upon the approach of danger, sound the trumpet to warn the people so that they may escape (Ezek. 33). This is the basic lesson of the book of Jonah (in all likelihood a product of the Persian or early Hellenistic period). Jonah declared in the name of the Lord, "In forty days Nineveh shall be destroyed." Forty days later Nineveh was *not* destroyed, not because Jonah was a false prophet but because the Ninevites had repented and God therefore could "repent" of his intention to destroy the city. The prophets spoke, as usual, on a national scale, but the lesson was true for the individual as well.

Thus humanity has free will to act, and God has free will to reward and punish. Some Jews were content with this system as outlined here. Josephus says that the Sadducees "do away with the (power of) Fate altogether. . . . They maintain that man has the free choice of good or evil, and that it rests with each man's will whether he follows the one or the other" (*Jewish War* 2.8.14, §164–165). Since the Sadducees denied the immortality of the soul, resurrection of the dead, and rewards in the hereafter, they probably believed (as Ezekiel did) that God punishes the wicked and rewards the righteous in this world.

But does humanity really have absolute free will? In many contexts the Hebrew Bible does not extend free will to kings and nations. The descendants of Abram will be slaves in Egypt for four hundred years, not because of any sin but because God willed it so (Gen. 15). God hardened Pharaoh's heart so that the exodus from Egypt would be a wondrous display of miracles and power. The Babylonian captivity will last seventy years (Jer. 25:12 and 29:10). And so on. In this conception sinfulness and righteousness, recidivism and repentance are irrelevant, since human destiny has been determined by God. This mode of thinking had a tremendous impact on the apocalyptic literature of the second temple. Daniel sees history unfolding as a sequence of four empires; other visionaries describe a greater or lesser number, or describe a series of ages instead. But they all agreed that the structure of human history was determined in advance by God, perhaps even at the creation. National repentance, which introduces an element of conditionality, has no role in this literature.

Many Jews of the second temple period thought that the actions of individuals, no less than those of nations, were, to some extent at least, predetermined by God. These Jews were influenced by the belief in astrology, which swept the entire Hellenistic world in the third century B.C.E., or were disturbed by the idea that God could so distance himself from the world as to allow humans the freedom to do whatever they pleased. According to Josephus the Essenes, in contrast with the Sadducees, declared that "Fate is mistress of all things, and that nothing befalls men unless it be in accordance with her decree," while the Pharisees said that "certain events are the work of Fate, but not all; as to other events, it depends upon ourselves whether they shall take place or not" (*Jewish Antiquities* 13.5.9, §172–173). Josephus' use of the term "Fate" (in Greek *Eimarmenē*) probably reflects this idea of predeterminism. The Essenes claimed that all human actions are determined by fate, while the Pharisees claimed that life is governed jointly by fate and free will. The Qumran scrolls, many of which, in all likelihood, are documents of the Essenes (see chapter 5), confirm that these pietists believed that God created two different types of people, those who were destined to become the sons of light and the supporters of truth, and those who were destined to become sons of darkness and the supporters of wickedness. A new member was accepted when the group determined that it was his "lot" to join the righteous remnant of Israel. But the Essenes' confidence in their status as the predetermined elect was not so strong as to eliminate the need for piety, good deeds, and repentance. In the Qumran hymns (*Hodayot*) confidence born of predeterminism is absent. They are dominated instead by the sense of gratitude that the penitent feels toward God, because God has chosen him, though unworthy and sinful, to be his servant. The rabbis were well aware of the paradox of combining human free will with divine predeterminism. In the words of R. Aqiba's pithy maxim (*Chapters of the Fathers* 3.15), "Everything is foreseen [by God] but free will is granted [to humans]." Clearly the Pharisees and the Essenes of Qumran did not agree on the extent to which predestination controlled human events, but they agreed in principle that human events are the product of free will and determinism.

But if God is partly responsible for human actions, is he not responsible for the evil that humans perform? If he is, how can humanity be held accountable for its actions? If he is not, whence humanity's inclination to sin? Josephus implies that these were the questions which impelled the Sadducees to deny that God has any share in determining human actions: "They remove God beyond not merely the commission but the very sight of evil" (*Jewish War* 2.8.14, §164). The more common way to answer these questions was to posit some force that, while created by God, nevertheless was separate enough from God to explain human sinfulness. This force was Satan (or his equivalent) and the evil hosts under his command (see above). In some of the Qumran texts, the cosmic struggle between the Spirit of Truth and the Spirit of Perversity is mirrored in a struggle within each person. The rabbinic version of this idea is that humans were created with two inclinations, the good and the wicked, and that life is a continuous struggle of the good inclination against the wicked. The wicked inclination is always suggesting various ways to sin that a person must resist. Some texts connect the origins of sin with the fall of Adam and Eve.

In much of the literature, then, there is the recognition not only that "there is no person who does not go astray" (1 Kings 8:46), but that an intrinsic part of being human is to be sinful. Why God created humanity in this way was a mystery, although the End would bring a new creation in which sin would have no place (see below). These conceptions had different consequences in Christianity and rabbinic Judaism. For the former the power of sin can be overcome only through faith in Christ. Without the intercession of Jesus humans are incapable of "salvation" (the forgiveness of sin). Rabbinic Judaism, in contrast, while recognizing the power of sin, believes that even without any intercessory figure, humanity is capable of finding favor in God's eyes. The means to this end are repentance, prayer, Torah study, and good deeds.

Redemption

The third paragraph of the *Shema* ends with the declaration that God redeemed the Israelites from Egypt: "I am the Lord your God, who brought you out of the land of Egypt, to be your God" (Num. 15:41). The Mishnah therefore calls this paragraph "the exodus from Egypt," and sees redemption as its theme. Just as God once redeemed his people from the oppression of Egypt, so too would he redeem them again. In the previous section (on Reward and Punishment) I discussed theodicy as far as it applied to the individual, and I focused on the notions of resurrection, immortality, and repentance. Much of that discussion is relevant here, although the theme of this section is theodicy as far as it applies to the nation. The distinction between nation and individual is useful because it separates the constituent elements of Jewish eschatology, but it must not be overdrawn, since the Jews of antiquity were not always sensitive to it. Many of the most personal prayers are couched in the first-person plural in the rabbinic prayer book. The notion of individual responsibility is always joined with corporate responsibility. As if to underscore this point, the first paragraph of the *Shema* is written in the second-person singular, the second and third paragraphs in the plural.

The basic problem that had to be answered was the same as that discussed above. Why evil? Why has God given dominion to the gentile nations? Even if it be conceded that the Jews are sinful and that God is using the nations of the world as the staff of his anger in order to punish them, why must the punishment last so long? Why must it be so severe? When will it end? And, most distressing of all, aren't the nations also sinful, even more sinful than the Jews who are the bearers of the holy Torah? Why doesn't God punish them too? These are the questions which are heard in one form or another throughout our period in the wake of the events of 587 B.C.E. (the destruction of the first temple), 167 B.C.E. (the persecution of Judaism and profanation of the temple by Epiphanes), 63 B.C.E. (the Roman conquest of Jerusalem), 70 C.E. (the destruction of the second temple), and 135 C.E. (the fall of Bar Kokhba). The Psalter is filled with "national laments" that are obsessed with these questions (although the dating of these psalms is usually uncertain). Here, for example, are excerpts from Psalm 79, ascribed by many scholars to the Maccabean period:

> O God, the heathen have come into thy inheritance; they have defiled thy holy temple; they have laid Jerusalem in ruins. . . . We have become a taunt to our neighbors, mocked and derided by those round about us. How long, O Lord? Will you be angry for ever? Will your jealous wrath burn like fire? Pour out your anger on the nations that do not know you, and on the kingdoms that do not call on your name! . . . Why should the nations say, "Where is their God?" . . . Return sevenfold into the bosom of our neighbors the taunts with which they have taunted you, O Lord!

Much external evidence confirms the psalmist's lament that the Jews have become a mockery among the nations. Pagan anti-Jewish writers (notably Apion) used the political subjugation of the Jews to prove that Judaism is a worthless religion, and this argument was developed even further in Christian anti-Jewish polemic. Just as the righteous had to endure the taunts of the wicked, Israel had to endure the taunts of the nations.

For some Jews, however, the injustice of the status quo was caused not only or not chiefly by the gentiles but by their fellow Jews. As I shall discuss more fully in chapter 5, one of the hallmarks of "sectarian" ideology is exclusivity; only the members of the group are righteous in God's eyes and only they properly understand God's will. In the present, wicked Jews control the temple and all the other apparatus of state and religion, and the members of the sect must suffer abuse and harassment. In this conception the polarity of Jew vs. gentile is accompanied, if not replaced, by the polarity of the righteous (that is, the sect) versus the wicked (all the other Jews and, apparently, the gentiles as well). Sects suffer from both persecution and a persecution complex, which uses the sufferings of the present to prove loyalty to God. Alienated from the rest of society, they create in their minds (that is, the heavens) an ideal world that in the end time would be realized on earth and vindicate them in the eyes of their opponents. The classic exponents of this perspective from later second temple times are the Jews of Qumrar and the early Christians.

The distinction between national and sectarian salvation is not always clear, however. One of the major problems posed by the numerous eschatological descriptions from second temple times is their social setting. Is the visionary speaking for a specific group or for the nation as a whole? Usually the texts, with their vague refer ences to the righteous and the wicked, do not provide enough data to answer this question. In order to simplify matters, in the following discussion I shall use the terms "nation," "Jews," "the righteous," as synonyms, even if some of the original texts might distinguish among them.

The present, then, is a time of trial in which God's righteous are persecuted. Why God allows this situation to persist is the eternal question of the existence of evil, to which the Jews gave varied answers as I discussed above. But even if they could not satisfactorily explain the present, they *knew* that justice would be established in the future. The righteous dead would be resurrected to glory (or otherwise rewarded), and the nation of Israel would be restored to that state of preeminence which it deserves.

The prophets already spoke of "the day of the Lord" and of "the end of days," but these prophecies did not address the questions that bothered the Jews of the second temple period. The prophets assured their contemporaries that after undergoing the punishments threatened by God they would see much better times. In the future the world will be at peace; lions shall lie down with lambs, and men shall beat their swords into plowshares. A shoot shall come forth from the stump of Jesse and shall rule righteously (Isaiah 2 and 11). These beautiful images contributed mightily to the conceptions that developed subsequently, but they are not motivated by a desire to explain the triumph of evil and the abuse of Israel at the hands of the gentiles. Also, for the prophets the "end of days" is simply a day in the future; it is neither the "end" of history nor the inauguration of a new order. The later literature, with its portrayal of cosmic battles between the forces of good and the forces of wickedness, with its emphasis on the "otherworldly" nature of the end time, with its developed angelology and wealth of detail, has a different atmosphere entirely from its prophetic antecedents. In addition, the literary form of much of these later works differs in many important respects from that of classical prophecy, a point to which I shall return in chapter 6 below.

What exactly would transpire in the end time (the *eschaton*, hence the term "eschatology," doctrine of the end time) was the subject of intense and varied speculations. The book of Daniel thinks that the troubles inflicted on the Jews by Epiphanes will be resolved by a battle between Epiphanes and the Ptolemaic king of Egypt. After the battle "shall arise Michael, the great prince who has charge of your people. And there shall be a time of trouble, . . . but at that time your people shall be delivered, every one whose name shall be found written in the book" (Dan. 12:1). These events will be followed by the resurrection. That the events of the end time will be preceded by a great battle was a widespread belief, although who exactly was supposed to fight whom was never clear. In Daniel one gentile king assaults another; neither the Jews nor the angelic hosts have any role in the battle (Michael's task is to protect his people, the Jews). Much more frequent is the depiction of a battle between Jews and gentiles, in which the former are led by a messiah, an "anointed" king. In the Qumran *War* scroll, however, the final battle is not so much between humans as between the supernatural forces of Good (the sons of light) and Evil (the sons of darkness). This speculation is a development of Ezekiel's description of the attack of "Gog" against the people of Israel (Ezek. 38–39). Ezekiel was describing the attack of a human king, but the text readily lent itself to a cosmic interpretation (cf. Rev. 20:7–10). According to Ezekiel, at this final battle, the Israelites are merely spectators to the display of God's might, since it is God who destroys the enemy. The

Israelites do nothing except clean the battlefield and bury the corpses.

Perhaps because it has neither a final battle involving the righteous nor a judgment scene, Daniel 12 does not mention a messiah. Similarly, the Qumran *War* scroll, in which most or all of the fighting is accomplished by supernatural, not human, forces, has no need for a messianic figure. Many other texts, however, attribute to a messiah (or to an equivalent figure with a different title; cf. the "son of man" in Daniel 7) the task of destroying the forces of evil, either in battle or in judgment. The messiah can be either a general or a judge or both. He serves as God's agent to punish the wicked and reward the righteous. The messiah is a human who has been "anointed" by God in order to implement his will in the end time. Some texts refer to *two* messiahs, the messiah from the tribe of Levi (a priestly messiah) and the messiah from the tribe of Judah (a royal messiah), or the messiah of Aaron and the messiah of Israel, but their separate functions are not described. In the vast majority of these accounts the messiah is definitely a human figure. Two Jewish texts of the first century C.E. (or are these Christian interpolations?), however, describe "the Chosen One" as a being who existed before the creation of the world, who sits on his glorious throne in heaven, and who shall judge both mortals and "spirits" in the end time (*1 Enoch* 45–57 and 4 Ezra 14).

Daniel also omits (or takes for granted) many other elements that were standard features in the eschatological speculations of his contemporaries and successors: the renewal of Jerusalem (perhaps through the replacement of the earthly city with the heavenly Jerusalem), the ingathering of the exiles, the reestablishment of the Davidic kingship, the veneration of God by the gentiles (presumably those gentiles who were not killed in the final war), and the renewed creation of the cosmos. These ideas too were developed in a bewildering variety of ways.

This complex of beliefs rests on assumptions both stated and unstated. Justice must triumph because the God of history is the God of justice. God has a covenant with his people and the covenant must be fulfilled. God also has covenants with the Davidic house and the Aaronide line that cannot be abrogated. The future chastisement of the nations, the glorification of Israel, and the triumph of peace were all predicted by the prophets, and those prophecies must be fulfilled. God controls human events and has determined in advance the exact stages of history: the triumph of the wicked empires and of the powers of sin, the crisis of the end, and its resolution. This process is not affected by repentance since its course is inevitable. Just as God redeemed his people in the past from various disasters (from Pharaoh, from the Babylonian captivity, etc.), surely he will come to their aid yet again, since their current situation is at least as difficult, if not worse, than those from which they were rescued previously. The end time is not merely some undetermined day in the future, as the prophets said, but is the end of history itself, the end of normal existence. It is a new creation in which evil has no place.

The impact of these ideas on the behavior of the Jews varied. Just as a firm belief in immortality and resurrection does not necessarily make one eager to die, so too a firm belief in the messiah and redemption does not necessarily make one eager to see the eschaton. As if to emphasize this point, many works highlight the troubles and disasters which will presage the arrival of the end (cf. Amos 5:18–20). In addition, since the end time is predetermined, nothing that the Jews would say or do could affect the time of its coming. This was the perspective which was emphasized in rabbinic piety. A redeemer will come to Israel, but the time of his coming cannot be hastened by human action. After the disastrous defeats in 70 c.e., 115–117 c.e., and 132–135 c.e., this was sound advice indeed. But many Jews, especially in the first century c.e., felt that they were living on the edge of history and expectantly awaited the promised deliverance. Usually this was understood to mean deliverance from the Romans, a mentality that is evident clearly in the Gospels, and less clearly in Josephus' portrayal of the revolutionary factions of the war of 66–70 c.e. In any case, the apocalyptic literature that is extant, even the literature that ascribes an active role to the righteous in the final battle, is not the work of political revolutionaries. At the Red Sea, Moses told the Israelites, "The Lord will fight for you, and you have only to be still" (Ex. 14:14). The apocalyptic visionaries told the Jews that the Lord will fight for them yet again.

Some Jews, however, understood the deliverance as a more personal and spiritual experience. For them the "kingdom of heaven" was to be realized by individual transformation on earth. Such Jews were to be found in the early Christian community and, a millennium later, among the Jewish mystics of the Middle Ages. Once again we see the connection between the salvation of the individual and the salvation of the group.

Conclusion

The major development in the Judaism of the second temple and rabbinic periods is the democratization of religion. Of course, pre-exilic piety often focused on the individual Israelite and second temple piety often focused on the community as a whole, but the shift in emphasis remains. The central institution of worship in the pre-exilic period was the temple, and the central feature of the cult was the sacrifice of animals. The individual Israelite had little role, since the priests, the only ones allowed to enter the sacrificial area, officiated on behalf of the people of Israel. During the second temple period the temple was supplemented by the synagogue, a lay institution; the sacrificial cult was supplemented by prayer, a cultic practice open to all; and the priest was supplemented by the scribe, the learned teacher.

During the pre-exilic period the prophets denounced the people for their sins and proclaimed that catastrophe was unavoidable unless the nation as a whole returned to God and repented of its evil ways. But beginning in the sixth century B.C.E., the doctrine of sin, retribution, and repentance was individualized. It no longer referred only to the people as a whole; it also, and perhaps primarily, referred to the individual citizens. Jeremiah and Ezekiel, representatives of the new conception, argue that the sins of the fathers are *not* visited upon the children. Righteous individuals will be saved even if the nation as a whole is guilty. These ideas intensified during the second temple period. Repentance became a virtue to be practiced by every Jew; the Day of Atonement became a day of repentance for all Jews, not just a day for the high priest to cleanse the altar of its accumulated pollutions (Ex. 30:10 and Lev. 16). The blessings of the end time were now thought to include not merely peace and prosperity for the nation but also reward for the righteous individuals of Israel, including the ultimate reward, resurrection.

The democratization of religion had as its goal the sanctification of daily life. Every act and every moment was to be in the service of God. The new regimen of study, prayer, ritual, and ethics was incumbent not upon some priestly or monastic elite but upon the entire community. All (male) Jews were equally obligated.

Theological developments are no less dramatic but much less focused. One of the major issues throughout the second temple period was theodicy, and the question was approached in two different ways. The first tried to reassure the faithful that justice would triumph in the future; the second tried to explain why justice was not triumphant in the present. The first answer consisted of new eschatological doctrines. Reward and punishment are meted out after death. Righteous individuals are resurrected to eternal life (and wicked individuals are resurrected to eternal punishment). The nation of Israel (or a group of the righteous within the nation) too will receive its due in the future. This future time, which would be inaugurated by the appearance either of God and his heavenly agents or of some specially designated mortal (the "messiah"), or both, was generally conceived as a new creation, in which the natural order would differ markedly from that now in effect. The second answer consisted of new theological speculations. Fallen angels, Satan, and other malevolent supernatural forces have corrupted God's creation and are responsible for humanity's inclination to sin and the apparent ascendancy of evil.

Although "theology" figures prominently in the literature that is extant from the period between the Maccabees and the Mishnah, Judaism was defined more by its practices than its beliefs. Probably all those who were known as Jews and who called themselves Jews believed in the one God who created the world, chose the Jews to be the bearer of his message, revealed his will to Moses (and the prophets), and controls the events of the world in general and of the Jews in particular. But all of these theological tenets were susceptible to diverse interpretations, and no one in antiquity thought to promote any single interpretation or set of interpretations as exclusively correct. In other words, no Jew of antiquity gave a creedal definition of Judaism.

When discussing the nature of God, Jewish thinkers in antiquity defended a series of conflicting truths that they did not even attempt to resolve: God was the Lord of the entire universe, and yet was also the national God of the Jews (universalism vs. particularism); God was One and Unique, and yet was also served by myriads of angels and opposed by a impressive array of powers (monotheism vs. polytheism); God was "in" the world, abiding among his people, and yet was also the Lord of the cosmos, enthroned in the distant heavens (immanence vs. transcendence); God was the eternal, immutable, immovable prime mover of the universe, and yet was also capable of anger, pity, and other human qualities (the God of the philosophers vs. the God of the Bible). The discussions of theodicy sometimes centered on another set of conflicting truths: God allows humans absolute free will to do as they please, and yet God also controls human events in accordance with his desire (free will vs. predetermination). To us moderns these pairs appear to be mutually exclusive, but to the Jews of antiquity they were simultaneously true. Some texts emphasize one aspect of God rather than another, but the fundamental tensions are never resolved.

4

The Community and Its Institutions

Introduction

Except for the brief interval of Maccabean success the Jews of antiquity never enjoyed political independence. They depended on the sufferance of their conquerors. And although they lived under a wide variety of empires, the treatment they received from their rulers was, for the most part, uniformly good. They were granted religious freedom and political autonomy. Not only were they allowed to observe their ancestral religion, they were allowed to form political bodies that controlled (or attempted to control) the internal affairs of the Jewish community. These political organizations were the *public* institutions of communal life (the temple, the sanhedrin, *politeumata*). They were supplemented by a wide variety of *private* organizations that, at least at the local level, were probably the real center of communal life (sects, schools, and associations). The distinction between public and private should not be pressed too rigorously, however, because some institutions, notably the synagogue, cannot be pigeonholed so easily.

The Public Institutions of the Land of Israel

As a province in an empire, the land of Israel (called Judea in Persian times, Coele Syria in Hellenistic times, Judea in early Roman times, and Palestine after the defeat of Bar Kokhba) was governed like any other province. It had its share of governors and administrators, tax collectors and generals, cities and villages. But the Jews of the country, who were a substantial part of the population, were a "nation" or "religious community" that was recognized by the state and was allowed to have its own institutions and jurisdiction. As a result, throughout the second temple and rabbinic periods, the Jews of the country were citizens of two parallel political systems. The first was the "civil" administration of the state, which was implemented on the local level by cities and villages, and on the provincial level by governors (for example, the procurators of the first century C.E.) or vassal kings (for example, Herod the Great and Herod Antipas). The second was the "national" or "religious" administration of the Jewish polity, which, for most of the second temple period, was implemented by the high priest. In some matters the two systems overlapped, creating a degree of confusion and uncertainty (see, for example, the Gospel accounts of the trial and execution of Jesus).

When the Jews returned to Judea in the sixth century B.C.E., the Persians established a dyarchy, a division of power between a governor, who was at first chosen from the old royal family (Zerubbabel, of the Davidic line), and a high priest (Jeshua son of Jozadak). The elevation of the high priest to a position of prominence was an innovation, since he had not been a powerful figure previously. During the period of the first temple he served at the pleasure of the king and only seldom emerged from obscurity to become an independent figure (notably 2 Kings 11). By the time of Ezra and Nehemiah (mid-fifth century B.C.E.) the royal family had disappeared and the high priest was emerging as the leading political figure. Ezra was neither governor nor high priest; he enacted his reforms on the basis of the authority granted him by the Persian king as special minister for the Jews of Judea (Ezra 7). Nehemiah was governor of the province and enforced his reforms by the civil authority of the state. But both Ezra and Nehemiah recognized that the high priesthood was the major source of opposition to their program.

By the fourth century B.C.E. at the latest, the high priest was the uncontested head of the Jews, not merely the head of the temple. In Hellenistic times the office was filled by an appointee of the king. He was responsible for the collection of taxes. "Civil" and "religious" power were combined in one person. The wars of the Maccabees in large measure revolved around this office. The high priests installed by Antiochus Epiphanes initiated the radical Hellenization, looted the temple, and may even have supported the persecution. In order to cement their victory the Maccabees had the Jews elect them the new high priestly family. With the Roman conquest in 63 B.C.E., civil power was vested in the Romans and their agents, and only religious authority was left to the high priests. When the great rebellion of 66–70 C.E. broke out, the revolutionaries vented their anger as much, if not more, against the high priests as against the

Romans. They appointed a new high priest to take the place of the one appointed by their enemies. Thus, by converting the high priesthood into a powerful office the Persians shaped the politics of the entire second temple period.

The two major institutions controlled by the high priest were the temple and the sanhedrin. Let us examine each of these briefly.

The Temple

As the focal point of the religion, the temple was the central communal institution not just for the Jews of the land of Israel but also for those of the diaspora. The half shekel contributed annually by diaspora Jews and the pilgrimages undertaken for the festivals bound together the entire Jewish community (see chapter 1). The ideology of the temple also served as a binding force: it represented monism and exclusivity. Only one place was suitable for God's home on earth, and that place was the temple mount in Jerusalem. During the second temple period, at least three other temples were erected, but none of them competed effectively with the temple of Jerusalem. The first was the temple built by the Jews of Elephantine (in upper Egypt) in the sixth century B.C.E., which was completely forgotten by later Jewish tradition and is known only through an archive discovered in Egypt at the end of the nineteenth century. The second was the temple of the Samaritans, erected on Mount Gerizim about the time of Alexander the Great. This temple, which became the focal point of the Samaritan schism (see chapter 5), was later destroyed by John Hyrcanus. The third was the temple built in Heliopolis (or Leontopolis) in Egypt by Onias, a scion of the high priestly family who fled from Jerusalem during the Antiochan persecution. Whatever Onias' intention, this temple did not gain the support or recognition of the Jews of Egypt; Philo does not even mention it. Diaspora Jews respected the exclusivistic claims advanced by the temple of Jerusalem. It represented the unity of God and the unity of Israel. "One temple for the one God," explains Josephus (*Against Apion* 2.23, §193).

The temple not only unified Jewish society, it also was the power base of the (or a) ruling class. As the exclusive ministers of God in the temple the priests enjoyed enormous power and prestige. Josephus, a priest himself, emphasizes that the priests carefully guarded their pedigree and were expert custodians of the sacred scriptures. In Josephus' view the ideal constitution for the Jews is a *theocracy*, the rule by God over his people, which translates into rule by God's representatives the priests. Josephus is not alone in this adulatory attitude. The Jews of Qumran created a hieratic society controlled in large part by "the priests the sons of Zadok." Many texts speak of a priestly messiah who will come at the end of days. Even after the Roman conquest in 63 B.C.E., the consequent loss of most of its civil jurisdiction, and the elevation of social nobodies to the office by Herod and the Romans, the high priesthood still enjoyed prestige and power through the first century of our era. Even after the destruction of the temple the priests continued to assert their privileged status within Jewish society, thereby competing with the rabbis for authority.

The priesthood consisted of high priests (the term includes the men who officiated as high priests in the temple as well as the families from which they were chosen) and simple priests, a division which resembles that between the upper and lower clergy in prerevolutionary France. All priests claimed descent from Aaron the brother of Moses, but the lineage of the high priests was superior to that of the simple priests. The high priestly families and the lay families with whom they intermarried were the real aristocracy of late second temple times. The social turmoil which preceded the outbreak of the war in 66 C.E. shows that the tension between the simple priests and the high priests was as great as that between the lay masses and the high priests. All priests were entitled to receive tithes and officiate in the temple, but only the high priests enjoyed the full measure of power that such a position could bestow.

The high priest and the priestly establishment were in charge of the temple and its cult, but their power was not unchallenged. The Jewish vassal kings (like Herod the Great) and the Roman governors of the country during the first century C.E. kept a careful watch on the temple to ensure that it would not become the focal point of unrest. The great rebellion of 66–70 C.E. began in the temple, and the temple remained the center of revolutionary activity until its destruction in 70 C.E. Many sects dreamed of purifying the temple and controlling it (cf. Mark 11:15–19). Rabbinic texts claim that the high priests, who belonged to the Sadducean group, had to obey the legal rulings of the rabbinic sages. I shall return to this theme in my discussion of sectarianism in chapter 5. The temple was a source of both power and power struggles within Jewish society.

The Sanhedrin

One of the most elusive institutions of the second temple period is the *sanhedrin* (a Hebrew word from the Greek, meaning literally "a sitting together," that is, "session" or "assembly"). According to the Gospels and Acts the sanhedrin was a supreme court chaired by the high priest and composed of members drawn from various groups (Sadducees, Pharisees, priests). It had authority to try cases that involved serious violations of religious law (for example, if someone claimed to be king of the Jews or if someone brought a gentile into the temple precincts). According to rabbinic tradition, the sanhedrin was a legislative as well as a judicial body, which was chaired by a pair of rabbinic sages and was composed entirely of members of the rabbinic elite. Josephus' incidental references to the sanhedrin show it to have been not a permanent body but an ad hoc committee assembled by the high priest whenever he needed advice on difficult cases. (Josephus knows a permanent council in Jerusalem that he calls by its proper Greek name *boulē.*) Scholars have been trying for centuries to sort out these conflicting testimonies about the body which is said to have played such an important role in the life and death of Jesus.

All the sources agree, however, that the Romans allowed the Jewish community a good deal of autonomy in matters of internal jurisdiction. Josephus and the New Testament agree that the high priest was the chairman of the Jewish polity and that the sanhedrin served him, and this claim is probably correct. With the destruction of the temple in 70 c.e., the Jerusalem sanhedrin disappeared and the Jewish community was left without a central organization. This was the lacuna which the rabbis gradually filled. Instead of the high priest, the head of the autonomous community of Jews in the land of Israel was now the *patriarch,* and instead of a priestly sanhedrin, the supreme judicial and legislative body was now a council of rabbis (often called, as before, the sanhedrin). It was not until the last part of the second century that the Romans recognized this state of affairs. By the year 300 c.e. or so the patriarch was claiming authority over all the Jews of the Roman empire, just as the temple once claimed the allegiance of all Jews everywhere. I shall return to these developments in the last chapter. The rabbinic version of the pre-70 sanhedrin is probably the result of projecting the conditions of rabbinic times upon the second temple period.

The Public Institutions of the Diaspora

The Jews of Palestine were subject both to their own internal government and to the government of the state. In similar fashion the larger communities of the diaspora in Hellenistic and Roman times were governed by two different political structures. First, like everyone else, they were subject to the local municipal and provincial administrations. Second, they were members of their own ethnic communities, which enjoyed a good measure of internal autonomy. An autonomous ethnic community in a Greek city was known as a *politeuma* (in plural *politeumata*). Other ethnic groups too had their own *politeumata,* but because of the troubles between the Jews and the "Greeks" in Alexandria in 38–41 C.E. we are best informed about the Jewish *politeuma* of that city.

The Jewish *politeuma* of Alexandria was led by a board of directors one of whom was the chief of the community. It had its own archives and courts. The numerous synagogues of the city belonged to the Jewish community and were extensions of the central organization. All the Jews of the city were citizens of the community. They also regarded themselves as "Alexandrians," a term that could mean either citizens or residents of the city of Alexandria. The clarification of this rather technical and seemingly insignificant ambiguity provoked a series of violent incidents. The Alexandrians resented the Jewish *politeuma* because it was a body that was *in* but not *of* the city. It was legally separate from the city and therefore a diminution of the city's own autonomy and self-esteem. The Alexandrians therefore wanted the Jewish *politeuma* to be dissolved. The Jews, by contrast, wanted the city government to recognize all the members of the community as citizens of the city of Alexandria. Municipal citizenship was a privileged status that conferred various material benefits (including lower taxes and lighter punishments for crimes) in addition to prestige. Apion, the leader of the anti-Jewish party, countered that if the Jews wished to be citizens of Alexandria they should worship the gods of the Alexandrians (see chapter 2). The Jews countered that they had been regarded as "Alexandrians" ever since the days of Alexander the Great himself. And the battle was joined. Exactly who or what started the battle is no clearer to us than it was to the emperor Claudius when, after four years of riots and bloodshed, he told the Jews and the Alexandrians to stop causing unrest and to live with each other in peace. Similar struggles took place in Caesarea (in Palestine), Antioch (in Syria), and the cities of Ionia (in modern-day western Turkey) during the first century, and their recurrence probably caused the conflagration that all but destroyed the Jewry of Egypt, Cyrene, and Cyprus in 115–117 C.E.

Three Greek inscriptions from Berenice (modern-day Benghazi, Libya) give a vivid glimpse of the life of a Jewish community during settled times.[1] The first inscription, dated to 8–6 B.C.E., is a resolution passed by the *politeuma* and its seven directors in honor of one Decimus Valerius Dionysius, apparently a Jew with a Greco-Latin name, who plastered and adorned the community's "amphitheater." The community therefore resolved to erect the inscription in the amphitheater in his honor, to free him from various communal obligations, and to crown him publicly at every assembly and at every new moon. The second inscription, dated to 24/5 C.E., records a resolution of the *politeuma* and its nine directors, voted at the festival of Tabernacles, to honor a Roman official who had been sent to the district and who showed great courtesy to both the Jews and the Greeks. He too was to receive an inscription in the amphitheater, and was to be praised publicly at every assembly and at every new moon. The third inscription, dated to 56 C.E., is a resolution of the community (here called not *politeuma* but *synagōgē*) commemorating monetary donations made by nine directors, one priest, and eight private individuals, for the repair of the synagogue.

These inscriptions show that the Jews of Berenice were organized as one large community (called *politeuma* in the first two inscriptions and *synagōgē* in the third) headed by seven or nine directors; that the community owned a building, called an "amphitheater" in the first two inscriptions and a "synagogue" in the third (on the meaning of the word "synagogue" see below); that the community met at regular intervals (at the new moon and apparently on Jewish holidays); and that the very organization which protected the legal rights and cultural distinctiveness of the Jews of Berenice was thoroughly Greek in conception and form (it owned an "amphitheater," passed resolutions, erected honorary inscriptions, and awarded crowns).

Not all Jews, however, lived in communities that had a central organization. The Jews of the western part of the Roman empire and of the towns and villages of the East did not form communities recognized by the state. Since there was no central communal organization, the synagogues of these localities were independent of each other. The Romans assured the Jews the right to assemble publicly for worship wherever they lived throughout the empire, and each synagogue created under this right was considered by the Romans a "club" or "association" for religious purposes. Thus the Jews were always able to worship freely, but they were not always able to form a corporate body that would be recognized by the state as "the Jewish community" of a given place. In smaller settlements that had only one synagogue the distinction between "central community" *(politeuma)* and "local community" (the synagogue) did not matter, but in larger settlements with many synagogues the distinction was substantive. In the third and fourth centuries of our era the Jews of Rome maintained at least eleven different synagogues, but there is no indication that in the aggregate all the synagogues formed a single Jewish community. Each synagogue had its own name and board of officers. Perhaps the Jews of the city, for their own convenience, had some sort of board supervising all the synagogues and looking out for matters of general concern, but this board, if it existed at all, had no legal standing in the eyes of the state. This type of organization ensured freedom of religion no less than the *politeuma* did, but it did not provide much communal autonomy. In these localities the synagogue was the essential unit of communal organization.

The Synagogue

The synagogue is a tripartite institution: a prayer-house, a study hall or school, and a meeting-house. In all likelihood, each of these parts was once a separate institution, each with its own history, and only after a long and complicated process were the three combined. The best evidence for this process is nomenclature. The Greek-speaking Jews of the diaspora, when referring to a specific place or building that had a communal function, generally used the rare Greek word *proseuchē* (in plural, *proseuchai*), which literally means "prayer." They used the common Greek word *synagōgē* in its literal sense of "congregation" or "assembly." The Jews of Palestine, in contrast, generally avoided the term *proseuchē* and used the word *synagōgē* to refer to a place or building that had a communal purpose. Thus the Jews of the diaspora had "prayer-houses," while Palestinian Jews had "meeting-houses." In several passages Philo remarks that the *proseuchai* resemble "schools," because their essential purpose is to teach the laws of Moses and the words of God. The rabbis, too, often associate the *bet midrash* ("school" or "academy") with the *bet keneset* ("meeting-house" or "synagogue"). The variety of these terms indicates that the fully formed synagogue was not the creation of a single person or even a single generation. How the three functions came to be combined is the subject of the following brief discussion. (For a discussion of daily prayer and Torah study, ideas that form the background to the emergence of the synagogue, see the previous chapter.)

The earliest extant references to a synagogue are two nearly identical inscriptions from Upper Egypt dated to the reign of Ptolemy III Euergetes (246–221 B.C.E.).[2] The first one reads, "For King Ptolemy and Queen Berenice, his sister and wife, and for their children, the Jews (have dedicated) the prayer-house *(proseuchē)*." The second commemorates the dedication of another prayer-house to the same king and queen by "the Jews of the city Crocodilopolis." The Jewish communities of these small towns obviously did not constitute formal communities *(politeumata),* but these inscriptions testify to some kind of communal organization. The prayer-houses were built by "the Jews" and dedicated to the reigning monarchs, a practice that is attested elsewhere in Egypt and Cyrenaica in the third and second centuries B.C.E. These buildings are called *proseuchai,* strongly implying that their primary function was to serve as houses of prayer.

It is probably not a coincidence that the earliest Jewish "prayer-houses" are attested in the diaspora. Far removed from the temple and its cult, diaspora Jews needed an alternative means for regular communion with God. They did not want to build temples or offer sacrifices, so they created a new institution in which the community would gather for prayer. Many scholars believe that such an institution is the product of the sixth century B.C.E., when the Babylonian exiles sought a replacement for the temple which had been destroyed. Although the suggestion is plausible, it is unsupported by any evidence and seems to put the custom of daily (or regular) prayer much earlier than the evidence will allow. A more likely conjecture is that the prayer-house is a product of the Hellenistic diaspora. In any case, the synagogue as *proseuchē* is first attested in Egypt in the third century B.C.E.

At least two hundred or two hundred and fifty years have to elapse before a synagogue is attested in the land of Israel. Most of the numerous works of the later second temple period virtually ignore the synagogue. Antiochus Epiphanes profaned the temple and persecuted the Jews, but no source accuses him of abusing synagogues, apparently because they did not yet exist in Palestine (although many scholars contend that Ps. 74:8 refers to the destruction of synagogues by Epiphanes). The earliest attestations are all from the first century of our era. The Gospels, of course, refer to various synagogues in Galilee. Jerusalem had synagogues of freedmen, Cyrenians, Alexandrians, and Cilicians, according to Acts 6:9. In his narrative Josephus refers to synagogues in several Palestinian cities. In the Herodian fortresses Masada and Herodion archaeologists have discovered meeting rooms that may have served as synagogues. The most important testimony, however, is the following Greek inscription from Jerusalem, in all likelihood of the first century C.E.:[3]

> Theodotus, son of Vettenus, priest and archisynagogue, son of an archisynagogue, grandson of an archisynagogue, built the synagogue for the reading of the Law and the teaching of the commandments, and the guest house and the rooms and the water supplies as an inn for

those who come from abroad; which [synagogue] his fathers had founded and the elders and Simonides.

Theodotus was a third-generation archisynagogue, the "ruler of the synagogue," an office that is mentioned several times in the New Testament (for example, Mark 5:35–38 and Acts 18:8, 17) and in numerous other inscriptions. Theodotus also calls himself a "priest," although neither his father nor his grandfather is so designated.

How do these Palestinian synagogues compare with their diaspora equivalents? Theodotus explains that his synagogue is to serve for "the reading of the Law and the teaching of the commandments." In the synagogues of Galilee Jesus' primary activity is teaching, just as it is Paul's in the synagogues of Asia Minor. As I mentioned above, Philo emphasizes the didactic function of the synagogues. The study of scripture, then, is an activity that the synagogues of Palestine and the diaspora have in common. Otherwise, however, they are very different. The Palestinian synagogues are not *proseuchai*, prayer-houses. Theodotus does not mention prayer in the description of his synagogue. Presumably both pilgrims and natives of Jerusalem would pray at or near the temple, but Jews of Palestine who lived more than a day's journey from Jerusalem—where did they pray? Daily or even weekly prayer at the temple was as impractical for them as it was for their co-religionists in the diaspora. Surely they prayed in their local synagogues, but it is striking that only one text refers to a *proseuchē* in Palestine (Josephus, *Life* 277, 280, and 293, describing the synagogue in Tiberias), and that only one text (Matt. 6:5) explicitly locates regular prayer in Palestinian synagogues (but perhaps Matthew means "gatherings" rather than "synagogues"). In the passage that uses the term *proseuchē*, Josephus describes how the people of Tiberias assembled in their prayer-house on the Sabbath, but instead of praying they seem to spend their time having a town meeting about the war. Only at a special fast decreed for a few days later do the Tiberians turn to prayer (although that too is soon interrupted by political debate). Where did they pray? Perhaps in the city square, perhaps out in the fields (see again Matt. 6:5). There is no easy solution to this question.

In those parts of the land of Israel that had substantial numbers of gentiles (the city of Caesarea, for example), the local synagogue probably played the same role in communal organization that it did in the diaspora. But in the Jewish areas its role will have been very different. Tiberias was a Jewish city, and Josephus implies that the prayer-house was a municipal building. Rabbinic legislation about the synagogue also assumes it to be a municipal structure. In Jerusalem, by contrast, there is no indication of any municipal synagogue. Here the synagogues were private affairs, just like clubs or associations. This is strongly implied by the names of the synagogues listed in Acts 6:9 and by the Theodotus inscription. Whatever the identity of "the elders and Simonides," the inscription shows that the synagogue was virtually the private possession of the Theodotus/Vettenus family for over three generations. In this respect the Theodotean synagogue is not unique. Some synagogues of the later centuries, to judge from their inscriptions, were the private foundations of their dedicators; they were open to the community, of course, but owned or at least run by a private party. Archaeology has revealed many synagogues that originally were private homes and later were converted to sacred use.

In sum: the synagogue is an amalgamation of a prayer-house, which apparently originated in the diaspora in early Hellenistic times; a study house or school, which apparently originated in Israel also in early Hellenistic times (see below); and a meeting-house, which served the different needs of diaspora and Palestinian Jewry. By the first century C.E. these diverse elements had not yet united to form a single type. In fact, even by the end of late antiquity the synagogue did not attain a single definition. The sources from the third to the seventh centuries C.E. present radically different portraits of the synagogue. The rich archaeological evidence from both the land of Israel and the diaspora documents a wide variety of synagogue types, and scholars no longer even try to trace a single line of development that will tie them all together. The synagogues revealed by the archaeologist, with their carvings, mosaics, and paintings, are not the sort of buildings that rabbinic evidence had led us to expect. I shall return briefly to these problems in the last chapter.

Two important historical conclusions follow from this reconstruction. First, many scholars and textbooks use the word "synagogue" as if the word described a single, consistent, and well-defined phenomenon. But in reality there were many kinds of synagogues, during both the second temple and rabbinic periods, with varying functions, architecture, religious rituals, and social settings. There was no United Synagogue of Antiquity that enforced standards on all the member congregations. The word "synagogue" covers a wide variety of phenomena, and a definition that fits one place and time may not be appropriate for another. Second, since the synagogue grew from diverse and complex origins, it is most unlikely that any single group or office controlled all the synagogues of antiquity. The synagogue was not a Pharisaic invention and there is no reason to assume that all pre-70 synagogues, even in the land of Israel, were under Pharisaic control (in spite of Matt. 23:2 and 6). Perhaps the rabbis after 70 consolidated their power over some of the synagogues in the land of Israel, but since synagogues were in the hands of local communities, and sometimes in the hands of local individuals, the rabbis certainly did not have the means to establish rapid and effective control over all the synagogues of the Roman world. That was a long and slow process. Both of these points militate against the widely accepted belief that the Jewish-Christian split was finalized when the rabbis, in about 90–100 c.e., incorporated into the synagogue liturgy a benediction (actually a malediction) against Jesus and the Christians. Even if the rabbis did incorporate such an anti-Christian prayer, a point which is by no means clear, they would have had no way to ensure its acceptance in any synagogue outside of their direct control (see further chapter 7).

Private Organizations

The society of the pre-exilic period was organized by tribe. Each tribe was an agglomeration of clans, and each clan was an agglomeration of families. There were twelve tribes in all; a thirteenth, the tribe of Levi, was in charge of sacerdotal functions. With the exile of the northern kingdom in 722 b.c.e. and the southern in 587 b.c.e., the tribal structure was destroyed beyond repair. When the Jews returned from Babylonia to Judea in the sixth century b.c.e. their reconstituted society consisted of clans, not tribes (Ezra 2 and Neh. 7). The tribe of Levi now consisted of two clearly distinguished elements, priests and Levites, and the rest of the people were called simply Israelites (for example, Ezra 10:25; the other subdivisions in the population need not be considered here). The memory of twelve tribes was still alive (Ezra 8:35), just as it would remain alive throughout the second temple and rabbinic periods, but the memory did not shape the new social order. Priestly and aristocratic clans played an important role throughout the second temple period, but in the population at large by the Hellenistic period the clans had dissolved, or at least had lost their hold on their constituent families.

The breakdown of the tribe into the clan, and the clan into the family, mirrors the breakdown of the belief in corporate responsibility and the emergence of a doctrine of theodicy based on the individual. The eschatological speculations and the religious doctrines of the period treated the individual not merely as a member of a family, clan, or nation, but as an independent being whose ultimate reward and punishment depended on his or her own deeds alone (see chapter 3). New organizations were created to give the individual a place within society commensurate with his or her new importance. The model for these new organizations was the association.

In Greco-Roman society associations (or "guilds" or "clubs," *collegia* in Latin and *koina* in Greek) were extremely popular. They gave the individual both a secure refuge from the stresses of the world and a convenient place in which to find friendship and recognition. These associations were of many types: religious, economic, fraternal, and so on. Many groups were administered in accordance with written rules or laws, and practically all of the groups were led by various functionaries with high-sounding titles. The groups were run as if they were miniature cities *(poleis)*, thus providing the membership a sense of power and control that usually eluded them in the real world.

Jewish society too had its share of private associations. As I discussed in the previous section, the synagogue, at least in the western diaspora, was a private association for religious purposes. The word "synagogue" in non-Jewish Greek sometimes means "association," and even the title "archisynagogue" is attested in the sense of "head of the association." The synagogue was more than just a club, but its growth was certainly aided by the increased popularity of associations during the Hellenistic period. The synagogue was the most common form of Jewish association, but it was not the only one.

Sects

The Latin word *secta,* which gives us our English word "sect," means "mode of life," hence "school" or "school of thought." It is the equivalent of the Greek word *hairesis,* which in turn gives us our English word "heresy." In English usage "sect" and "heresy" often have negative valence: a sect is a "deviationist" group, and a heresy is an "incorrect" doctrine or practice. In the next chapter I shall discuss "orthodoxy" and "heresy" in ancient Judaism, and shall return to a fuller discussion of separatism, exclusiveness, and other concepts implied by the English words "sect" and "heresy." In this chapter my concern is neither theological authenticity nor social popularity, but group structure. I use "sect" as a neutral term of description for various groups in ancient Judaism that separated themselves from the community at large and were distinctive and coherent enough to receive special epithets from outsiders and/or to bestow special epithets upon themselves ("Essenes," "Christians," "Pharisees," etc.).

The clearest example of a sect is the group that lived at Qumran and is usually identified with the Essenes described by Philo and Josephus. The two major Qumran documents that outline the structure of the sect are the *Covenant of Damascus* (especially the second half) and the *Rule of the Community* (sometimes called the *Manual of Discipline,* especially 5:1–6:23), but the two descriptions do not coincide exactly (and neither coincides with the eschatological descriptions of the community contained in other works). The *Covenant of Damascus* describes a group that lives in "camps" among other Jews. They marry, have children, own property and slaves, and must be wary of contacts with both gentiles and Jewish nonsectaries. Their leader is the Overseer (in Greek translation the title would be *episkopos* or "bishop"), who is assisted by a priest and a panel of ten judges. All members (apparently), both new and old, must take an oath of loyalty to the laws of Moses.

The *Rule of the Community,* by contrast, presupposes a different social setting and a much more rigorous separation from the world. The members live a communal life, with little or no contact with outsiders. They do not own property; all goods are surrendered to the group upon acceptance. Nor are they married. Once again the Overseer figures prominently in the leadership of the group, but "the priests the sons of Zadok" are even more prominent. The text also describes the "Session of the Many," a general assembly that discusses various matters, notably the admission of new members, and which is presided over by the Overseer, the priests, the Levites, and the elders. Potential members underwent a probation process lasting three years, at the beginning of which they swore an oath of loyalty to the sect. After completing their catechism, if they were approved by the Session of the Many, they could join the sect and partake of its communal meals. Every year all members of the sect renewed the covenant in a ceremony based on Deuteronomy 27–28. Thus while the organization envisioned by the *Damascus Covenant* resembles that of the *Rule of the Community* (emphasis on purity, separation from sinners, obedience to authority, oaths of loyalty), the two texts emphasize different points and disagree on many matters of detail.

The content and literary form of these rules closely resemble the regulations of Greco-Roman associations. Sociologically considered, the Qumran sect is an association whose goal is to create a utopian society for its members. The *Covenant of Damascus* is still set in the real world, but the *Rule of the Community* mandates a society without women, children, private property, discord, falsehood—in sum, an ideal society which never existed but which was dreamed about by many political thinkers in antiquity. The utopian elements are also prominent in the descriptions of Philo and Josephus, whose accounts are nearly identical with each other. Both writers say that the Essenes numbered four thousand people and lived in villages and towns throughout the land of Israel. Neither writer highlights the group's exclusiveness and hieratic character. These points accord well with the social setting envisioned by the *Covenant of Damascus*. The tension between the ideal and the real is reflected in Josephus' statement that some Essenes were celibate, and that others married in order to have children. In general, however, both Philo and Josephus emphasize the utopian elements which recur (in different detail) in the *Rule of the Community*. They uphold the Essenes as wondrous exemplars of the philosophic life.

Many of the utopian or "sectarian" features of the Qumran Essenes can be found in other groups as well. The Essene community bears striking similarities to the community of early Christians as described in the opening chapters of the book of Acts. Property is held in common, violators of the rules are punished, the group is controlled by a board of leaders, lots are used in the selection process, entrants into the group require "conversion," and so on. These parallels are in addition to those of attitude (both are eschatologically oriented), doctrine (both see the current world as under the control of wicked forces), and practice (both lay great importance upon ablutions or "baptisms").

Not quite as close to the Qumran Essenes is the *haburah* ("fellowship" or "brotherhood"), described in the Mishnah (*Demai* 2:2–3) and related works. This was an association of those who pledged to observe the laws of purity at all times, even if they had no plans to enter the temple or bring a sacrifice. Many Jews slighted the laws of the priestly tithes, but the members of the *haburah* pledged to observe them punctiliously. As a result, they were unable to eat with anyone outside of their group. Like the *Covenant of Damascus*, the rabbinic legislation envisions a society in which members of the group come into daily and intimate contact with nonmembers, both Jewish and gentile. Like the *Rule of the Community*, the rabbinic legislation requires an oath of all those entering the group and outlines a novitiate of three years in the course of which the novice gradually attains the rank of a full member. As in the Community Rule, his elevation in status is indicated by his ability to share the food and drink of the other members.

Many scholars believe that this *haburah* is a "sectarian" body, since membership requires separation from the larger community, and ascribe its origins to the Pharisees, a group whose name seems to mean "separatists." Whether or not the *haburah* is Pharisaic, its "sectarian" character is uncertain, because the rabbinic legislation, our sole source for the *haburah,* does not clearly state whether the *haburah* is a tight organization or a loose association of religious elitists. Furthermore, while the *haburah* promotes separation from the masses, it is unclear whether the separation is the consequence of a claim to exclusive possession of the truth, like the claims advanced by the Essenes and the Christians. Without a claim to exclusive truth, a group is not a sect (see the next chapter). At Qumran, the sectarians are righteous and therefore pure; everyone else is wicked and therefore impure. The rabbinic legislation seems to be based on the opposite logic. The members of the *haburah* are pure and therefore righteous; everyone else is impure and therefore wicked. In any case, no matter what social reality may be lurking behind the rabbinic legislation about the *haburah,* the affinity with the Qumran legislation shows that separatism based on purity laws was a powerful idea in ancient Judaism that extended even beyond clearly sectarian groups.

Professional Guilds

Unlike synagogues and sects, professional guilds have a long history in the ancient Near East. Craftsmen's and merchants' guilds played an important role in the economies of Babylonia, Assyria, and Egypt. The evidence for the activity of guilds in Palestine is not abundant, but is sufficient to indicate their existence throughout the second temple and rabbinic periods. When rebuilding the wall of Jerusalem, Nehemiah assigned some of the work to (one of) "the goldsmiths" and to (one of) "the perfumers" (Neh. 3:8, 31). The first book of Chronicles refers to "families" of scribes (2:55) and weavers (4:21). Josephus and the New Testament refer to many craft workers (including scribes), but give no indication of how they were organized. Rabbinic texts, however, refer to guilds of wool dealers, dyers, bakers, muleteers, shippers, butchers, and weavers. A Jewish inscription of the second century C.E. from Joppa mentions a guild of fishermen.[4] According to another rabbinic tradition one "family" during second temple times was responsible for baking the showbread for the temple, another "family" for preparing the incense. One day they went on strike and did not return to work until their wages were doubled. From these and other indications it is likely that professional guilds were part of the social fabric of ancient Judaism. Other nonreligious associations probably existed too, but they are nowhere mentioned.

Schools

A different sort of organization altogether is the school. According to rabbinic tradition, either Simeon ben Shetah (first century B.C.E.) or Joshua ben Gamla (first century C.E.) decreed compulsory education for all children, but it is not likely that either tradition has historical value.[5] A few Greek cities in Hellenistic times instituted free public education for children (usually as the result of a grant from a wealthy citizen), but there is no indication that the Jewish community of either Palestine or the diaspora during second temple times maintained public schools for either children or adults. Josephus and Philo, who boast that all Jews, even children, know the laws of Moses, emphasize the custom of the public reading of the Torah (in the synagogues) and do not mention separate schools. In all likelihood elementary education was the responsibility of the family. Wealthy (or ignorant!) people might hire a tutor for their children, but generally in the ancient world elementary education did not go beyond paternal instruction in a craft.

Advanced study, beyond the public reading and explication of the Torah every Sabbath in the synagogue, was almost exclusively the prerogative of the wealthy and the privileged, since only they had the means and the leisure (in Greek, *scholē*, whence Latin *schola* and English *school*) to pursue higher education instead of trying to make a living (cf. Ben Sira 38:24–39:11). What sort of school could one attend? The English word "school" conjures up the image of a corporate, perpetual institution housed in a large building filled with teachers, students, and offices. The ancient world did not know any schools of this type. The Athenian schools founded by Plato, Aristotle, Epicurus, and Zeno in the fourth and third centuries B.C.E. were perpetual institutions—the Epicurean school still flourished in the second century C.E.—with graded ranks of students and faculty, but were much smaller and more informal than the modern word "school" would suggest. Academies of the Athenian sort did not exist (as far as we know) in the Jewish society of either Palestine or the diaspora in the second temple period, although Josephus describes the Pharisees, Sadducees, and Essenes as if they were "schools" (see chapter 5). Josephus means by the comparison that the doctrines of the Jewish sects resemble those of their Greek counterparts, but perhaps he also is drawing a parallel in organizational structure. Following Josephus' lead, many modern scholars have observed that the utopian organization of the Essenes resembles that of the "school" of the Pythagoreans. But most schools were not brotherhoods of people living in common, and normal schools of the Athenian pattern did not emerge in Palestine until the rabbinic period.

A different type of school is the disciple circle, a handful of disciples grouped around a master. The disciples were apprentices who learned by constant attendance upon the master. They watched his every action and listened to his every word. The disciple circle existed as long as the master remained active; upon his death or retirement the school died with him. Hence these schools were neither corporate bodies nor perpetual institutions. Disciple circles were the normal pattern for higher education in both Jewish and Greco-Roman antiquity.

The first solid evidence for the institutionalization of higher education in the period of the second temple is provided by Ben Sira (ca. 200 B.C.E.), who writes (51:23–28):

> Draw near to me, you who are untaught, and lodge in my school. Why do you say you are lacking in these things, and why are your souls very thirsty? I opened my mouth and said, Get these things for yourselves without money. Put your neck under the yoke, and let your souls receive instruction; it is to be found close by. See with your eyes that I have labored little and found for myself much rest. Get instruction with a large sum of silver, and you will gain by it much gold.

Ben Sira is encouraging his readers, who were the well-to-do, to emulate his example and submit to the yoke of wisdom. He invites them to "lodge in my school," *bet midrashi* (literally "sit in my house of inquiry"). This school was, presumably, a circle that met in Ben Sira's house. The book of Proverbs, an older representative of wisdom literature, also presumes a didactic setting (note all the second-person addresses to "my son"), but contains no reference to a specific educational setting like the *bet midrash*.

In rabbinic literature the *bet midrash* figures prominently, although the rabbis never define precisely the nature of the institution. Sometimes the *bet midrash* appears to be a place where a master and his disciples gather for study, sometimes it appears to be an actual building. A recently discovered inscription from the Golan states "This is the *bet midrash* of R. Eliezer HaQappar," a rabbi of the second century.[6] (Unfortunately the rest of the building has disappeared without a trace.) One rabbinic text of the second century refers to "the *bet midrash* at Ardaskus," another to "the *bet midrash* at Lod."[7] These texts imply that by the second century the *bet midrash* was becoming a permanent institution in some localities. As a rule, however, the rabbis of the second century did not need a special place for the instruction of their disciples, because the disciples were always with the master. They would live, eat, sleep, and travel with him. They would listen to his discussions with other rabbis and watch him decide legal cases. There was little privacy for either party in this relationship; even on his wedding night R. Gamaliel was attended by his faithful disciples. The master was sometimes addressed as "father," because he was the father to his disciples. According to rabbinic law a student's obligations to his master are similar to those of a son to his father: he had to stand up in his presence, to greet him, and perhaps even to bow down before him. He could not stand or sit in his place, speak in his presence, contradict him, or respond sharply to him. This was the way of Torah. In effect, joining a disciple circle was like joining a new family (cf. Mark 3:32–35; 10:29–31).

These small communities of devoted disciples gathered around a revered master have many analogies, of course, to the earliest community of the followers of Jesus. One of Jesus' major activities, as remarked above, was to teach, and the apostles were his beloved disciples. Jesus was not only a teacher, however; he was also a prophet and a healer, and the traditions about him clearly derive in part from the biblical record about Elijah and his disciple Elisha. In contrast, the rabbis of the second century did not claim to be holy men or miracle workers (although some rabbis of the third and fourth centuries did). Another difference is that Jesus' followers consisted mostly of the poor, while the rabbinic following in the second century seems to have come mostly from higher classes (this changed in the third century). The first Christians depended upon gifts for their support (Matt. 10:9–11; 1 Cor. 9; 2 Cor. 7:10–11; Phil. 4:10–20), the rabbis did not. Although the social settings are very different, the disciple circle of Jesus closely resembles the disciple circles of the rabbis in the second century.

The historical implications of this reconstruction resemble those stated above at the conclusion of the discussion of the synagogue. Schools were private, not public, institutions. No single organization supervised schools or "authorized" teachers. Both Palestine and the diaspora must have seen a large variety of people who were called *didaskalos* or *rabbi* by their followers (cf. John 1:38). Not all of them were Pharisees or members of that select fraternity which produced the Mishnah and related works, and not all of them taught the same interpretation of Judaism.

Conclusion

Jewish society of the second temple and rabbinic periods was in many respects a typical ancient society. It consisted mostly of the poor and the very poor. The aristocracy and the learned elite, who wrote most of the extant literature and figure prominently in the historical narratives, were a small percentage of the population. The "silent majority" included not only the poor but other powerless groups as well (notably women and slaves). The poor hated the rich with a hatred that occasionally flared into violence. The country dwellers envied and/or hated the city folk, since the city was the home of tax collectors, landlords, and decadence (that is, culture). The Maccabean rebellion was the triumph of simple priests from the country over high priests from the city. The war of 66–70 was in large part a civil war between the lower priesthood and the high priesthood, between the poor and the rich, and between the country and the city. In all these respects Jewish society typifies ancient society as a whole.

What made Jewish society "Jewish" was Judaism and its institutions. Everywhere in Greco-Roman society there were to be found priests and temples, associations and schools, but the peculiarities of Judaism made the Jewish versions of these institutions, for all of their similarities to their Greco-Roman counterparts, essentially Jewish. No other religion in antiquity developed either the monism and exclusivism of the Jerusalem temple or the democratization and mass participation of the synagogue or the exclusivism and polemical stance of the sects. Even the *politeuma,* a creation of Hellenistic public law, was used by the Jews primarily to defend their rights and ensure freedom of worship. The spirit of Judaism was expressed not only in its practices and beliefs but also in its institutions.

5

Sectarian and Normative

Introduction: Definitions and Terminology

When describing the reign of Jonathan the high priest (the mid-140s B.C.E.), Josephus remarks (*Jewish Antiquities* 13.5.9, §171–173):

> Now at this time there were three schools of thought among the Jews, which held different opinions concerning human affairs; the first being that of the Pharisees, the second that of the Sadducees, and the third that of the Essenes. As for the Pharisees, they say that certain events are the work of Fate, but not all; as to other events, it depends upon ourselves whether they shall take place or not. The sect of Essenes, however, declares that Fate is the mistress of all things, and that nothing befalls men unless in accordance with her decree. But the Sadducees do away with Fate, holding that there is no such thing and that human actions are not achieved in accordance with her decree, but that all things lie within our own power. . . .

When describing events in Judea a century and a half later, Josephus describes the same three "schools of thought" in almost the same language. These accounts of Josephus are puzzling and raise many questions. What is a "school of thought" (*hairesis* in Greek)? When and why did the three "schools of thought" arise? What is their history? What is the meaning and origin of the names Pharisees, Essenes, and Sadducees? Was the eternal question of fate vs. free will the central item of debate among these "schools"? Did Judaism have only three "schools of thought," and did all Jews necessarily subscribe to one of them? Neither Josephus nor any other ancient author directly addresses these questions. I begin my answer with a discussion of the terms "sect," "heresy," "orthodoxy," and "normative." In this section I use a phenomenological approach in order to explain the concept of "sectarianism" in the abstract; I assume for illustrative purposes that the Pharisees, the Samaritans, the early

Christians, and the Jews of Qumran were "sects," or at least were groups with marked sectarian features. In making this assumption I am anticipating the results of the body of this chapter, the historical survey of sects in antiquity.

"Sect" and "Heresy"

The English words "sect" and "heresy" usually convey a negative meaning. A "sect" is a group that "deviates" from the norm and separates from the church; a "denomination," by contrast, is a legitimate subgroup of a church. A "heresy" is an "inauthentic" or "illegitimate" doctrine; a "tenet," by contrast, is an "official" or "essential" doctrine. In other words, "sects" and "heresies" are religious groups and doctrines of which we disapprove. In their original usage, however, the Latin word *secta* and its equivalent Greek word *hairesis* lacked any negative connotation and were neutral terms for "school" (a collection of people) or "school of thought" (a collection of ideas). When Josephus labeled the Pharisees, Sadducees, and Essenes *haireseis*, he was not dismissing them as "sects" or "heresies" but was presenting them as "schools" or "schools of thought" that could be appreciated by his Greek readers. *Secta* came to mean "sect" and *hairesis* came to mean "heresy" in the writings of the church fathers who used these terms to denigrate their opponents.

In this chapter I use the word "sect" in another sense entirely. (I avoid the term "heresy," as I shall explain below.) Here is my definition:

> A sect is a small, organized group that separates itself from a larger religious body and asserts that it alone embodies the ideals of the larger group because it alone understands God's will.

This definition is a modern one and is derived from the sociology of medieval and modern Christianity. Although scholars debate which characteristics are essential for a sect and which are only incidental (like obscenity, a sect is more easily recognized than defined), I think that any "minimal" definition would resemble the one that I have given.

A sect must be *small* enough to be a distinctive part of a *larger religious body*. If a sect grows to the extent that it is a large body in its own right, it is no longer a sect but a "religion" or a "church." The precise definition of "large body" and "church" is debated by sociologists, but that question need not be treated here. In the period under review in this book two Jewish sects (or sect-like groups) outgrew their sectarian origins to become independent religions. Out of the Christian sect came Christianity, and out of the Pharisaic sect came rabbinic Judaism, also known simply as "Judaism."

A sect must be *organized*. Sects usually have an administrative structure, a process of initiation for new members, rules for proper conduct, and the threat of expulsion for members who are recalcitrant. In many sects new members are acquired only through "conversion," not birth. (Of course, this is sometimes true of "religions" as well. Tertullian, a church father of the late second century, boasted that "Christians are made, not born.")

A sect *separates itself* from the community, but the separation can take various forms. The members of the sect might flee to the desert or some other isolated place. Or they might live among, but not with, their nonsectarian co-religionists. They create taboos ("boundaries") that inhibit normal social intercourse between members of the group (the "pure," "righteous," "elect," etc.) and nonmembers (the "impure," "wicked," "damned," etc.). No matter what form the separation takes, it is generally caused by a sense of alienation from the rest of the community, especially from the community's central institutions. In many cases (as at Qumran) a dualistic theology, which divides the supernatural realm between God and Satan (see chapter 3), mirrors a dualistic social perspective, which divides humanity between the sons of light and the sons of darkness. Social alienation might also express itself in intense eschatological speculation, by which the sect reassures itself that its current status of powerlessness is only temporary. In the future the sect will be glorified and its enemies will be discomfited.

A sect asserts that *it alone embodies the ideals of the larger group*. In Jewish terms this means that a sect sees itself as the true Israel. At best all other Jews are sinners; at worst they hardly deserve the name "Israel" at all. The contrasting perspectives of the sect and the larger community are revealed by the appellations that each has for the other. The sect might use self-designations that are elitist (for example, "the elect of Israel," "the righteous remnant," "the blessed of God," "the sons of light") or pietist (for example, "the repenters of Israel," "the righteous ones," "the pious ones," "those who have entered the new covenant"), or might simply call itself "Israel" (as the Samaritans and the Christians did—and do). The rest of the Jews are dismissed as "the wicked," "the oppressors," "the sons of darkness," and so on. In return, the opponents of the sect might bestow on it all sorts of uncomplimentary epithets in order to deny its legitimacy. The sect has "sundered itself" from the rest of Israel (the name "Pharisee," in all likelihood, was originally an opprobrious epithet meaning "separatist"), and advocates an "intrusive" or "illegitimate" ideology.

The sect's claim to be the exclusive embodiment of the ideals of the larger community is based on its claim that *it alone understands God's will.* This assertion was buttressed by a variety of means. A sect might claim that it or its leader is privy to a new revelation from God which was unknown to or unappreciated by outsiders. Or it might claim that it is the bearer of an ancient tradition, or that it has rediscovered the true religion which had been forgotten or corrupted by the majority. Or it might claim that only it properly understands the sacred scriptures or that only it has correctly selected the books which belong in the canon. In sum, the sect contends that only its authority figures can speak on behalf of God, because those of the larger community do not have access to the truth.

In the final analysis, what makes a sect a sect is its separation and exclusivity. Guilds, clubs, synagogues, and schools resemble sects in that they are small voluntary associations, but as long as they neither separate themselves from the community nor claim exclusive possession of the truth, they are not sects. In some instances a group can separate itself from the majority and still not be a sect; the "orders" of the Catholic church are the classic examples. The Benedictine order is a small organized group that separates itself from the community and conducts itself in accordance with a rule (The Rule of St. Benedict) that resembles the Qumran Community Rule in both form and content. But the Benedictines are not a sect because they see themselves, and are seen by the church, as an elite, not as the sole possessors of Christian truth. They admit that non-Benedictine Christians who live a righteous life will attain salvation. They derive their legitimation not from some proprietary revelation or sacred text (Benedict is a saint for the entire church), but from the same pope who presides over all other Catholics.

The Focal Points of Jewish Sectarianism

Sects feel alienated from the rest of the world. They feel that the traditional values and practices of society have been corrupted, or are no longer adequate; that society is irredeemably sinful; that society has not granted a particular individual or group (usually the sect itself) deserved recognition, or that it has granted a particular individual or group (some other sect) undeserved recognition. As a result of these feelings the sect concludes that its only option, until the heavenly forces inaugurate a new order of things on earth, is to separate from society and to create a more perfect community. By the time a sect has separated itself and become a distinct group, it is difficult to determine the original cause of its alienation, because the feelings that were its *cause* are now reinforced or superseded by feelings that are its *effect.* For example, in a (still unpublished) letter the leader of the Qumran community (the Teacher of Righteousness?) says to his opponents (the Wicked Priest?) that their failure to properly observe various purity laws and temple rituals compels the group to separate itself from the rest of Israel. Does this letter reveal the *causes* of the sect's alienation, or its *effects?* If the latter is correct, as seems likely, this document does not end the search for the reasons that impelled the Jews of Qumran to abandon their co-religionists and to seek their salvation on their own. But whether as a cause or an effect of its alienation, a sect rejects or, at least, harshly criticizes the institutions and practices venerated by the rest of society. In ancient Judaism the targets of sectarian polemics were primarily three: law, temple, and scripture. I shall treat each of these separately.

Law as Focal Point

Christianity is a creedal religion, and Christian sectarianism too is creedal. The vast majority of the sectarian debates of early Christianity centered on theological questions, especially the nature and interrelationship of the first two persons of the Trinity. Judaism, however, was not (and, in large measure, is not) a creedal religion. The "cutting edge" of ancient Jewish sectarianism was not theology but law. Of course sects often advocated peculiar doctrinal views, but these did not play the formative role that the legal positions did. Abundant evidence makes this point clear: the proto-sectarianism of the Persian period; the critique of Jewish society contained in the *Rule of the Community* and the *Damascus Covenant* of Qumran; the letter of the Teacher of Righteousness (mentioned in the previous paragraph); Josephus' assertion that the Pharisees accept the validity of "the ancestral traditions" while the Sadducees do not; the New Testament's account of the debates between the Pharisees and Jesus; and the rabbinic accounts of the debates between the Pharisees and the Sadducees. All this material emphasizes the legal character of the debates among the sects and ignores or slights philosophical and theological matters.

There is some evidence on the other side, to be sure: Josephus' portrait of the Pharisees, Sadducees, and Essenes as philosophical "schools" that debate the eternal questions of fate, free will, and the immortality of the soul; and the New Testament's view that the distinguishing characteristic of the Sadducees is their denial of the resurrection of the dead (a perspective shared by one stray rabbinic text). The two sources written in Greek (Josephus and the New Testament) support both the legal and the philosophical interpretations of Jewish sectarian dispute, while the sources written in Hebrew (Qumran scrolls and rabbinic texts) support the legal interpretation exclusively. I conclude that sectarian dispute focused primarily on legal questions, a pattern that continued in the Jewish sectarianism of the Middle Ages, and that the Greek sources advanced the opposite perspective for the benefit of their intended non-Jewish audience.

Three areas of law in particular were the subjects of debate: marriage; Sabbath and festivals; temple and purity. In the view of the sect the ruling elite (or society at large) has contracted illegal marriages. Either they do not properly understand the intricacies of the table of forbidden relations given in Leviticus 18 and 20 or they marry "foreign" women. By denouncing these marriages and thereby delegitimating the offspring of their opponents, the sectarians not only confirm their belief that only they practice Judaism properly, they also erect a barrier that prohibits marriage between themselves and the rest of society. The Sabbath and the festivals were celebrated communally both in the temple and outside it, and by advancing a peculiar interpretation of these rituals the members of the sect distanced themselves from the common patterns of religiosity. At Qumran this separation reached an extreme form; the sect advocated not only a particularly severe mode of observance for the Sabbath, but also a peculiar calendar that was not followed by the rest of the community. The day the Jews of Qumran celebrated as the Day of Atonement was a regular workday for all other Jews.

Last, the laws governing temple and purity always figured prominently in sectarian self-definition. The purity laws are outlined in Leviticus (especially the first half) and Numbers (especially Num. 19). Impurity is contracted chiefly through contact with a human corpse, an "impure" animal, or a sexual discharge (from either a man or a woman). The laws are complex because so many variables are involved: the source of the impurity; the means by which the impurity is transferred to persons, foodstuffs, and objects; the degree of the impurity; and the method of purification. Each of these variables was treated by the Torah, and each was analyzed at great length in second temple times (especially at Qumran) and in rabbinic times. The English words "pure" and "impure" may create the impression that these laws are either hygienic ("pure" for "clean," and "impure" for "dirty") or metaphoric ("pure" for "righteous" or "good," "impure" for "wicked" or "bad"), but this impression is wrong. Leviticus does not care whether certain animals (for example, pigs) are dirty, since that fact is irrelevant to their status of impurity, nor does Leviticus include obvious sources of "dirt" (for example, feces and urine) among the sources of impurity. Leviticus 16:30 equates atonement with purification, but for the most part in Leviticus "sin" is not the cause of impurity, and righteousness is not synonymous with purity. (The term *ritual* impurity used by many modern scholars emphasizes this fact.)

According to Leviticus and Numbers, anyone and anything that enters the "camp," the abode of God, must be pure. That which is impure must be expelled from the camp. The camp includes all the children of Israel: the tabernacle, the priests and Levites, and the twelve tribes. It was not until the period of the second temple that the full implications of this conception were actualized. Pietists and sectarians observed all the purity laws, because God was in the "camp." Purity was a matter of daily life. The food on one's table was akin to meat on the altar; a priest's obligation to observe the purity laws when entering the sanctuary was no greater than that of the Jew who lived in the "camp." The Jews of Qumran, the Pharisees, and the "fellowship" *(haburah)* described in the previous chapter exemplify this way of life. It was probably fear of impurity that impelled the Essenes of Qumran to prohibit women from their midst. For most Jews of the second temple period, however, the sanctification of daily life was not implemented to such a radical degree. They felt, as the majority of rabbis did later as well, that "the camp" included only the temple and the temple mount. Jews who wished to enter the temple or bring a sacrifice purified themselves. Archaeological excavations at the temple mount in Jerusalem have revealed a whole series of baths adjacent to the steps leading to the main entrance of the temple. Here the faithful would bathe before entering the sacred precincts. Away from the temple, however, most Jews saw no need to observe the purity laws since they were no longer in the "camp" described by Leviticus.

Even more than the laws of marriage and the Sabbath, the laws of purity prevent normal social intercourse between those who observe them and those who do not. Those who observe the laws cannot share the table, utensils, or food of those who do not. They must avoid physical contact (for example, a handshake) with those who are impure. It is natural then for a sect to develop its own idiosyncratic purity regulations in order to give concrete expression to its sense of alienation and exclusivity. The sectarian community is a place of purity that not only rivals the temple but also supplants it. The temple is polluted, the priests corrupt, and the rituals debased. The temple is a site of *impurity* and must be purified of its contagion before it can resume its rightful place in the divine order. This is the attitude of a sect, and it is to this attitude that I now turn.

Temple as Focal Point

Throughout its existence the second temple enjoyed a status which in paradoxical fashion was both substantially higher and substantially lower than that of the first. No longer under the thumb of the monarchs, no longer the target of the polemics of the prophets, no longer rivaled seriously by "high places" and other temples, the second temple and its cult gained a centrality and importance that the first temple never achieved. The priesthood became the aristocracy and the high priest became the leader of the country. With the growth of the diaspora the temple became the recipient of donations and the goal of pilgrimage for Jews throughout the world. After being rebuilt by Herod the Great, Jerusalem became one of the most famous cities of the East and its temple was the object of universal admiration.

But the newfound importance of the temple could not hide several difficult problems. Built by a Davidic king, authorized by a prophet, and authenticated through the miraculous manifestation of God (a cloud of smoke and, according to Chronicles, fire from heaven), the first temple was the splendid achievement of a splendid reign. The second temple, by contrast, although authorized by the prophets Haggai and Zechariah, was built by a gentile king and was never authenticated by an overt sign of divine favor. Second Isaiah, in his prophecy announcing God's selection of Cyrus the Great to be his "anointed one" to free the Jews from the Babylonian captivity and to build the temple, is aware that some Jews do not approve of God's plan ("Woe to him who strives with his Maker, an earthen vessel with the potter! Does the clay say to him who fashions it, 'What are you making'?" Isa. 45:9). The old men who had seen the first temple in its glory cried at the dedication of the second (Ezra 3:12)—apparently tears of sadness, as they contemplated the puny temple that was before them. In the second century B.C.E., the temple's problematic status was revealed to all. The high priests were corrupted and the temple was profaned by a gentile monarch. Even after it was regained and purified by pious Jews, there was no prophet to approve their work and no miracle to assure them that the temple was once again the abode of God. The Maccabees installed themselves as high priests although they were not of the high priestly line. When the Romans conquered Jerusalem in 63 B.C.E. they entered the sacred precincts, polluting them with their presence. Herod the Great rebuilt the temple magnificently, but his detractors viewed him as a "half-Jew." He completely debased the high priesthood, appointing men who had even less claim than the Maccabees to be the legitimate successors of Aaron.

Thus although the second temple emerged as the central symbol and institution of Judaism, and although the priesthood, especially the high priesthood, emerged as the new aristocracy of the Jewish polity, both temple and priesthood, especially after the Maccabean period, had serious ideological weakness. How could the Jews be sure that the institution and the people who claimed to mediate between them and God were really authorized to do so? The sects argued that the temple and the priests did not find favor in God's eyes. The exclusive claims to truth advanced by the temple—"one temple for the one God," as Josephus puts it (*Against Apion* 2.23, §193)—were arrogated by the sect itself. Instead of the polluted temple and the corrupt priests, the sect and its leaders offer the only access to God. Either explicitly or implicitly the sect sees itself and its authority figures as the replacements for the temple and its priests. This self-perception is well attested at Qumran and in early Christianity (for example, 1 Cor. 3:16–17; 6:19; 2 Cor. 6:16; Eph. 2:19–22; 1 Peter 2:1–10), the major distinction between them being that the Jews of Qumran saw their community as the *temporary* replacement for the temple, since God would erect a new temple in the future, while (some of) the early Christians argued that their community was its *permanent* replacement (Rev. 21:22). The daily observance of purity laws by laypeople, a practice that characterized Pharisees, Essenes, and various others, was an arrogation of laws that originally applied to the temple alone.

The close connection between the temple and sectarianism is also shown by the fact that the important stages in the development of Jewish sectarianism coincide with the important stages in the history of the second temple. Sects appeared in inchoate form in the Persian period when the newly built temple was trying to establish its legitimacy. They emerged fully developed in the second century B.C.E. after the temple had been profaned by Epiphanes and purified by the Maccabees. Sects disappeared after 70 C.E., because the destruction of the temple removed one of the chief focal points of sectarianism.

Scripture as Focal Point

By the time the Jews returned from Persia, classical prophecy of the sort perfected by the prophets of the eighth and early sixth centuries B.C.E. was on the wane. The Jews recognized that they were living in a postclassical age. The prophets who persisted in seeing heavenly visions and hearing heavenly voices saw and heard in a manner very different from those of earlier times. As a consequence (cause?) of the cessation or permutation of prophecy, the Jews began to seek the word of the Lord not from people but from texts. The sacred traditions of the past were compiled and redacted, and the Torah was created. The words of the great prophets of the past were similarly compiled and redacted. This process, whose ultimate result was the formation of "the Bible" (see next chapter), raised two important questions. First, which books were to be considered "canonical" (in the sense of "authoritative")? Second, how were the canonical books to be interpreted, and who was "authorized" to interpret them?

A canon includes certain works and excludes others. In Christianity the selection of the canonical books of the New Testament was a battleground between "orthodoxy" and "heresy." One "orthodox" church father of the late second century refuted the "heretics" by appealing to the Christian canon: only four Gospels are true (canonical); no other Gospel is a valid source for church doctrine; therefore anyone who reveres any other Gospel is not a member of the holy and true Catholic church.[1] In contrast, the formation of the biblical canon did not play a role in the sectarian debates of ancient Judaism. In second temple times the biblical canon was very fluid. All Jews regarded the Torah as authoritative, and all Jews except the Samaritans regarded the prophetic books as authoritative. But the nature and degree of the authority that was ascribed to these books, and the identity of the other books which also were to be regarded as authoritative, varied greatly from community to community. The Essenes of Qumran criticized the religious behavior of their fellow Jews, but failure to respect the Essene writings is not among their complaints. No ancient source implies that the constitution of the canon was a focal point of sectarian dispute. There is no evidence that any central body (for example, the temple priesthood) tried to impose on the population a unified canon. Thus, the formation of the biblical canon was an integral part of the sectarian debate in Christianity, but in Judaism it was not. Jewish sects composed and/or preserved works that they alone considered authoritative, but this activity was not apparently essential either to their self-definition or to the way in which they were defined by their opponents.

A clearer focus of sectarian debate was the interpretation of the Bible. Since the word of God no longer was revealed through the prophets, as in the old days, the Jews turned to the exegesis of holy writ. Through interpretation the eternal verities of the texts could be discovered and made relevant to the contemporary situation. Torah study became a fixed part of the liturgy, and a class of learned sages arose whose claim to prominence was based on their erudition and expertise in scriptural interpretation (see chapter 3). Sects too claimed to derive their doctrines and practices from scripture, with the added claim, of course, that only their interpretation was correct. Biblical interpretation was an essential part of sectarian self-definition. Origen, a church father of the mid-third century, explains that "the variety of the interpretations of the writings of Moses and the sayings of the prophets" was one of the major factors that caused Jewish "sects" (Origen uses the term *haireseis*) to come into existence.[2] This explanation is surely as correct for Jewish sects (in the sense used in this chapter) as for Jewish "schools of thought."

The Israelites of the pre-exilic period had to struggle with the problem of distinguishing the true prophet from the false. Both the true and the false proclaimed, "Thus speaks the Lord," but only one of them was true. The Jews of the second temple period still had to contend with the problem of false prophecy, but in great measure this problem was replaced by a new one: how was one to distinguish the "true" (that is, authoritative, canonical) books and the "true" (that is, correct) scriptural interpretations from the false? The sects provided clear answers to this question, and these answers were part of their sectarian self-definition.

"Orthodox" and "Normative"

Throughout this book I avoid the terms "orthodox" and "normative" (and their antonyms "heretical" and "schismatic"). In this section I explain why.

The Greek word *orthodoxia*, the ancestor of the English "orthodoxy," means "right opinion," just as the Latin word *norma*, the ancestor of the English "normal" and "normative," means "standard of behavior." The terms therefore imply the "rightness" of the religious variety to which they are applied. "Orthodox Judaism" is Judaism which is *true*—that is, revealed by God and sanctioned by tradition. "Normative Judaism" is the *dominant* form of Judaism—

that is, the form practiced and revered as legitimate by the largest number of Jews. The two meanings overlap but are not identical. To define one variety of Judaism as "orthodox" is to make a theological judgment, a confession of faith not susceptible to rational inquiry. Whether the Judaism of the Pharisees is "truer" than that of the Sadducees, and whether the Judaism of Gamaliel is "truer" than that of Jesus and Paul, are questions that a historian cannot answer. A historian therefore must not describe any variety of Judaism as "orthodox" unless he or she is clearly writing from a confessional perspective.

To define one variety of Judaism as "normative" is a historical judgment, a statement that this variety was more widely practiced than others, but here too the notion of "rightness" almost invariably intrudes. In the period of the first temple, if we may believe the tirades of the prophets, most Israelites went whoring after foreign gods, sacrificing to them on every hilltop and under every tree. The religion of the masses and, at certain times, of the state as well, was syncretistic: the God of Israel was worshiped alongside other gods. Shouldn't we call Israelite syncretism "normative"? We do not do so because the biblical prophets and historians, who are deemed by both Judaism and Christianity to have been the bearers of the word of God, roundly condemned such practices. Thus even the term "normative" conveys a notion of "rightness" and is best avoided. (Appropriate substitutes are "popular" or "dominant.")

This issue can be approached from a different perspective. What is "Judaism"? Is it the religious behavior of all people who call themselves and are known to others as Jews, Israelites, and Hebrews? Or is it an ideal set of beliefs and practices against which the practices and beliefs of real Jews are to be measured and judged? If the former, Judaism is a relativistic construct of human beings, and no variety of Judaism is any more "correct" or "authentic" than any other. This is the perspective of the historian. If the latter, Judaism is a body of absolute truths revealed by God and/or sanctioned by tradition, and those interpretations of Judaism which more nearly approximate these absolute truths are truer and more authentic than those which do not. This is the perspective of the believer. In this book I am a historian.

Another objection to the term "orthodoxy" is that it introduces a meaningless concept into ancient Judaism. The church councils of the fourth century prescribed the acceptable limits of Christian practice and belief, defined the canon, established creeds, and anathematized sects and heresies. In other words, these councils defined "orthodoxy." Indeed, it was during the fourth century that the term "orthodox" (and related words) began to be widely used by patristic writers in order to distinguish the "true" Christianity from the "false." The rise of the papacy made the process of self-definition even easier. Whoever was admitted to communion with the bishop of Rome was "orthodox"; whoever was not was a heretic. The party that triumphed in the fourth century, thereby becoming Christian "orthodoxy," saw itself as the representative of that Christianity which had been believed "everywhere, always, and by all."[3] The numerous other interpretations of Christianity during the early centuries were dismissed as "sects" and "heresies." Jesus and Paul established "orthodoxy," and all those sects which bedeviled the church in its infancy were corruptions of the one holy and true Catholic church. Thus the triumph of "orthodoxy" was accompanied by heresiology (the study and refutation of "heresies"), ecclesiology (the definition of the church community, reading certain people in and certain people out), and ecclesiastical historiography (the writing of church history from the perspective of the triumphant party).

Judaism, by contrast, has never had either a pope or church councils, and without these there is no objective criterion for the determination of "orthodoxy." The temple was the central authority against which sects defined themselves, but the high priests lacked sufficient power to be able to state which forms of Judaism were "orthodox" or to exclude from the temple those Jews whose practices they condemned. After the destruction of the temple in 70 C.E., the rabbinic movement gradually assumed the role of central authority, but that process took several centuries, and the rabbis were never unified sufficiently either to elect a pope or to convene synods. Judaism did not produce heresiology, ecclesiology, or ecclesiastical historiography until the Middle Ages, when the rabbis were confronted by the sect of Karaites within, and the militance of Islam and Christianity without. The rabbinic literature of antiquity contains, to be sure, isolated passages that attack various sects (notably the Sadducees), define the limits of tolerable practice or belief, and project upon the worthies of the past (for example, Moses "our rabbi") the values of rabbinic culture, but rabbinic literature lacks the coherent self-definition so abundantly attested in the Christian literature of the fourth century. The word "orthodox" was not applied to a variety of Judaism until the nineteenth century, when the opponents of reform organized themselves under the banner of "orthodox and Torah-true Judaism." These Jews, in order to delegitimate reform, adopted the historical perspective that the medieval rabbis had turned against the Karaites. "Orthodox Judaism" to this day still sees itself as the representative of that Judaism which has been believed "everywhere, always, and by all." The only way to avoid the accumulated theological and polemical baggage attached to "orthodox," "normative," and "heresy" is to avoid the terms and the concepts they convey.

Proto-Sectarianism in the Persian Period

During the period of the first temple there was no shortage of religious conflict—between prophets and kings, between prophets and priests, between priests and kings, between "true" and "false" prophets, between syncretists and monotheists, between those who advocated worship throughout the land and those who permitted it only in Jerusalem—but these conflicts did not produce sects. At no point did the prophets secede from the nation in order to form their own "sects" or "conventicles." Pre-exilic society provides only one example of a body that in any way resembles the sects of later times. This is the "house of the Rechabites," a clan (group?) that had been commanded by its "father" (founder?) Jonadab ben Rechab to refrain from drinking wine, building houses, and cultivating land (Jer. 35). By early medieval times the Jewish and Christian imagination had assimilated the Rechabites to the Essenes, but the Rechabites described by Jeremiah, even if they were not a clan but a group of pietists, lack all the distinguishing characteristics of a sect.

Why didn't the religious conflicts of the first temple period produce sects? There are many possible answers to this question, but I offer here one suggestion that develops a point made earlier. In the pre-exilic period the dominant component of Israelite identity was nationality. As I discussed in chapter 2, conversion to Judaism did not exist in pre-exilic times, because a society based on birth is incapable of establishing a regular process by which outsiders can be naturalized. The institution of conversion to Judaism presumes that citizenship in the Jewish polity is a matter of religion rather than birth. Sectarianism too defines citizenship in the Jewish polity in terms of religion. In the eyes of a sect, because most native-born Jews do not observe Judaism correctly, they have lost their status as Jews; they are no longer "Israel." The transition from identity based on nationality to identity based on religion facilitated the emergence of both conversion and sectarianism. Each is completely absent from the pre-exilic period, begins to emerge in the Persian period, and reaches full development only in the second century B.C.E.

The religious disputes within the Jewish communities of Babylonia and Israel during the Persian period were many and varied. Out of these disputes arose groups that in many ways prefigure the sects of later times. After briefly discussing the activities of Ezra and Nehemiah, I shall examine the three best-attested proto-sects: "the congregation of the (returned) exile," mentioned in the book of Ezra; the group represented by Nehemiah 10; and the group represented by Isaiah 65.

Ezra and Nehemiah

Law, temple, and scripture, the three focal points of Jewish sectarianism, are also the focal points of the activity of Ezra and Nehemiah. As the later sects would, the two reformers attacked the manner in which the larger society was observing the laws relating to marriage; the Sabbath and festivals; and the temple and purity. Both Ezra and Nehemiah enforced the prohibition of intermarriage, which had been violated primarily by the priesthood and the aristocracy. Nehemiah enforced the observance of the Sabbath laws, and rearranged the system of the tithes and temple offerings. He also purified the temple precincts, a procedure that involved the expulsion of Tobiah "the Ammonite" who had been domiciled in one of the temple chambers at the invitation of the high priest (Neh. 13:7-8).

The major targets of all the actions of Ezra and Nehemiah were the priests and their allies. Ezra read to the public "the book of the instruction *(Torah)* of Moses" and, assisted by the Levites, explained its meaning (Neh. 8). In effect, Ezra "published" the Torah by making it accessible to the masses. This was a direct threat to the political hegemony of the priesthood. The word *Torah* means instruction, but in pre-exilic times the primary meaning of the word was "priestly instruction" (for example, Jer. 18:18). Ezra, however, tried to remove the priest as the intermediary between the people and the sacred traditions by giving the people direct access to "the book of the Torah." The Romans regarded the publication of the Twelve Tables in 451 B.C.E. (a date which, by curious coincidence, is nearly identical with that of Ezra) as a significant step in the gradual dissolution of the power of the patricians, because a law that is fixed and publicly available reduces the potential for arbitrary and capricious rulings by the magistrates. By giving the masses free access to the Torah, Ezra was curbing the power of the priestly magistrates. He was aided in his work by the Levites, a group that was at odds with the priesthood throughout the second temple period (Nehemiah too was aided by the Levites), and read the Torah not in the temple itself but at the water gate, probably because the temple priests wanted no part of Ezra's reforms.

What gave Ezra and Nehemiah the authority to oppose the priests, dissolve their marriages, eject their friends from the temple, and rearrange the temple offerings and sacrifices? Both Ezra and Nehemiah were officials in the Persian bureaucracy and therefore supported by the power of the state. Ezra was the recipient of a special charter from the king, which appointed him minister in charge of Jewish affairs (Ezra 7), while Nehemiah was the governor of the district of Judea. In addition to this external legitimation, Ezra's authority was confirmed internally as well. He is said to have been a priest of the high priestly line (Ezra 7:1–5), but nowhere does this fact play a role in the narrative. Perhaps because he did not serve as high priest he was willing to act against the interests of his class.

More important for the legitimation of Ezra's authority was his status as "a scribe skilled in the instruction (Torah) of Moses" (Ezra 7:6). Throughout the ancient Near East, scribes were the functionaries who ran the government, administered the civil service, and prepared correspondence and contracts. Ezra was a "Jewish" scribe whose expertise derived not from the common law of the ancient Near East but from the teachings of Moses. His authority, then, was based on erudition. He was able to teach the Torah and to determine the validity of the marriages contracted by the aristocracy because of his superior expertise. Nehemiah was neither a priest nor a scribe, but we may presume that he too sought an internal legitimation for his authority in his superior expertise and piety. Even the priests in the temple were subject to him, because they did not know as well as he how to administer the temple in a way that would find favor in God's eyes.

Like the sects of later times, Ezra and Nehemiah emphasize the laws of marriage, Sabbath, temple, and purity; attack the power of the priests, especially the high priests; and justify their authority by appeal to their superior expertise in the Torah of Moses. Although they regard the priesthood as incompetent or corrupt, they venerate the temple and place it at the center of their religion. For the biblical narrator the Jews who supported Ezra and Nehemiah constituted not a separate group but the Judean community as a whole. This is not the place for a full discussion of the actions of Ezra and Nehemiah or for an assessment of the correctness of this view. What is relevant here is the fact that the narrative, against its own thesis, shows that Ezra and Nehemiah were the leaders not of all but only of some of the Jews, and that these followers were members of a distinctive group. I now turn to these proto-sectarian organizations of the Persian period.

"The Congregation of the Exile" and Nehemiah 10

The book of Ezra uses the terms "the exile," "the members of the exile," and "the congregation of the exile," to refer to the people who returned from Babylonia to Israel in the days of Zerubbabel and Ezra (that is, they are not Jews *in* the exile but *from* the exile). The author sees "the congregation of the exile" as an organized and disciplined group, the embodiment of authentic Judaism (in other words, "the church"). These Jews rebuild the temple, rebuff the "adversaries of Judah and Benjamin" (4:1), dedicate the temple, celebrate the Passover (6:19–20), and offer sacrifices on behalf of the twelve tribes of Israel (8:35). Their ranks are augmented by those who "joined them and separated [themselves] from the pollutions of the peoples of the land to worship the Lord, the God of Israel" (6:21), a reference to "converts" (gentiles? Jews?) who joined their community. When it is reported to Ezra that certain members of "the exile" have married foreign women, a proclamation was issued for all "the members of the exile" to gather at the square in front of the temple; whoever did not obey within three days was to have his property confiscated and he himself was to be excluded from "the congregation of the exile" (10:7–8). Over one hundred people were discovered to have intermarried, and they were ordered to divorce their foreign wives and their children. (Whether they obeyed is not entirely clear.)

Although the book of Nehemiah does not use the term "the exile" in this sense, it is familiar with a similar type of group. Nehemiah 8 describes the reading and teaching of the Torah to "the people" by Ezra. Nehemiah 9 is the record of a public fast and atonement service which was prompted by the Torah reading, just as the discovery of the book of Deuteronomy a century and a half earlier was the occasion for public repentance and atonement. (Scholars debate whether the connection between Nehemiah 8 and 9–10 is original or secondary; Ezra is the major figure in Nehemiah 8 but is not mentioned in Nehemiah 9–10.) The highlight of that service was a long penitential prayer, in the first-person plural, which culminates in Nehemiah 10 with a "covenant" or "pledge." The co-signers of this document, listed by name and speaking still in the first-person plural, obligate themselves to follow the teaching (Torah) of God and to observe all his commandments, specifically, to avoid intermarriage with "the peoples of the land"; not to have commercial dealings with "the peoples of the land" on the Sabbath; to observe the seventh year ("the year of release"); and to support the temple and its priesthood through a wide variety of offerings (money, wood, first fruits, firstborn, dough, and crops).

Like "the congregation of the exile," the signers of this document claim to be the embodiment of authentic Judaism and are viewed by the biblical narrator as "the church" which represents the entire people (rabbinic texts refer to the signatories as "the men of the great assembly"). The list of signatures concludes with "the rest of the people, the priests, the Levites, the gatekeepers, the singers, the temple servants, and all who separated themselves from the peoples of the lands to follow the teaching of God" (Neh. 10:29). Like "the congregation of the exile," this group too was augmented by outsiders (Jewish? gentile? compare Ezra 6:21). While "the congregation of the exile" is associated with Ezra, the group behind Nehemiah 10 is associated with Nehemiah, the first and most prominent of the signatories. The covenant highlights laws that are modifications or extensions of those Nehemiah enforced during his second tenure as governor (in 432 B.C.E.): the elimination of intermarriage and the expulsion of foreigners from the temple (Neh. 13:1-9, 23-30); support of the temple and its clergy through tithes and offerings (13:10-14, 30-31); and the avoidance of commerce on the Sabbath (13:14-22). (The covenant's concern with "the year of release" perhaps reflects an act of Nehemiah during his first tenure in office in 445 B.C.E., the cancellation of debts recounted in Nehemiah 5.)

Both of these groups are proto-sects. "The congregation of the exile" regards itself as the authentic expression of Judaism; its opponents are the "adversaries of Judah and Benjamin." Jews (that is those who venerate the God of Israel) outside the group are regarded as foreigners and therefore unmarriageable by members of the group. (The twin facts that priests, who are obsessed with genealogical purity, married the daughters of these outsiders, and that some of these outsiders had Jewish names like "Tobiah," imply that these people were not real foreigners at all, in spite of the polemical application of the adjectives "Ammonite," "Moabite," etc.) Those who violated the group's discipline were subject to expulsion. Nehemiah 10, the "covenant" of a related group, resembles in form the Qumran Community Rule. It states the reason for the group's existence ("to walk in accordance with God's teaching") and emphasizes the rules which are especially important for the group's self-definition. These rules, like those of later sectarianism, center on marriage, Sabbath, and the temple offerings (only the purity rules are missing).

Isaiah 65

A different sort of proto-sect is the group that stands behind Isaiah 65. The anonymous author of the last chapters of the book of Isaiah is known to modern scholarship as Third Isaiah (or Trito-Isaiah). Isaiah 63–64 is a psalm of lament that bewails the destruction of Jerusalem and beseeches God to relent from his anger. In chapter 65 God (or the prophet speaking on his behalf in the first-person singular) responds. God has called out to his people but they have refused to listen.

> I was ready to be sought by those who did not ask for me; I was ready to be found by those who did not seek me. I said, "Here am I, here am I," to a nation that did not call on my name [or: to a nation that is not called by my name]. I spread out my hands all the day to a rebellious people, who walk in a way that is not good, following their own devices; a people who provoke me to my face continually. (Vs. 1–3)

This is followed by a description of their abominable acts: they eat swine and perform many forbidden (idolatrous) rituals. Therefore God shall destroy them, but not all of them.

> For my servants' sake (I will) not destroy them all. I will bring forth descendants from Jacob, and from Judah inheritors of my mountains; my chosen shall inherit it, and my servants shall dwell there. . . . But you who forsake the Lord, who forget my holy mountain, . . . I will destine you to the sword, and all of you shall bow down to the slaughter. . . . Behold, my servants shall eat, but you shall be hungry; behold, my servants shall drink, but you shall be thirsty; behold, my servants shall rejoice, but you shall be put to shame. . . . You shall leave your name to my chosen for a curse, and the Lord God will slay you; but his servants he will call by a different name. (Vs. 8–15)

This is followed by a promise "to create new heavens and a new earth" for "my people," who shall live a utopian existence around God's holy mountain.

The idea that God punishes the Israelites because of their sins, and discriminates between the righteous and the wicked, is scarcely novel. But the stark contrast between God's "servants" and the people as a whole; the prophet's satisfaction that the mass of the people will be destroyed because of their wickedness; the virulent condemnation of the people by the prophet; the implication that God's "servants" and "chosen" are not merely a status but a group; and the idea that the future will vindicate the claims of the righteous against the wicked—all of this is new, and all of this anticipates the perspective of later sectarianism. (It is no surprise, therefore, that this chapter is frequently cited or alluded to in the Qumran scrolls and in early Christianity, for example, Rom. 10:20–21.) God is angry at his people, who are no longer called by his name, that is chosen by him, because they refuse to heed his message. Only his servants, the chosen ones, will receive his blessings and will be vindicated in the (near) future.

The issues that agitated the author of this chapter and the extent to which the "servants" and the "chosen" formed distinct groups, cannot be determined with any certainty. Several scholars have suggested that Third Isaiah was a member of a prophetic "school" that advanced for the Jerusalem temple and the restoration community of the Persian period a program which was rejected by the priesthood. The repeated emphasis on the openness of the temple to gentiles (Isa. 56:6–7; 60:1–14; 66:12–24) suggests that this was an issue over which the "school" and the community differed. Ezra and Nehemiah complained that the priests of the temple were too inclusive in allowing "gentiles" to marry Jews and enter the holy precincts; the group represented by Third Isaiah complained that the priests of the temple were too exclusive in prohibiting gentiles from serving the Lord in his temple. After being rejected by the priests, the prophetic "school" predicted the destruction of the larger community and dreamed of the time when it would be rewarded by God.

Thus the Persian period provides three good examples of proto-sectarianism. The "congregation of the exile" and the "covenanters" of Nehemiah 10 anticipate the strict organization and legal emphases of later sects, while the prophetic "school" of Isaiah 65 anticipates their social alienation and eschatological dreaming. All three groups see the temple as the center of their religion but oppose the regime of the priesthood. They assert that they know better than the high priest how to administer the temple and find favor with God. None of these groups fits the definition of sect given above, since we may doubt whether any of them was either highly organized or clearly separate, but each is a harbinger of what is to come.

Pharisees, Sadducees, and Essenes

The heyday of Jewish sectarianism was from the middle of the second century B.C.E. to the destruction of the temple in 70 C.E. In several passages Josephus describes the three "schools of thought" found among the Jews at that time, the Pharisees, Sadducees, and Essenes. The Josephan evidence about these three groups is supplemented by the testimony of the New Testament, the Qumran scrolls, and rabbinic texts. (Philo and one or two pagan writers provide some additional evidence about the Essenes; see below.) I shall survey each body of evidence separately, and then present a synthetic portrait of the three groups.

Sources Written in Greek: Josephus

In order to distinguish the Pharisees from the Sadducees, and the two of them from the Essenes, Josephus highlights three areas in which the sects differed from each other. These areas are philosophy, social standing and politics, and way of life.

Philosophy

Josephus calls the three groups *haireseis*, "schools of thought" or "philosophical schools." Each advocates certain doctrines about fate, free will, and immortality—precisely the questions that should be addressed by philosophical schools. Josephus explicitly compares the Pharisees with the Stoics and the Essenes with the Pythagoreans, and implicitly compares the Sadducees with the Epicureans. The Sadducees do not allocate "Fate" any role in human affairs, and they deny both immortality of the soul and resurrection; the Essenes ascribe all human actions to the power of Fate and believe in both immortality and resurrection; the Pharisees adopt a middle course, ascribing power to both Fate and human free will, and believing in immortality and resurrection (but apparently in a way different from the Essenes—this point is not clear).

In all likelihood, as I remarked above, Josephus' presentation of the three groups as "philosophical schools" was for the benefit of his non-Jewish readers, who would have had little interest either in the real Pharisees, Sadducees, and Essenes or in the issues that divided them. The three "schools" probably did debate theological and philosophical questions, but we may doubt whether these debates were central to their sectarian identity.

Social Standing and Politics

These "schools" also engaged in politics. After supporting the Pharisees, John Hyrcanus shifted his allegiance to the Sadducees. On his deathbed Alexander Jannaeus, who had faced revolt from many quarters of the population, counseled his wife and successor, Salome Alexandra, to befriend the Pharisees "because these men have so much influence with their fellow Jews that they can injure those whom they hate and help those to whom they are friendly; for they have the complete confidence of the masses" (*Jewish Antiquities* 13.15.5, §401). Alexandra heeded his advice and gave the Pharisees free reign. They killed many of their opponents, especially the aristocrats who had supported Jannaeus. Salome's son Aristobulus opposed the Pharisees and resented the influence they had over his mother. When Herod came to power, Pollio the Pharisee counseled the people to accept Herod as their leader; as a result Pollio and the Pharisees, who numbered six thousand, were respected by Herod. Josephus further records that the Pharisees had special influence over the women of Herod's court. The last time the Pharisees appear in a political context is in the year 66 c.e., when, just before the outbreak of the revolt, they joined the "principal citizens" and the chief priests in beseeching the revolutionaries not to begin a war that they could not win. Their advice was ignored. During the first year of the war, the Pharisee Simon ben Gamaliel was a member of the revolutionary presidium in Jerusalem, and three other individual Pharisees are mentioned in his company.

Thus "the Pharisees" appear as a "political party" in the time of John Hyrcanus (137–104 b.c.e.), Salome Alexandra (76–67 b.c.e.), Herod the Great (37–34 b.c.e.), and in the first year of the great revolt (66–67 c.e.). Several politically important individuals from the time of Herod and the outbreak of the revolt are called Pharisees. The Sadducees, in contrast, appear only once as a political party, when Hyrcanus joins them and abandons the Pharisees, and only one individual is ever called a Sadducee, a high priest of the first century c.e. The Essenes never appear as a political group, although individual Essenes are occasionally mentioned. One Essene predicted to his disciples the murder of the brother of Aristobulus (104–103 b.c.e.). Another accurately forecast the career of Herod the Great, and a third interpreted a significant dream of Herod's son after the death of his father. John the Essene led some military campaigns in the early phases of the war of 66–70. Three of these four Essenes, then, were "holy men" or "prophets," rather than politicians.

The Pharisees have "the complete confidence of the masses." This idea is expressed even more strongly in another passage. The Pharisees "are extremely influential among the masses; and all prayers and sacred rites of divine worship are performed according to their exposition. . . . Whenever the Sadducees assume some office, though they submit unwillingly and perforce, yet submit they do to the dictates of the Pharisees, since otherwise the masses would not tolerate them." The Sadducees are supported only by "the people of highest standing" (*Jewish Antiquities* 18.1.3–4, §15–17). The Pharisees, who in the time of Herod numbered six thousand, are the party of the masses, while the Sadducees are the party of the aristocracy. Thus according to Josephus the Pharisees had a great deal of power in Jewish society from the last part of the second century B.C.E. until the outbreak of the great revolt, while the Sadducees did not. It may be significant that these claims of Pharisaic power appear only in the *Jewish Antiquities*, which was completed in 93/4 C.E., and not the *Jewish War*, which was completed between ten and fifteen years earlier. The Essenes, who numbered only four thousand, were apparently not a political party at all.

Way of Life

"Philosophical schools" in antiquity were often as conspicuous for the way of life affected by their adherents as for their tenets. In his long descriptions of the Essenes, which were summarized in chapter 4, Josephus emphasizes the ascetic and pietistic character of their communal life. Although he provides no parallel description of the communal life of the Pharisees and Sadducees, Josephus mentions one important point over which the two groups differed (*Jewish Antiquities* 13.10.6, §297–298):

> The Pharisees handed down to the people certain regulations from the ancestral succession and not recorded in the laws of Moses, for which reason they are rejected by the Sadducean group, who hold that only those regulations should be considered valid which were written (in Scripture), and that those which had been handed down by the fathers need not be observed. And concerning these matters the two parties came to have controversies and serious differences.

Since the Pharisees follow "the tradition of the fathers," they show deference to their elders, while the Sadducees by contrast are very argumentative with their teachers. Josephus nowhere gives an example or defines the meaning of "the tradition of the fathers," so that it is difficult to know precisely what is intended. It is hard to accept the notion that the Sadducees followed "only those regulations which were written (in Scripture)," since a life lived in accordance with scripture alone is a life filled with obscurities and contradictions (see the next chapter). This problem aside, the passage shows that the Pharisees were known for their dedication to the ancestral tradition which supplemented the written Torah, and that the Sadducees were known for their denial of the Pharisaic tradition.

The Evidence of Josephus

Josephus describes the Pharisees, Sadducees, and Essenes from three different perspectives, but does not explain how the perspectives are to be fitted together. What is the connection between the fact that the Pharisees attribute power to both fate and free will and the fact that they affirm the validity of the ancestral traditions? What is the connection between either of these facts and the fact that they enjoy the support of the masses but not of the aristocracy? The same problem applies to the description of the Sadducees. Even if these descriptions are accurate, they certainly are not coherent.

One point which is clear is that Josephus does not regard any of these groups as a "sect" in the sense given above. Both the *Jewish War* and the *Jewish Antiquities* view the Pharisees as the most prominent of the three groups, but the latter work adds the important claim that the Pharisees are the leaders of the masses, whose support is essential if any government over the Jews is to succeed. The Sadducees were the aristocratic opponents of the Pharisees. The Essenes were a group of religious and philosophic virtuosi, living a utopian life of the sort that would provoke the admiration of Jews and non-Jews alike. Josephus mentions their three-year catechumenate, their oath of loyalty to the group, their separation from their fellow Jews, their emphasis on purity and ablutions, but he regards them not as a "sect" but as a pietistic elite.

Sources Written in Greek: The New Testament

The New Testament, especially the Gospels, has abundant material on the Pharisees, but little on the Sadducees and nothing on the Essenes. The references can be divided under the same three headings which I used when discussing the evidence of Josephus: philosophy, social standing and politics, and way of life.

Philosophy

The Sadducees deny the resurrection of the dead, the Pharisees affirm it. This fact is known both to the Gospels (Matt. 22:23–33 and parallels) and to Acts 23. Acts adds that the Sadducees also say that "there is no angel or spirit," which probably means that heavenly beings do not communicate directly with people (Paul claimed they did). This denial is attested nowhere else. Aside from this, the New Testament has virtually nothing about the theological tenets of the Pharisees and Sadducees.

Social Standing and Politics

Josephus says explicitly that the Pharisees have the support of the masses and carry great weight in public religious matters, and that the Sadducees are supported by the aristocracy alone. The same point is made implicitly by the New Testament. Although the Sadducees are the party of the high priest and his associates (Acts 4:1; 5:17), the primary targets of the polemic of the Gospels, especially Matthew, are not the Sadducees but the Pharisees. It is they, often in the company of "scribes," who confront Jesus and his disciples and, in return, are severely denounced for their hypocrisy and other sins (Matt. 23).

> The scribes and the Pharisees sit on Moses' seat; so practice and observe whatever they tell you, but not what they do; for they preach, but do not practice. They bind heavy burdens . . . and lay them on men's shoulders; but they themselves will not move them with their finger. They do all their deeds to be seen by men; for they make their phylacteries broad and their fringes long, and they love the place of honor at feasts and the best seats in the synagogues, and salutations in the market places, and being called "rabbi" by men.

The charge of hypocrisy is probably the result of intrasectarian polemic, but the passage clearly shows that in the circles that shaped and transmitted the Gospels, especially Matthew, the Pharisees were a prominent, if not the most prominent, Jewish group. Even the Gospel of John, whose favorite appellation for the Jewish authority figures is the term "Jews," frequently uses "Pharisees" as an equivalent (and never mentions scribes).

Thus, according to the New Testament, the Pharisees were a powerful group in Jewish society. The source of their power, however, was not their control of the institutions of the state. That is, both Pharisees and Sadducees sat on the sanhedrin, but neither group was a political party. Pharisees (and Sadducees) are conspicuously absent from the passion narratives in all four Gospels. The power of the Pharisees was an extension of their piety and knowledge. They sit on the seat of Moses because they are the authentic exponents of Judaism (even if they are alleged not to practice what they preach).

Way of Life

Even if we dismiss, or at least discount, the Gospel accounts of the hypocrisy, ostentatiousness, and greed of the Pharisees, because these charges are the unverified and unverifiable attacks of one

Jewish group against its major rival, the Gospels also present some useful data about the way of life that distinguished the Pharisees from their fellow Jews. (Although Christians are warned to be wary of the "leaven of the Sadducees" as well as that of the Pharisees, the Gospels have virtually nothing to say about the practices of the Sadducees.)

The Pharisees are known for their dedication to "the tradition of the elders," and for their meticulous observance of the laws. The Pharisaic "tradition of the elders" is attacked by Jesus in Matthew 15 (paralleled by Mark 7). When Paul boasts of his zeal for the ancestral traditions (Gal. 1:14), he is probably boasting of his former Pharisaic piety. That piety included not only loyalty to the tradition but also the punctilious observance of the laws. Within a space of four chapters the Paul of Acts proclaims three times that he was or still is a Pharisee. One passage refers to the debate between the Pharisees and the Sadducees on the resurrection of the dead (Acts 23:6). The other two ignore the Sadducees and boast of Paul's Pharisaic zeal for the law. The first is Acts 22:3:

> I am a Jew . . . brought up in this city at the feet of Gamaliel, educated according to the strict manner [or: educated in the minutiae] of the law of our fathers, being zealous for God as you all are this day [or: educated at the feet of Gamaliel, and zealous for the ancestral law of God as you all are this day].

Gamaliel, of course, was a well-known Pharisee (Acts 5:34). The second is Acts 26:5, "according to the strictest party *(hairesis)* of our religion I have lived as a Pharisee." These boasts are confirmed by the Paul of the epistles who rehearses his qualifications, "circumcised on the eighth day, of the people of Israel, . . . as to the law a Pharisee, . . . as to righteousness under the law blameless" (Phil. 3:5–6).

In a few passages in the Gospels the Pharisees question Jesus about his messianic status, but for the most part they question him or his disciples about their legal practices. The topics of these legal disputes are the Sabbath (plucking grain and healing), purity (washing hands before eating, dining with impure people, purification of utensils), oaths, and divorce. When Jesus criticizes the Pharisees, he invariably criticizes their legal practices. Matthew 23:15–26 provides an inventory of Pharisaic practices of which Jesus disapproves: proselytism, distinction between various kinds of oaths, and emphasis on tithes and purifications. Here then is a glimpse at some of the laws which comprise the "tradition of the elders" and which the Pharisees observe so punctiliously.

The Evidence of the New Testament

According to the New Testament, institutional power in Judea in the first century was wielded by high priests, priests, scribes (a group Josephus all but ignores), and elders. The Essenes apparently are too insignificant to rate even a mention. The Sadducees are a school of thought that denies the resurrection of the dead and is supported by the high priests and the aristocracy. The Pharisees are a much more influential group and are accorded great respect by the masses. They are known for their allegiance to "the tradition of the elders" and their punctilious observance of the law. The laws that were debated between the Pharisees and the followers of Jesus are in large part the same items that were on the agenda of the followers of Nehemiah: Sabbath, purity (and tithing), and marriage (in this case, divorce). A new feature is the debate concerning the validity of oaths. That the Pharisees (or Sadducees) constituted a "sect," there is not the slightest hint.

I have interpreted Jesus' attack on the Pharisees' hypocrisy, etc., as the consequence of intense rivalry and disagreement between the Pharisees and the early followers of Jesus, who transmitted (invented?) and edited these sayings and stories. Some scholars have suggested that the Christian polemic is the result not so much of sectarian competition as of the hostility that the masses often feel toward their authority figures. There is probably some truth to this view as well, which results in a paradox widely attested in the history of religions. The religious elite is both revered and despised, honored and disobeyed, by the masses. Rabbinic texts show that many Jews had this oxymoronic attitude toward the rabbis of the second and third centuries (see chapter 7), and the New Testament suggests that some Jews already had this attitude toward the Pharisees in the first century.

Sources Written in Hebrew: Qumran Scrolls

The Works in the Qumran "Library"

The scrolls discovered in the Judean desert (also known as the Dead Sea Scrolls) are at once the richest and the most puzzling sources for ancient Jewish sectarianism. The scrolls were discovered in caves adjacent to a settlement at Khirbet Qumran (hence the name Qumran scrolls). Pottery fragments link the scrolls found in the caves to the settlement, so that the vast majority of scholars agree that the scrolls constitute the library of the group that lived in the settlement, and that some of the scrolls were actually written at Qumran.

What is the origin of the literature preserved by the scrolls? This question is much more difficult. The library contains: (1) works, of whatever origin, that were widely read and widely available in Jewish society; (2) works that originated in esoteric, pietistic, or sectarian circles outside of Qumran; and (3) works that were the product of the Qumran sect itself. I think that all scholars would accept this tri-partite classification, but would debate which works belong in category (2) and which in category (3). The simplest category is (1), which includes the books of the Bible (in Hebrew, Aramaic, or Greek) and works like Tobit and Ben Sira. No one will argue that Leviticus or Isaiah was composed at Qumran even though many copies of these works were found there! *Jubilees, Testament of Levi,* and *Enoch* probably belong to category (2); they appear to be eso-teric works, but give no indication of their origins and, in all likeli-hood, were not composed at Qumran (or, if they were composed at Qumran, do not reflect the distinctive history and ideology of the group). Category (3) in turn consists of two types of works. Some works composed at Qumran reflect the distinctive history and ideol-ogy of the Qumran group, and have a marked sectarian character. The *Rule of the Community,* the *Damascus Covenant,* the *War of the Sons of Light Against the Sons of Darkness,* the Commentary *(Pesher)* on Nahum, and the Commentary on Habakkuk—all of these works reflect a strong sense of contrast between members of the group and outsiders, even if they disagree on various other matters. But other works, like the *Temple Scroll,* the Hymns, and the angelic lit-urgy, which fit Qumranic theology and practice so well that they probably are of Qumranic origin, reflect no sectarian self-con-sciousness at all.

Scholars have only begun to try to sort this out. A more precise identification of the origins of the works that belong in category (2) would greatly illuminate the relations of the Qumran sectarians to their predecessors in the third century B.C.E. (when the book of *Enoch* was written). A more precise identification of the two different types of works that belong to category (3) would greatly illuminate the history of the sect. Perhaps the works which show a marked sectarian self-consciousness are later than those which do not, or perhaps their intended audiences are different. (One scholar has recently argued that the *Damascus Covenant* contains within it the remains of a "missionary" work designed to convince other Jews to join the sect.) These are some of the questions that are the subject of current research. A further complication is the fact that many important texts remain unpublished. In sum, the number of items on the scholarly agenda is enormous, and this is certainly not the place for a full discussion. In chapter 3 I cited many of the Qumran texts in order to illustrate the Jewish religion of the period, and in chapter 4 I described the social organization of the Qumran community. Here I focus on the connections between the Essenes and the Qumran scrolls.

Qumran and the Essenes

The group that produced the *Rule of the Community* (also called the *Manual of Discipline*) shares many features with the Essenes described by Josephus and Philo: commonality of property, a three-year probationary period, an oath at initiation, sacred meals, an emphasis on purity (including the wearing of white garments), strict organization and discipline, celibacy, and the belief in predestination. It is likely, therefore, that the *Rule of the Community* represents the Essenes, and the numerous links between that document and other Qumran texts make it likely that the Qumran community was a community of Essenes. This identification will explain even some of the marked contrasts between various Qumran documents. The *Rule of the Community* envisions a society of celibate men living in isolation from their fellow Jews, while the *Damascus Covenant* envisions a community of men, women, and children living among Jews (and gentiles!) who are not members of the group. Similarly, in the utopian society envisioned by the *Temple Scroll* women may live in the cities throughout the country but not in the temple city, which they may visit but not inhabit. No sexual relations are permitted in the temple city. Josephus and Philo state that the Essenes lived throughout the country, but two pagan authors of the first century of our era place the Essenes near the Dead Sea, precisely the location of Qumran.[4] After noting that the Essenes are celibate, Josephus remarks that some Essenes do marry in order to procreate. Thus according to both the Qumran scrolls and the historical record, some sectarians were celibate, others not; some lived in isolation near the Dead Sea, others not. The Jews of Qumran were Essenes.

The "sectarian" scrolls of the Qumran library also show that Josephus and Philo omit many of the essential characteristics of the group, not least of which is its sectarian nature. The Qumran group celebrated its festivals according to a solar calendar of 365 days, while the rest of the Jews followed a lunar calendar of approximately 354 days. (Some scholars have argued that the Qumran scrolls testify to several different solar calendars.) The group denounced its fellow Jews as sinners and "sons of darkness," and strengthened its dualistic social perspective with a dualistic theology. Living in a period when sin was triumphant, the Qumran Jews regarded the Jerusalem temple as polluted and its priesthood as sinful. In the end of days the world would be purged of evil, the sinners would be destroyed, a new temple would be built, and the sect would rise to glory. In the interim, the sect itself was a surrogate temple, and its liturgy a surrogate sacrifice. The group, unlike the Jerusalem temple, was led by true priests, the sons of Zadok. All of these features are omitted in whole or in part by Philo and Josephus. The only clue that the Essenes may have been a "sect" is Josephus' remark that "although they send votive offerings to the temple, they do not offer sacrifices (there), because of the difference in the purity regulations which they practice. For this reason they are barred from [or: they avoid] the temple precincts of the community and perform their rites (or: sacrifices) by themselves" (*Jewish Antiquities* 18.1.5, §19). The Greek of this passage is very difficult, perhaps corrupt, but this is the closest that Josephus comes to noticing the separation and exclusivism that characterized the Essene worldview.

The Evidence of the Qumran Scrolls

The sectarian scrolls of Qumran well illustrate the three focal points of sectarian dispute discussed in the earlier part of this chapter. The Essenes attacked the legal practices of their fellow Jews (especially their observance of the laws governing marriage; Sabbath, festivals, and calendar; and purity), denied the sanctity of the Jerusalem temple, and interpreted the Bible in their own peculiar fashion (and accepted as authoritative certain books known only to themselves). Some of their biblical commentaries, notably the commentary on Nahum, give a history of the group, but the history is in code. The cast of characters includes "the Wicked Priest," "the Teacher of Righteousness," "the Lion of Wrath," and "the Seekers After Smooth Things." Scholars have labored long and hard to attach names to these phrases (thus "the Wicked Priest" is, perhaps, Jonathan the Hasmonean; "the Lion of Wrath" is Alexander Jannaeus; "the Seekers After Smooth Things" are the Pharisees), but this problem is best left to the cryptanalysts of the CIA. The "Teacher of Righteousness" is a figure who is mentioned in some of the scrolls, and seems to be the title of the founder of the group. Unfortunately little hard data is given about either the Teacher or his archenemy, the Wicked Priest. The crucial point, which is not explained in the Qumran scrolls, not even in the still unpublished letter of the Teacher of Righteousness (?) to the Wicked Priest (?), is why the group felt that it had to secede from the rest of society. The attacks on the temple and on the legal practices of their co-religionists mask the real source of alienation, which is never mentioned explicitly.

Last, sectarians do not see themselves as sectarians, and the Jews of Qumran never refer to themselves as "Essenes" or "Essaeans." They are the chosen of God, the elect of God, the community, the many, the community of God, the repenters of Israel, the members of the covenant, the members of the new covenant, Judah, Israel, and so on, but not "Essenes." (The meaning of the name "Essene" is unknown, as I shall discuss below.) But the Jews of Qumran certainly were a sect in the sense described above, and that important fact, hidden by Josephus and Philo, is clearly revealed in the Qumran scrolls.

Sources Written in Hebrew: Rabbinic Texts

Like the Essenes of Qumran, the group that produced the Mishnah and related works does not give itself an identifying label. Rabbinic texts refer to Pharisees, Sadducees, and assorted other groups (but never to "Essenes"), but at no point do the rabbis explicitly declare that they are, or regard themselves as, the descendants of this or that group of second temple times, and at no point do they refer to any named individual as "X the Pharisee" or "Y the Sadducee." Nevertheless, virtually all scholars see the rabbis as the descendants of the Pharisees. Like the Pharisees described by Josephus and the New Testament, the rabbis are loyal to the "ancestral tradition" (sometimes called the "oral law") and are punctilious about the observance of the commandments, notably the laws regulating purity, Sabbath, festivals, and marriage. They believe in resurrection and in a combination of destiny and free will. The rabbis claim to be (and to have been) the leaders of the masses, and they look upon the Pharisees of the second temple period as their heroes. The house of Gamaliel, known from Josephus and the New Testament to be Pharisaic, assumed the leadership of the rabbis around the year 100 c.e. Therefore, the pre-70 Pharisees must have had some intimate connection with the post-70 rabbis, but this connection does not mean that the two groups were identical in all respects or that the rabbinic group consisted of Pharisees alone.

The rabbinic evidence about the Pharisees and Sadducees is of two sorts. The first consists of texts that explicitly refer to either of these two groups; the second consists of texts that describe the conditions of the second temple period or attribute sayings to people who lived at that time. I shall survey each of these in turn.

Explicit Evidence: Pharisees vs. Sadducees

In rabbinic Hebrew the word *parush* (plur. *perushim*), whose literal meaning is "separatist," often is used with a negative valence. For example, the liturgical condemnation of heretics, mentioned briefly in chapter 4 and to be discussed again in chapter 7, is called in one rabbinic document "the blessing against separatists *(perushim)*."[5] Occasionally the word appears with the meaning "pietist" without negative overtones. In other passages, however, the word *perushim* is used as the name of a group, and that group is the same as that which Josephus and the New Testament call Pharisees. Here is an excerpt from the chief mishnaic passage about Pharisees and Sadducees (*Yadayim* 4:6–7):

> The Sadducees say, We cry out against you, O Pharisees, for you say "The Holy Scriptures render the hands unclean but the writings of Homer do not render the hands unclean." . . .
>
> The Sadducees say, We cry out against you, O Pharisees, for you declare pure an unbroken stream of liquid (which connects a pure vessel to an impure). The Pharisees say, We cry out against you, O Sadducees, for you declare pure a channel of water which flows from a burial ground.
>
> The Sadducees say, We cry out against you, O Pharisees, for you say, "If my ox or my ass have done an injury, I (the owner) am culpable, but if my bondman or bondwoman have done an injury I (the owner) am not culpable."

This passage (as well as related ones) illustrates the rabbinic perspectives on the Pharisees and the Sadducees. (1) The position attributed to the Pharisees is always that of the rabbis themselves. In these debates the Pharisees are always the victors, the Sadducees always the losers.

(2) The topics of debate are always legal, sometimes (as here) of the most technical and trivial sort, and for the most part center on temple cult and purity. Nowhere do the rabbinic texts posit a fundamental principle that separates the two groups; they do not even support Josephus' contention that the Sadducees deny the ancestral traditions affirmed by the Pharisees. One rabbinic passage, which purports to give a history of the origins of the Sadducees and Boethusians (a mysterious group mentioned only in rabbinic literature),

asserts that these groups "broke away from the Torah" because they erroneously concluded that there is no reward and punishment in the next world and no resurrection of the dead.[6] The perspective of this passage is close to that of the New Testament, which sees the Sadducees primarily as a "philosophical" school that denies immortality and resurrection, but everywhere else the rabbis see not theology but law as the focal point of the disputes between the groups. The "Sadducees" who participate in some of these legal debates are not always the priestly aristocrats known to the Greek sources but sometimes are the Zadokite priests of the Qumran community (see below).

(3) The Pharisees are not a "sect" but the exponents of authentic Judaism to whom even the Sadducees (and the Boethusians) must yield. Public rituals in the temple were performed in such a way as to flout the rulings of the Sadducees and the Boethusians. Three stories tell of the deaths of high priests (in two cases by supernatural means, in one by an angry mob) who refused to follow the practices enjoined by the rabbis-Pharisees and endorsed by the masses.[7] Thus the rabbis confirm the report of Josephus: the Sadducees are powerless because they must submit to the rulings of the Pharisees. (But the rabbis go even further than Josephus. They claim that the sanhedrin was constituted of, and controlled by, rabbinic sages, whereas the New Testament and Josephus say that it was constituted of members of diverse groups and controlled by the high priests.)

Implicit Evidence: The Rabbinic Version of the Past

The mishnaic tractate *Chapters of the Fathers* opens with a chain of tradition that links Moses to the rabbis of the second and third centuries. Rabbinic tradition was transmitted through the generations from masters to disciples. The first master was God and the first disciple was Moses. Moses in turn was Joshua's teacher, and so on. Since the Mishnah regards rabbinic Judaism as the only authentic form of Judaism that ever existed, it imagines that it had proponents in every generation and that these proponents were the nation's leaders. The Mishnah (and rabbinic tradition generally) knows very little about the pre-rabbinic sages who are alleged to have lived during the second temple period. Some of them, notably Hillel and Shammai (approximately the time of Herod), are the heroes of anecdotes of dubious historicity, but none of them, not even Hillel and Shammai, figures prominently in the legal tradition that forms the core of the Mishnah. Hillel, Shammai, and all the rest are disembodied names whose function is to bridge the gap between the prophets of the Bible and the rabbis of the Mishnah. Although no rabbinic text ever calls any of these people Pharisees, it is striking that some of the individual Pharisees who appear on the pages of Josephus and the New Testament can be identified with links in the rabbinic chain of tradition. The Pharisee Gamaliel known to the New Testament and the Pharisee Simon ben Gamaliel known to Josephus are certainly identical with the rabbinic figures of the same names.

If the individuals of the pre-70 period are bare names for the Mishnah, the "house of Hillel" and the "house of Shammai" are substantial entities that are cited frequently. The word "house" is probably the equivalent of "school," although no rabbinic text describes the social organization behind this term. The two houses are cited numerous times in the Mishnah, almost always in tandem, and almost always in debate. The major focal points of the debates between the houses were the laws of purity, Sabbath, festivals, and table fellowship (What is the proper procedure for the eating of a meal? Which blessings must be recited and in what order? What are the rules of etiquette that must be observed? How should the purity rules be implemented during a meal?). In all these matters, if the house of Shammai says "impure" or "forbidden," the house of Hillel can be counted on to say "pure" or "permitted."

Most scholars view the two houses as wings or factions of the Pharisees, because the profile of their interests is consistent with what is known elsewhere of the Pharisees specifically and of Jewish sects generally (with the notable addition of table fellowship and near omission of temple law). But the very identity of these interests is a serious problem, for how can the Pharisees disagree among themselves on the same issues over which sects disagree? If the Pharisees reject the purity rules of the Sadducees, how can the house of Hillel reject the purity rules of the house of Shammai without engendering further sectarian division? The Mishnah assures us that the houses did not split into separate factions (*Yebamot* 1:4):

> Although these forbid what the others permit, and these declare ineligible (for marriage) those whom the others declare eligible, yet (the men of) the house of Shammai did not refrain from marrying women from the house of Hillel, nor did (the men of) the house of Hillel refrain from marrying women from the house of Shammai. Despite all the disputes about what is pure and impure, wherein these declare pure what the others declare impure, neither refrained from using anything that pertained to the others in matters concerned with purity.

Although each of the houses advanced its own marriage and purity laws, nevertheless, the Mishnah insists, they lived together as one big happy family. How were the houses able to accomplish this? Why did the disputes between the Pharisees and the Sadducees create social barriers while those between the houses did not? What was the relationship between the houses and the Pharisees? None of these questions is addressed, much less answered, by the Mishnah or any other rabbinic text. Rather than repeat the oft-repeated assertion that the Pharisees consisted of two schools or wings, one progressive or liberal (the house of Hillel) and the other conservative or strict (the house of Shammai), I prefer to admit ignorance. We know neither the social reality that the houses represent nor the relationship of the houses to the Pharisees.

The Rabbinic Evidence

The rabbis of the second century and later did not look upon themselves as members of a sect, either because they were not, or because members of a sect never see themselves for what they really are. Nor did the rabbis see their ancestors as sectarians, but as the legitimate leaders of the Jewish people and as the exponents of authentic Judaism. The *haberim*, "associates," that group of pietists who carefully observed the laws of tithing and purity (see chapter 4), is nowhere in rabbinic tradition connected with the Pharisees or regarded as a sectlike organization. The Sadducees and the Boethusians "break away from the Torah" and debate the rabbis on various legal matters, mostly concerning purity and temple cult, but have little impact because they flail helplessly against the masses and their leaders, the rabbis. In the debates with the Sadducees and the Boethusians, the Pharisees represent the position that the rabbis themselves accept as correct. To some extent, therefore, the rabbis identify themselves with the Pharisees of second temple times. This identification is confirmed by implicit evidence (the rabbis of the Mishnah have many features in common with the Pharisees described by Josephus and the New Testament) and by the prominence in both traditions of Gamaliel and his son.

If the rabbis really were the descendants of the Pharisees, it is remarkable that they know (or choose to reveal) so little information about their ancestors. Few legal opinions and few narratives of any historical value are attributed by rabbinic tradition to the individual masters of the second temple period. Virtually all modern scholars agree that much of rabbinic Judaism derives from second temple times, but the rabbis are not interested in documenting this fact.

Only the houses of Hillel and Shammai are cited abundantly, and these shadowy groups debate primarily the laws pertaining to purity, Sabbath and festivals, and meals.

The Names of the Pharisees, Sadducees, and Essenes

The names of the Pharisees, Sadducees, and Essenes provide only slight additional evidence. Practically all scholars now agree that the name "Pharisee" derives from the Hebrew and Aramaic *parush* or *perushi* (in the plural *perushim*), which means "one who is separated," but whether the separation is from the gentiles (as Ezra and Nehemiah speak of those who "separated themselves from the impurity of the nations of the lands"; compare 1 Macc. 1:11), from sources of ritual impurity, or from irreligious Jews, is not as clear. It is likely that the term was first used by the group's opponents in order to denigrate it ("separatists!" they cried), and that it never became part of the group's self-definition. At least it never so appears in the Mishnah or in the bulk of rabbinic tradition.

Most scholars now agree that the name Sadducee derives from the Hebrew *Zeduqi* and means "a descendant of Zadok the priest." "The priests the sons of Zadok" is a regular turn of phrase in the last chapters of Ezekiel. Presumably this is a self-designation. Sadducees see themselves as the descendants of Zadok the priest, that is, as the true priests who are to officiate in the temple. Two different groups of "Zadokites" are known. The first is the Qumran community, which accorded prominence and power to the priests the sons of Zadok. The second is the aristocratic and priestly social stratum called "Sadducees" by Josephus and the New Testament. Some of the rabbinic texts that mention "Sadducees" seem to refer to the aristocratic priests of the Greek sources, while others seem to refer to the sectarian pietists of Qumran. For example, the Sadducees who argue in the Mishnah quoted above that impurity can be transferred through an unbroken stream of liquid are the Zadokite priests of the Qumran community. The rabbinic texts do not distinguish between different types of Sadducees, but the Qumran texts allow this point to be established with some certainty. (The same ambiguity is true of the Boethusians, a group known only from rabbinic texts. In some contexts they are an aristocratic priestly group like the Sadducees; in others they are extreme pietists, whose practices are identical with those of the Qumran sect.)

The name of the Essenes, like the group itself, remains mysterious. Since it does not appear in any Hebrew source, its original pronunciation and even its original language (is it Greek, Aramaic, or Hebrew?) are unknown. Philo and Josephus transcribe the name either as "Essene" or as "Essaean," and the guesses by modern scholars include "pious ones," "healers," and others. Etymology and meaning remain disputed.

Summary: From the Persian Period to the Pharisees, Sadducees, and Essenes

After its reconstruction in the Persian period the temple became not only the center of worship in Judea but also the center of society. The priests were not only the ministers in the temple but also the official leaders of the Jews. But the temple's new status was offset by the sense that it was not as authentic as the one built by Solomon. The priests' new status was offset by the sense that they were not sufficiently pious. The dissonance between social reality and religious perception gave the impetus to the rise of sectlike groups which affirmed the validity of the priests and the temple but which attempted to supplement them or control them. "The congregation of the exile" and the covenanters of Nehemiah 10 supported the temple but subjugated priestly authority to their own. They taught the Torah in public, adopted marriage laws much stricter than those followed by the priests, and observed the laws of purity and tithing in accordance with their own interpretations. These Jews probably justified their actions by appeal to their superior erudition and piety. Ezra was a scribe learned in the Torah, and therefore was the ultimate authority for his supporters. Another group, the prophetic school of Third Isaiah, was equally disenchanted with the ways of the priests and the restoration community, but instead of attacking the political hegemony of the priests, dreamed of the day when a new creation would dawn, the temple in Jerusalem would become a true house of God, and the chosen ones (the members of the community) would finally be vindicated.

What happened to these groups in the Hellenistic period is not known. The high priests of Jerusalem were still very much in control, but the democratization of religion (discussed in chapter 3) proceeded apace. Prayer, Torah study, the daily performance of the commandments, the promise of individual reward in the hereafter —all these became the distinguishing characteristics of Judaism, and all these minimize, or at least reduce, the centrality of the temple and the priesthood. The third century B.C.E. witnessed the emergence of the scribes, a group of laypeople learned in the sacred writings, although their precise social function is obscure. The dual result of this process was the creation of new social organizations (synagogues and sects) which took the place of the temple, and new social elites (teachers, sages, and "rabbis") who took the place of the priests. Synagogues appear in Egypt in the third century B.C.E., in the land of Israel in the first century C.E. Sects emerge in the Maccabean period.

The desecration of the temple and the persecution of Judaism by Epiphanes, the overt corruption of the high priesthood, the Maccabean revolt and the reclamation of the temple through force of arms, and the usurpation of the high priesthood by Jonathan the Hasmonean, all these highlighted the problematic status of the temple. Was it legitimate? Was it the real house of God? Even if the temple had been legitimate before, how could one be sure that its purification was efficacious in the eyes of God? The dissonance between the real and the perceived was greater now than before. Through vigorous propaganda the Maccabees sought to legitimate both themselves and the temple they had regained, but many Jews were not convinced. Those who were least convinced formed sects.

The first such group was the *Hasidim*, "the pious ones," who supported the Maccabees in their struggle against Epiphanes and the corrupt priests of Jerusalem. After the great victory and the rededication of the temple, they ceased to fight the Seleucids because they had no desire to further the dynastic pretensions of the Maccabees. These are virtually all the known facts about the Hasidim. Many modern scholars have suggested that the Hasidim were the ancestors of both the Pharisees and the Essenes, but the suggestion lacks any supporting evidence. Even if it were true, it would not help much because so little is known of this group. Whether or not it was a sect is unknown.

Josephus refers to the three sects for the first time during the reign of Jonathan, who had been appointed high priest by one of the pretenders to the Seleucid throne, and archaeology confirms that the Qumran community was founded in the middle of the second century B.C.E. Prominent among the Essenes at this early stage were "the priests the sons of Zadok," that is, "true" and "legitimate" priests. They complained that, among other things, the temple was polluted, the temple priests were illegitimate, the temple cult was not conducted in accordance with the correct calendar or the correct purity laws, and the Jews were not observing the Sabbath properly. They believed that they were living in a time of wrath when the forces of evil were on the ascendant, but that at some point in the near future the forces of light would triumph and the sect would conquer its enemies. Some of the less extreme of their number lived among the larger community, raising families and involved in the affairs of the world. The more rigorous ones dwelt in isolation; avoided contact with women, gentiles, and non-sectarian Jews (all of them sources of impurity); read, composed, copied, and studied a wide variety of works, both esoteric and exoteric; and joined their prayers to those of the angels while they awaited the great war. The end of the Qumran community did come in a great war, but probably not in a way imagined by the Essenes. In 68 c.e. the community was destroyed by the Romans.

Other Zadokite priests were probably the ancestors of the group known in the first century as Sadducees. Their history is most obscure. For Josephus and the New Testament the Sadducees are high priests and aristocrats who deny the resurrection of the dead. There must have been more to the Sadducees than just this, certainly in the time of their origins, but our sources do not reveal it. Not all priests, high priests, and aristocrats were Sadducees; many were Pharisees, and many were not members of any group at all.

By the first century of our era the Pharisees were priests and laypeople who believed that the ancestral tradition was as binding as the written Torah of Moses. The ancestral tradition included observance of the purity laws (that is, priestly piety transferred to the laity), tithing (another matter of interest to priests), and numerous details in the laws of oaths, Sabbath, and marriage. According to the New Testament the Pharisees were closely associated with the scribes, a profession grounded on expertise in the laws. The crucial historical question is the relationship of the Pharisees to general Jewish society. Were they a sect? an elite? a "movement"? an order? Each of these possibilities has been defended by modern scholars. None of the ancient sources views the Pharisees as a sect, and there is no sign that the Pharisees of the first century had that exclusivistic ideology, strict organization, and group-oriented eschatology which characterize sects. But the name Pharisee, which means "separatist"; the emphasis on the laws of purity and table fellowship (if indeed the houses of Hillel and Shammai were Pharisees); the rabbinic association of *haberim* (if indeed this is a relic of Pharisaic times); their relatively small numbers (six thousand in the days of Herod)—all these imply that the Pharisees were a distinctive group that abstained from normal social intercourse with other Jews. Perhaps, then, they were pietists who, in order to attain a higher level of purity and religiosity, separated themselves to some extent from their co-religionists, but who saw themselves, and were seen by others, not as exclusive bearers of the truth but as virtuosi and elites.

Of course, the New Testament, Josephus, and rabbinic literature would have us believe even more. The New Testament would have us believe that the Pharisees sat on the seat of Moses, were given seats of honor in synagogues, and were called "rabbi" ("my master") in the streets. Josephus would have us believe that the Sadducees could accomplish nothing because they had perforce to obey the Pharisees. The masses supported the Pharisees to such an extent that anyone who sought to govern the Jews had to obtain the support of the Pharisees. The rabbis would have us believe that wicked high priests who flouted the rulings of the Pharisees were struck dead by God or pelted to death by the masses. The Pharisees-sages controlled the sanhedrin and all the trappings of state.

How much truth there is in this portrait of Pharisaic power is an extremely difficult question. On the one hand, it is striking that all these sources were written after the destruction of the temple in 70 C.E. and may therefore be projecting the conditions of their own time back upon previous generations. After 70 the sects disappeared and the rabbinic movement, which consisted in large part of the heirs of the Pharisees, emerged. In the *Jewish Antiquities*, completed in 93/4 C.E., Josephus emphasizes Pharisaic power, but in the *Jewish War*, completed ten or fifteen years earlier, he does not. Many scholars have argued that much of the anti-Pharisee polemic of the Gospels appears in post-70 additions to earlier material. Perhaps then the unanimous testimony of the three sources tells us much about the status of the rabbis, the inheritors of the Pharisees, after 70 C.E., but little about the Pharisees before 70 C.E. On the other hand, it is difficult to believe that all three sources, especially Josephus and the New Testament, are inventing out of whole cloth. Perhaps they are exaggerating, but it is likely that their reports contain at least some truth. The Pharisees must have been an important group even before 70 C.E. They did not control the institutions of the state, and their ability to enforce their opinions (their "power") was limited. But they clearly had "power" in a nonpolitical sense, because they were influential and highly respected.

These were the Pharisees of the first century C.E. The picture of their ancestors of the second and first centuries B.C.E. is even more blurry. Josephus, who is unaware of the possibility that the sects might have developed in the course of two centuries, presents the Pharisees of the Hasmonean times as identical with those of the first century. They observe the ancestral traditions, are influential with the masses, and so on. The only novelty is their political activism. When given an opportunity they enforce their ancestral traditions and assassinate or expel their opponents. From the same period we have the polemic of the Qumran scrolls against "the seekers of smooth things," probably the Pharisees, but unfortunately the scrolls are cryptic and provide little hard data. Perhaps the early Pharisees dedicated themselves to the ancestral traditions because they believed that the temple cult alone was no longer adequate, and in the flush of youth tried aggressively to enforce their program on the people. This is the picture suggested by Josephus, but we have no way of knowing whether it is correct.

Other Sects and Groups

I have devoted a great deal of attention (perhaps too much!) to the Pharisees, Sadducees, and Essenes, because of their prominence in the ancient sources and in modern scholarship. However, Judaism in the period between the Maccabees and the destruction of the temple in 70 c.e. had many more than three "sects" or "schools." Josephus himself mentions a "fourth philosophy" and various other revolutionary groups. He also mentions once (unless the passage is an interpolation) "the tribe of Christians." He refers to the Samaritans on many occasions, although never as a "sect" or "school." Philo describes a group of Therapeutae in Egypt. I shall briefly discuss each of these.

"Fourth Philosophy," Sicarii, and Zealots

After describing the Pharisees, Sadducees, and Essenes, Josephus turns to a fourth school of philosophy. While the first three were legitimate, the fourth, Josephus says, was "intrusive," an "innovation and revolution in the ancestral ways" (*Jewish Antiquities* 18.1.1, §9). The basic tenet of this group, which was founded by Judas the Galilean (or the Gaulanite) and Zadok the Pharisee, was "No king but God!" The slogan seems anarchic in character, since it justifies the rejection of all political institutions, but in practice Judas and his followers attacked only Romans and those Jews who supported or cooperated with Roman rule. The group first appeared in 6 c.e., when it rebelled against the Romans; the rebellion was crushed (Acts 5:37). For the next generation Judea was quiet. Even when Caligula threatened to erect a statue in the temple, no rebels were to be seen. But shortly thereafter the country was overrun by "brigands," and in his narrative of the events from the mid-40s c.e. to the outbreak of the war Josephus frequently mentions "brigands" and their deleterious effects. In the 50s c.e. a new type of rebel appeared, the "Sicarii" (literally, "dagger men"), who specialized in mixing with the crowds in Jerusalem and stabbing to death those Jews who supported Roman rule. With the outbreak of the war itself, especially from the summer of 67 C.E. until the destruction, another name begins to appear on the pages of Josephus, that of the Zealots.

Until recently most scholars assumed that the "fourth philosophy," the brigands, the Sicarii, and the Zealots were four different names for a single group of revolutionaries. Founded by Judas at the beginning of the first century, this group engaged in a continuous struggle against the Romans until the destruction of the temple in 70 C.E. and the fall of Masada in 73 or 74 C.E. For ease of reference these scholars used the name "Zealots" as a synonym for "revolutionaries." Recent scholarship, however, has emphasized that this interpretation is incorrect. It is likely that the Sicarii were the descendants of the "fourth philosophy" founded by Judas, but neither group should be identified with brigands, Zealots, or other groups. Each has its own history.

The Sicarii burst into prominence in the 40s C.E., were always an urban phenomenon, and restricted their murderous attacks to their fellow Jews, especially aristocrats and the well-to-do. For a brief period at the beginning of the war they commanded the revolutionary forces, but then were ousted from Jerusalem by their fellow Jews. They spent the rest of the war at Masada, and aside from raiding several Jewish towns for supplies did nothing to hinder or aid the war effort. In the end they slew themselves rather than be captured by the Romans. The Zealots, by contrast, first appear (except for three stray references in Josephus) in the events of 67 C.E., and consisted for the most part of peasants who fled to Jerusalem as the Romans swept southward from Galilee. The Zealots removed the aristocratic high priest and attacked, with equal intensity, other revolutionary groups, the aristocracy, and the Romans. Unlike the Sicarii and the Zealots, the "brigands" were not a "group" at all. Brigandage was a rural phenomenon found throughout the ancient world and was the consequence of economic stress and social dislocation. Many of the Jewish brigands were anti-Roman, because they hated the tax collectors and landlords supported by Rome, but most were not ideologically motivated. Their goal was to make money, and they did not much care whether the travelers and villagers whom they robbed were Jews or Romans, the supporters of peace or the fomenters of war. Like the word "terrorist" in contemporary political vocabulary, "brigand" is a relative term. One man's "terrorist" or "brigand" is another man's "freedom fighter" or "hero" (compare Robin Hood). Those people whom Josephus and the Romans denounced as "brigands" included real malefactors as well as real revolutionaries.

Sicarii, Zealots, and brigands were not the only revolutionaries who fought the Romans. The first act of rebellion was taken by some of the temple priests, and a priestly revolutionary party played an important role in the first half of the war. (These priests, some of them of the high priestly line, were the bitter enemies of the Zealots and the Sicarii.) Various noblemen joined in, each with his own band of retainers and supporters. A group of Jews from Idumea, the birthplace of Herod the Great, supported the Zealots for a while in their battle against the high priests and the aristocrats. In sum, the war was fought by a wide variety of groups and parties whose animosity for one another often surpassed their collective animosity for the Romans.

Were any of these groups sects? Clearly the question is relevant only to the more highly organized groups, notably the Sicarii. The evidence is insufficient to answer the question. We may be sure that the revolutionaries in general and the Sicarii in particular were motivated by religious goals (for example, to hasten or implement the arrival of the messianic age; to fight for God, Torah, and the holy land; to rid the holy land of foreign contagion; to be zealous for the Torah of God), although Josephus, because he cannot admit the possibility that revolution against Rome is a legitimate expression of Judaism, denies the fact. The slogan "No king but God!" must be the summary of a well-developed religious program. But even if the stated goals of the revolutionaries were religious in nature, there is little evidence that the competing revolutionary groups represent competing sectarian ideologies. Furthermore, it is likely that the *real* causes of the war lie elsewhere entirely. The war of 66–70 is a classic example of a social revolution that is also a native revolt against an imperialist power. It follows standard patterns and is not a uniquely Jewish phenomenon (see chapter 2). Jewish sectarianism probably did not play a dominant role.

Christians

This is not the place for a full discussion of early Christianity. I am interested here only in pointing to certain features which clearly locate early Christianity (that is, the postresurrection community) within the world of Jewish sectarianism.

The Christian community described in the opening chapters of Acts is a sect in the sense that it is "a small organized group that has separated itself from a larger religious body." The twelve apostles control the group; property is held in common, disbursements are made to the faithful from the common till, and disobedience to one's superiors is not tolerated (Acts 5:1–11). The group dines and prays together. New members are "converted" through baptism and repentance (Acts 2:38–42). Like the Essenes, the early Christians attempted to create a utopian community (and like Josephus' and Philo's portrait of the Essenes, Luke's portrait of the early Christians is highly idealized). A sense of alienation from the rest of society is apparent in the numerous calls for repentance and in the eschatological fervor of the group. (Other works in the New Testament canon, notably Ephesians and Colossians, have a dualistic view of the cosmic order, similar to that of the Qumran Essenes.) The leaders of the group reject priestly authority, and, although some of the Christians maintain their veneration for the temple (Acts 3:1), others vehemently reject it, forecasting its destruction (Acts 6–7).

One of the central themes of the book of Acts is that Christianity is a legitimate development of Judaism and that the Jews of that time (and later!) were wrong to reject it. But because the focus shifts quickly to the gentile mission (Acts 10–11), Luke never explains in detail the relationship of the new form of Judaism, known as Christianity (Acts 11:26), to the old. In Galatians and Romans, Paul addresses this question, but the two epistles do not agree (Galatians is a much more radical rejection of Judaism than is Romans). During the past thirty years, with the rise of ecumenism and the increased desire to free the New Testament of any charge of "anti-Semitism," many scholars have emphasized that Paul's rejection of Jewish law and, to some extent, of Judaism itself is directed to a *gentile* audience. Paul, these scholars argue, objected if a gentile wished to subject himself to the Jewish laws, but had no objection if a native-born Jew wished to continue observing the laws after receiving faith in Christ. These scholars further argue that Paul does not appropriate the title "Israel" for the gentile Christians alone but includes within this concept the Jews as well, Israel after the flesh. A similar interpretation of Paul was already advanced by the book of Acts, since the Paul of Acts never polemicizes against the law and often observes the requirements of Jewish ritual, including circumcision (Acts 16:3).

Even if this interpretation of Paul is correct, the fact remains that Paul believes, both in the epistles and in Acts, that the only true expression of Judaism includes faith in Christ, that is, Christianity. This is implied too in Luke's portrait of the first Christians. Faith in Christ was not to be an act of pietism for an elite, but was to be the new norm for Judaism. Those Jews who do not accept Christ are sinners. If this is not a sectarian perspective, it certainly is very close to it.

Belief in Jesus' resurrection and status as messiah was the focal point for the differentiation between Christian and non-Christian Jews. The failure of the larger Jewish community to realize the importance of the person who had just ascended to heaven caused the group of believers to feel alienated from the larger community. I have argued throughout this chapter that in ancient Judaism sectarian alienation, whatever its origin, generally expressed itself in polemics against the central institutions of society (notably the temple), its authority figures (notably the priests), and its religious practices (notably purity, Sabbath, and marriage law). The "cutting edge" of sectarianism was not theology but practice. Someone in the early community preserved (invented?) the debate stories in which Jesus attacks the religious practices of the Pharisees in precisely these matters, and preserved (invented?) the prophecy of the destruction and the re-erection of the temple. Faith in Christ surely led the early Christians to distinctive rituals (baptism, Eucharist) and practices (possession by the Spirit, speaking in tongues), and to distinctive interpretations of some of the Jewish observances (the feast of Passover, the feast of Pentecost, prayer). These distinctive and peculiar practices, more than the distinctive and peculiar theology on which the practices were based, made Christianity a "sect" or, at least, a separate group within Jewish society.

Early Christianity ceased to be a Jewish sect when it ceased to observe Jewish practices. It abolished circumcision and became a religious movement overwhelmingly gentile in composition and character. This process was accompanied by the elevation of Jesus to a position far higher and more significant than that occupied by any intermediary figure in Judaism. Its practices no longer those of the Jews, its theology no longer that of the Jews, and its composition no longer Jewish, the Christianity of the early second century C.E. was no longer a Jewish phenomenon but a separate religion. Small groups of Jewish-Christians (more accurately, Christian Jews) persisted through the first five or six centuries C.E., but they were regarded as "sects" by both the Jews and the Christians. As one fourth-century church father remarked, "they are not Jews because they believe in Christ, and they are not Christians because they observe the Jewish laws."[8] To what extent the rabbis were responsible for the expulsion of the Christians through the institution of the "benediction against heretics" is a question I shall consider in the last chapter.

Samaritans

The single best-known fact about the Samaritans is that Jesus mentions a good one (Luke 10:29–37), but the point of that parable is that Jews do not expect to be treated well by Samaritans because neither group regards the other with "neighborly" feelings. Like the history of early Christianity, the history of the Samaritans is too complex to be treated here in any detail.

First a note on nomenclature. The name "Samaritan" has two distinct meanings: an inhabitant of the district of Samaria (compare "Galilean," "Judean," "Idumean"), or a member of a religious community centered in Shechem and Mount Gerizim. In order to reduce the confusion, some scholars restrict the term "Samaritan" to the second sense and use the term "Samarian" in the first. In Greco-Roman times the city of Samaria, ancient Shomron, the erstwhile capital of the northern kingdom, was a pagan city, and much of the countryside was pagan as well. These pagans hated the Jews to their north and their south, and were involved in several violent incidents in the first century C.E. that turned out to be the prelude to the great revolt. The people who concern us here are not these pagans but the community that dwelt (and still dwells) in Shechem and venerated (and still venerates) Mount Gerizim.

The history of the group begins in the last part of the fourth century B.C.E. After the conquest of the country by Alexander the Great in 334 B.C.E., the city of Samaria rebelled against Macedonian rule. In retaliation, the city was destroyed, cleared of its former inhabitants, and resettled with pagans. Archaeological evidence suggests that the former inhabitants of Samaria fled to Shechem, where they established themselves. In all likelihood, the temple on Mount Gerizim was now built to serve the new community. The erection of the temple, however, did not signal a break with the Jews of Judea who venerated the temple in Jerusalem. There was tension, to be sure, between the two communities, but no "schism." The alphabet used by the Samaritans and the text form of their Torah are those which were widespread in Judea in the second century B.C.E. The decrees of Epiphanes applied to the Samaritans as well as to the Judeans, a fact which confirms that both groups were Jews in the eyes of the state. Unlike the Jews of Judea, however, the Samaritans accepted the king's program and dedicated their temple to Zeus. Perhaps in revenge for this act, John Hyrcanus destroyed the Gerizim temple in 129 B.C.E. and the city of Shechem in 109 B.C.E. This caused undying tension between the communities. The Samaritans created their own canon (which included only the

Torah), developed rituals and practices that in many areas agreed, and in many areas disagreed, with those of their fellow Jews, and elaborated their own eschatology (including the restoration of their temple on Mount Gerizim).

Who were these Samaritans who venerated Mount Gerizim? This was a question of great controversy in antiquity and still remains unresolved. Josephus gives several different answers. In one passage he says that the Samaritans were the descendants of the ten tribes of the northern kingdom. In another he says that they are the descendants of the Cutheans whose syncretistic cult is described in 2 Kings 17. (Josephus and the rabbis often call the Samaritans "Cutheans," *Kutim.*) He also tells the interesting story that in the time of Alexander the Great a brother of the high priest was expelled from Jerusalem because he had married the daughter of Sanballat, governor of Samaria. He fled to his father-in-law after being assured that he would receive a temple of his own. Other priests who had intermarried fled with him. Sanballat obtained permission from Alexander the Great to build the temple on Gerizim. This story implies that the temple on Gerizim, like the temple in Heliopolis in Egypt and like (perhaps) the sect of Qumran Essenes, was founded by runaway priests from Jerusalem. The Samaritans in Hellenistic times called themselves "the Sidonians who live in Shechem," that is, the offspring of Canaanites and Phoenicians. In a medieval work the Samaritans argue that only they are the true Israel because all the rest of Israel sinned when, under the leadership of the wicked priest Eli (1 Sam. 1), they abandoned Shechem and Gerizim in order to worship at Shiloh and later at Jerusalem.

Were the Samaritans a "sect"? On the one hand, they have many sectarian features. As long as their temple stood on Mount Gerizim they seem to have regarded themselves as part of the larger community of the worshipers of the God of Israel, but after their temple was destroyed they argued that the Jerusalem temple was completely unacceptable to God, because it was built on the wrong place, and that a new and true temple would someday be rebuilt on Gerizim. We may presume that they also delegitimated the Jerusalemite priesthood. In sum, they looked upon themselves as the true Israel. On the other hand, the Samaritans have many features that are decidedly nonsectarian: their mixed origins, their ethnic ties to Shechem and Mount Gerizim, and their widespread diaspora, which has been estimated by some scholars to rival that of the Jews. Sect or no, the Samaritans were a distinctive group or community that gradually emerged during the second temple period. Scholars now agree that the separation between the Jews and the Samaritans, like the separation between Judaism and Christianity, was not an *event* but a protracted *process*.

Therapeutae

Jewish sectarianism was a phenomenon restricted to the mother country. Alienation from the temple and the priests was required if sectarianism was to have a focus, and outside the land of Israel that focus did not exist, because all Jews were equally distant from the holy land and from contact with the sacred. All the sources that speak about the Pharisees, Sadducees, Essenes, and other sects, place them exclusively (except for occasional refugees from war or persecution) in the land of Israel, for the most part in Judea. (Paul became a Pharisee and studied with Gamaliel in Israel, not Tarsus.) The sole exception (aside from early Christianity) is a group described by Philo, the Therapeutae (Greek for "healers" or "attendants").

The Therapeutae were an Essene-like group that was scattered throughout Egypt and consisted of both men and women. They abstained from marriage, practiced moderation and self-mastery, and ate, prayed, and studied communally. They prayed every morning, and on Sabbath and holidays held more elaborate services that featured the singing of hymns, a communal dinner, an ecstatic dance, and the study of scripture. The members were classified according to seniority, the junior always deferring to the senior. They devoted their entire existence to the contemplation of God and truth. In various details the Therapeutae differ from the Essenes (the Therapeutae do not eat meat or drink wine, the Essenes do; the Therapeutae engage in daily fasts, the Essenes do not; the Therapeutae include both men and women in their rituals, the Essenes men only), but the overall resemblance of the two groups is striking.

At the very least, then, the Therapeutae were a pietistic group in Egypt that in some important ways resembled the Essenes. Its existence shows that the impulse to flee the world in order to pursue a life of holiness was to be found among Jews not only in the land of Israel but also in the diaspora, but there is no hint in Philo of any sectarian self-definition. Some scholars have suggested that the Therapeutae were the Egyptian branch of the Essenes, but the question cannot be decided.

Conclusion

Sects are elitist groups, small and selective. The social standing of their members is irrelevant; the members of a sect, whether poor or rich, plebeian or aristocratic, remove themselves from the social mainstream and make themselves special. The commonality of property among the Essenes and the early Christians enforces this point. It is their membership in the sect, not their prior economic or social status, which confers an elite rank on the members. The groups have priestly character; they consist in large part of priests and of laypeople who look upon themselves as priests. Their community is the temple, their liturgy is the sacrificial cult. They observe the laws of purity in order to distinguish themselves, the saved, from the rest. Alienated from society and disenchanted with the temple and the priesthood of Jerusalem, they arrogate to themselves the exclusive claim of truth which the temple still possessed for the rest of the community. Until the coming of the eschaton the sect alone is the path to God. In the first century C.E. the Essenes and the early Christians (and, perhaps, the Samaritans) were sects. The Pharisees, at least in the first century, seem not to have been a sect but a more amorphous group that remained distinctive while exerting great influence. And of course there were many other groups as well.

Sectarianism is the culmination of the democratization of Judaism. Its essential goal was to bridge the gap between humanity and God through constant practice of the commandments of the Torah and total immersion in the contemplation of God and his works. Sectarian piety supplants or supplements the temple cult through prayer, scriptural study, and purifications, and rejects or dilutes the power of the priesthood. The democratization (or the individualization) of religion was a process that affected all forms of Judaism in second temple times, as I discussed in chapter 3, but it affected the sects most of all.

Most Jews were not members of any sect. They observed the Sabbath and the holidays, heard the scriptural lessons in synagogue on Sabbath, abstained from forbidden foods, purified themselves before entering the temple precincts, circumcised their sons on the eighth day, and adhered to the "ethical norms" of folk piety. Whatever they may have thought of the priests and the temple, they went on pilgrimage to the temple a few times a year and probably relied on the priesthood to propitiate the deity through a constant and well-maintained sacrificial cult. If the "average" Jew of antiquity was anything like the "average" citizen of every other time and place, he or she was more concerned about rainfall and harvests than about theology and religion. For this "average" Jew the primary benefit of the democratization of religion was that it provided an additional means for serving God and thereby ensuring divine blessing. Sectarians and other pietists demanded a much greater reliance on individual piety and a much reduced reliance on the temple cult, but these insatiable demands were dismissed as the rantings of a fanatic few.

6

Canonization and Its Implications

Introduction

The Jews of the second temple period created the document which Christians call "the Old Testament" and which Jews call "Tanak"—an acronym for *Torah* (the five books of Moses), *Nebiim* (the Prophets), and *Ketubim* (the Writings)—that is, the Bible. In the Persian period the various strands of the Torah were woven together for the final time and the resulting product became the "constitution" or foundation document for all forms of Judaism. No one any longer dared to modify the older compositions (called by modern scholars J, P, E, and D) that it incorporated, not even to reconcile their numerous contradictions or to clarify their numerous obscurities. Nor did anyone ever try to "reopen" the Torah by discovering additional fragments of its constituent sources. Once the text of the Torah was firmly established in the last centuries B.C.E., no one (except the Samaritans) dared change it. Even the very parchment (or papyrus) on which the Torah was written became sacred.

In the Hellenistic period the words of the prophets underwent a similar process of selection and edition. The prophecies of Isaiah, Jeremiah, Ezekiel, and "the twelve prophets" had been augmented through the centuries by the words of numerous anonymous seers and interpolators, the most famous of whom are "Second Isaiah" and "Third Isaiah." Now, however, all these books were closed (even if their texts remained fluid for some time). Not only were the words of anonymous seers no longer added to those of the named prophets, no one any longer saw heavenly visions and heard heavenly voices quite like those of previous times. Prophecy continued, but its method and message were different from those of Isaiah,

Jeremiah, and Ezekiel, and its authors now hid behind pseudonyms or false identities (a practice known as "pseudepigraphy").

This process of selection, edition, and veneration of the books of the past is called "canonization" or "the formation of the biblical canon." The Greek word "canon" means "straight rod" or "bar," hence "rule," "norm," or "standard." In the Christian Greek of the second century c.e. it came to mean "rule of faith," the revealed truth of the church. By the fourth century the noun "canon" was used regularly by both Greek and Latin church fathers to designate the fixed selection of authoritative books that were believed to have been written under divine inspiration and therefore to constitute the sacred scriptures of the church ("the Old Testament" and "the New Testament"). Since heretics included among these scriptures (especially the New Testament) numerous works that in the eyes of the orthodox were neither sacred nor inspired, the definition of the canon of the Christian Bible became an important task for both heresy hunters and church councils.

Not all the works that were excluded from the canon were deemed heretical. Some were merely "of the second rank" or "among the apocrypha" (works that were "to be hidden away" because they were not to be read, at least not in the liturgy). For most church fathers "the apocrypha" was not a fixed selection but a fluid category for books of dubious status. In modern parlance the phrase *"the* Apocrypha" (or *"the* Apocrypha of the Old Testament") is often used to designate those Jewish books (Ben Sira, Wisdom of Solomon, 1 Maccabees, 2 Maccabees, Judith, Tobit, etc.) which are included in the Greek or Latin Old Testament of the church but are absent from the Hebrew Tanak of the Jews. This usage gained currency only when Martin Luther removed these books from the Old Testament and edited them as a separate collection under the title *"The* Apocrypha." (Catholics call these books, or at least the majority of these books, "deuterocanonical," and use the term "apocryphal" to designate those books which the church rejected from the canon altogether.)

The Jews of antiquity apparently did not have a word for "canon." Philo, Josephus, and the New Testament use the Greek terms for "scripture," "scriptures," "sacred scriptures," "the sacred books," and the like, and the rabbis use their Hebrew equivalents, but none of them has a word for "canon." The rabbis at least have a phrase that is the functional equivalent of the term "canonical." A book that "renders the hands impure" is "sacred" and, in our terminology, canonical; a book that does not "render the hands impure" is not sacred and, in our terminology, noncanonical. (The Sadducees protested the idea that sacred scriptures render the hands impure; see Mishnah *Yadayim* 4:6, quoted in the previous chapter.) Like the church fathers, the rabbis mention books that are or should be "hidden away," that is, not read at all, or at least not read in synagogue.

Perhaps, one might argue, the Jews of antiquity did not have a word for "canon" because the entire concept was foreign to them. This radical position is not without some support. In his *Jewish Antiquities,* a survey of Jewish history from Adam and Eve until the outbreak of the war in 66 C.E., Josephus does not distinguish between canonical books and noncanonical. He does not tell the reader when he is paraphrasing a biblical book and when a nonbiblical book. He does not give any indication that he has crossed some great divide when his account reaches the end of the biblical material. He utilizes exactly the same techniques for the paraphrase of both biblical and nonbiblical works. It is impossible to tell from the *Jewish Antiquities* whether Josephus has any notion of canon. These facts are remarkable because in another of his works Josephus provides the earliest extant description of the biblical canon (see below), a description that he ignores in his *Jewish Antiquities.*

The Jews of Qumran too do not have a clear sense of canon. That they regarded the Torah, the Prophets, and the Psalms as canonical is evident from the manner in which these books were cited and interpreted in their literature (although they did preserve the *Temple Scroll,* which seeks to be a replacement for the Torah), but there is no sign that they had any conception of a "Bible." The caves have yielded fragments of biblical and nonbiblical books, but it is impossible to tell from the physical remains of the scrolls whether the texts written on them were canonical or not. The writing material, the scribal techniques, the mode of preservation—all these are substantially identical for biblical and nonbiblical books alike.

In spite of the failure of the Jews of antiquity to use the word "canon" or an equivalent, and in spite of the absence of a biblical canon at Qumran and in the major work of Josephus, I think that most of the Jews of antiquity would have recognized the concepts that are conveyed by the words "canon" and "canonical." The definition of these words is very elusive, as we shall see, especially if we admit that not all Jews necessarily would have shared the same definition, but in the final analysis the terms do reflect some reality in ancient Judaism. In contrast I avoid the terms "apocrypha" and "apocryphal," although the rabbis use the latter expression, because the words invariably convey the impression of a fixed list of "deuterocanonical" books, a list that never existed in any form of ancient Judaism. (On the term "pseudepigrapha," see below.)

"Canon" and "Canonical"

A *canon* is a list of books. Unlike a regular list, a canon contains a fixed number of items (although it can be expanded or shortened from time to time). A *canonical* work is distinguished from a non-canonical one by three characteristics: it was created in a previous generation, usually long before it achieved its canonical status; its text is firmly established and is not open to changes of any kind (except those introduced by scholars seeking to produce an accurate text); and it is regarded as "authoritative" by a community. This definition of canon and canonical applies not only to the Tanak of the Jews and the Old and New Testaments of the Christians. All literate cultures produce canons and canonical literature, and even within Judaism and Christianity canonization of authoritative works persisted long after the creation of the Jewish and Christian Bibles. Furthermore, with a few modifications the definition applies not only to books but also to other products of human creativity (art, music, architecture, etc.).

All artistic creation is the product of imitation and originality. All painters, authors, sculptors, and composers imitate their predecessors even while they try to assert their own originality. Because artists imitate their predecessors, we can recognize certain styles that extend over considerable periods (for example, Baroque architecture, Romantic music). At a certain point in artistic development imitation ceases because it has become impossible. There is a sense that the old style has reached its limit and can no longer be imitated or developed. The old style is replaced by a new one, which may be the result either of a conscious rejection of the old ways (for example, the rebellion of the nineteenth-century French impressionists against the conventional modes of painting) or of a further incremental modification which only later is recognized as the culmination of the old and the introduction of the new (for example, the shift in musical style from Classical to Romantic). During the efflorescence of a given style, and more especially a generation or two after its decline, certain artists and works are recognized as the best representatives of their genres. They are deemed "classics" of enduring worth, and are studied or imitated. In other words, they are "canonical."

Jewish culture in the latter part of the second temple period was hardly unique, therefore, in selecting the best and the most enduring works of its literary patrimony and according them "canonical" status. Their contemporaries in the Greek world were engaged in a parallel process. In Greco-Roman antiquity the art of imitation was not left to personal whim; rhetorical manuals taught the orator, the historian, and the poet the approved manner by which he should imitate the great authors of the past, and gave the student lists of authors who were the models of perfection within each genre. The works of these authors were studied, imitated, and preserved; the works of other authors were neglected. In the fourth century B.C.E. (that is, the century after Ezra) Aeschylus, Sophocles, and Euripides, playwrights of the previous century, attained "canonical" rank: they were recognized as *"the* three tragedians." Around the year 200 B.C.E. (that is, about the same time as Ben Sira) one scholar in Alexandria selected nine lyric poets, all of whom lived centuries earlier, as the best of their genre. Scholars and rhetoricians in the following generations made selective lists in other genres (for example, the ten Attic orators) or modified the selections that had been made earlier. In every case, however, the selected authors, who in Roman times collectively received the Latin title *classici* (the best, those of the first class), lived long before the time of those who were making the selection.

The similarity of this selection process to that which produced the Tanak is so striking that scholars from the middle of the eighteenth century to the present have not hesitated to call the Greek selections "canons," although the Greeks themselves never used the term in this sense.[1] Both the Jews and the Greeks of the Hellenistic period realized that they were living in a postclassical age, and that the greatest expressions of their national literatures had already been written.

The canonization of the Jewish and Christian Bibles was but the first act of canonization within Judaism and Christianity. Both religions have a large number of "canonical" authors and texts which, no less than the Bible, and in many respects far more than the Bible, teach doctrine and practice to the faithful. In Christianity these authors are the church fathers of antiquity, the scholastics of the Middle Ages, and the leaders of the Reformation and the Counter-Reformation. In 1298 the Latin church introduced a feast day in honor of the four doctors (teachers) of the church (Ambrose, Jerome, Augustine, and Gregory the Great), and since that time the Catholic church has expanded this "canon" to include more than thirty authors. In rabbinic Judaism these works are the Mishnah, the two Talmudim (although with the decline in the fortunes of the Jewry of the land of Israel during the early Middle Ages, the Palestinian Talmud soon fell from the rabbinic canon), and their continuators in medieval and early modern times.

The Mishnah and other rabbinic works, and the books written by the doctors of the church, are canonical within their respective communities. They have shaped the religious traditions that follow them, and are venerated and studied. Christian doctrine (at least until the Reformation) has been shaped more by Augustine than by Paul (or, perhaps more accurately, more by Paul as understood by Augustine than by Paul himself), just as Jewish practice has been shaped more by the Mishnah than by the Torah (or, perhaps less accurately, more by the Torah as understood by the Mishnah than by the Torah itself).

This brief survey of the phenomenon of canonization shows that the canonical status of the Tanak and of the Christian Bible is not unique. It is amply paralleled in other cultures and in the Judaism and Christianity of later times. But from another perspective the canonical status of the Tanak and the Christian Bible *is* unique. The Bible clearly enjoyed (and still enjoys) a measure of authority unlike that of other canonical works, and that authority is to be connected with the Tanak's status as the revealed or inspired word of God. But what is the nature of the connection between the Tanak's special authority and its special status? Which is the cause and which the effect? Did the Tanak's status as the revealed or inspired word of God confer on it unusual authority, or did the Tanak's special authority engender the belief in its divinity? The answer is probably something between the two.

The Jews (and Christians) of antiquity believed that the books of the Tanak were authoritative because they were revealed or inspired by God. This belief is attested in the first century C.E. (see below) and was adopted by both Christianity and rabbinic Judaism. Whether or not this belief is correct is a question that a historian cannot answer. (Compare my discussion of "orthodoxy" and "heresy" in chapter 5.) Whether a belief by the Jews in a book's divinity is a sufficient condition to establish the book's claim to membership in the Tanak is a question that a historian can answer, and the answer is no. (Whether it is a necessary condition, I shall discuss below.) Many ancient poets and authors claimed inspiration from Apollo or the Muses. One Greek scholar in antiquity astutely observed that legislators routinely ascribed their laws to a deity in order to give their legislation greater authority. He illustrates this thesis by citing Minos the lawgiver of the Cretans, who ascribed his laws to Zeus; Lycurgus the lawgiver of the Spartans, who ascribed his laws to Apollo; and Moses the lawgiver of the Jews, who ascribed

his laws to "Iao."[2] Furthermore, many Jewish books outside the
Tanak, notably the apocalypses, claimed to be inspired or revealed
by God or some other heavenly figure. Some Jews, at least, regarded
this literature as authoritative, and perhaps accorded it "biblical"
status. Fourth Ezra (also called 2 Esdras), an apocalyptic work of the
first century C.E., implies that these books were even more authoritative than the twenty-four books of the Tanak (14:46–47). Pagan
books, pagan laws, and Jewish apocalypses claimed to be the reposi-
tory of divine revelation, and the parallel claim of the Tanak will not
set it apart from the crowd. What, then, makes the books of the
Tanak different from all other canonical books?

For the historian, the Tanak and the New Testament are special
neither because they were revealed or inspired by God nor because
they were believed to have been revealed or inspired by God, but
because they enjoy special status within their faith communities.
The canonical books of the Tanak possess existential value for the
Jewish community. They transcend the period of their origins and
respond to the community's needs by shaping its identity and en-
dowing its existence with meaning and purpose. The books are
"relevant" in a very immediate sense. They contain laws that are still
binding and must be obeyed; prophecies that present eternal verities which speak, even generations after they were first delivered, to
the present and the future; histories that are paradigms of reward
and punishment, model lessons in God's control of human affairs;
wisdom that is always salutary and ennobling; and hymns and
poems that bring the humanity of every generation closer to God.
No ancient source gives this definition—after all, no ancient Jewish
source even has a word for canon!—and not all Jews everywhere at
all times maintained this attitude toward their canonical literature,
but the "existential" definition does, I think, accurately reflect the
meaning of "biblical" within Judaism from ancient to modern times.

Because the Torah, the Prophets, and at least some of the books
of the Writings (notably the Psalms) were seen as eternally valid and
existentially meaningful, they were venerated far more than other
canonical works. The scrolls on which they are written are sacred
(as the rabbis say, they "render the hands impure"). The scrolls of
the Torah are more sacred than those of the Prophets, which in turn
are more sacred than those of the Writings—just as the Torah is
more authoritative than the Prophets, and the Prophets are more
authoritative than the Writings. The scrolls of the Mishnah, in contrast, have no sanctity whatsoever. (What degree of sanctity the Jews
of Qumran ascribed to their scrolls is unknown.) The sanctity of the
Torah scrolls was an important element in the Jewish piety of both

Israel and the diaspora. The emperor Augustus decreed that anyone caught stealing "the sacred books" of the Jews was to be punished severely; in the first century C.E. a Roman soldier in Judea desecrated a Torah scroll, and the only way the Romans could quiet the subsequent disorder that erupted among the Jews was to behead the offender.[3]

Since they are seen as eternally valid, the Torah and the Prophets provide lections for the weekly liturgy, although the Writings (and the Mishnah) do not. In theory, at least, the Torah was the ultimate authority, the record of God's revelation to Moses. Through the power of interpretation the Jews were able to free themselves from laws of the Torah which they found difficult, unethical, harsh, or unreasonable, but they would rarely admit that they were overturning the sacred text. They would insist that they were merely *interpreting* it (see below). The same attitude can often be found in the Talmud's approach to the Mishnah, but many rabbis, both in ancient times and later, had no qualms in rejecting outright some of the laws of the Mishnah, although they accepted the authority of the Mishnah as a whole and may have regarded it as containing the "oral law" which was revealed to Moses at Mount Sinai. The Mishnah is a "canonical" work but it is not eternally valid; its authority is not that of the "biblical" books.

The most important consequence of the canonization of the Tanak was that it was regarded as inspired or revealed by God. Perhaps the Torah and the Prophets (Isaiah, Jeremiah, Ezekiel, and the twelve minor prophets) became canonical (that is, were viewed as eternally valid and existentially meaningful) because they were regarded as divinely inspired, but for the rest of the biblical canon the sequence is almost certainly the reverse (canonization caused the belief in divine inspiration). Over half of the Hebrew canon consists of works whose authors do not claim to be inspired by God (Joshua–Kings, and virtually all of the Writings except Daniel), and it is likely that the belief in the divine inspiration of all these was derived by analogy from the Prophets and the Torah. By the first century C.E. many Jews believed that any ancient text which contained eternal truths must have been divinely inspired. In all likelihood the Writings became part of the Tanak before they were seen as divine, because divine origin is not a necessary condition for biblical status.

To summarize: In popular parlance "canonical" and "biblical" are synonymous terms, but I have distinguished between them. All literate cultures, including Judaism, produce "canonical" or "classical" texts that are admired, studied, imitated, and regarded as au thoritative. The phenomenon of "canonization" is not restricted either to Judaism or to antiquity. Canonical Jewish texts have been written from ancient to modern times, and will continue to be written for as long as Judaism remains a living culture. A select few of these canonical works, however, were chosen in antiquity to form the Tanak, "the Bible" or "scripture" or "the scriptures." These were regarded as *the* basic writings of Judaism, were especially venerated, and by the first century C.E. were believed by most Jews, if not by all, to have been inspired or revealed by God. Biblical books are distinguished by their higher level of authority. They are existentially meaningful and eternally valid. The authority of some other Jewish canonical works (like the Mishnah and the two Talmudim) may approximate that of the Tanak, but is decidedly inferior to it.

I turn now to the history of the canonization of the Bible. In order to minimize confusion I shall concentrate my discussion on the Tanak, the Hebrew Bible, and shall only briefly treat the Bible of the Greek Jews. I revert to common usage and use "canonical" as a synonym for "biblical," meaning "forming part of that special collection of works which are believed to be existentially meaningful and eternally valid."

The History of the Biblical Canon

The Torah

The core of the canon for all the Jews of antiquity was the Torah (literally, "teaching" or "instruction"), often called by Greek-speaking Jews "the law" or "the laws." (The term *Pentateuch*, "the five rolls," derives from the Greek church fathers.) The narrator of the first four books of the Torah (Genesis–Numbers) is anonymous; God often speaks to the patriarchs (in Genesis) and to Moses and the Israelites (in Exodus–Numbers), but the text nowhere identifies either its narrator or its author. Deuteronomy, by contrast, claims to be the work of Moses. It is a series of long orations in which Moses speaks about himself in the first person (although in some sections an anonymous narrator speaks about Moses in the third person). It is no accident that Deuteronomy, which began its career as a document discovered in the temple, has respect for writing and the written word. It refers to itself as "the book of the Torah" (for example, Deut. 29:20) and enjoins the king to write a copy of the Torah for himself (Deut. 17:18). The historical works written in the

Deuteronomic tradition (Joshua–Kings) frequently refer to a book called "the Torah of Moses" (for example, Josh. 8:31 and 2 Kings 14:6) and use expressions like "in accordance with what is written in the book of the Torah" (for example, Josh. 8:34) or "in accordance with what is written in [the book of] the Torah of Moses" (for example, Josh. 23:6 and 1 Kings 2:3). In these passages the word "Torah" retains its original meaning of "instruction" or "teaching" but is on its way to becoming a proper noun.

The Deuteronomic idea that Moses wrote a sacred book struck deep roots after the exile. In the literature of the Persian period, the expression "Torah of Moses" sometimes means simply "the teaching of Moses" (Mal. 3:22 enjoins the people to "Remember the Torah of my servant Moses") but usually indicates a book. This book is no longer Deuteronomy alone (as in Neh. 13:1, which refers to "the book of Moses") but the priestly tradition as well. "P" and "D" have been combined. Laws that are found not in Deuteronomy but in Leviticus are said to have been "written in the Torah of Moses the servant of God" (Ezra 3:2; 2 Chron. 23:18; 35:12). Ezra, "a scribe expert in the Torah of Moses" (Ezra 7:6), reads from "the book of the Torah of Moses" (Neh. 8:1), which is also called "the book of the Torah of God" (Neh. 8:18), and finds within it injunctions about the festival of Sukkot that are part of the priestly tradition (compare Neh. 8:15–16 with Lev. 23:40).

During the Persian period a book emerged which was known as "the Torah of Moses." It was the product of centuries of tradition, both written and oral, but now its various strands (J, E, P, D, and others) were intertwined for the final time, and editorial activity ceased. Interpretive glosses were no longer included within the work. The book was believed to be the work of Moses, and all who would worship God properly studied it and obeyed its commands. In other words, the canonization of the Torah had begun. The process was not yet complete, however. Its text was not yet firmly established and its authority was not yet above challenge.

Jewish tradition, represented by the Babylonian Talmud (*Sanhedrin* 21b) and by 4 Ezra, credits Ezra with having "edited" the Torah, that is, changing its script from the "round" script of Israelite times (usually called "paleo-Hebrew") to the "square" script still used today. This tradition is probably based on Ezra's status as "scribe" and on his activity as a teacher of the Torah. Whether Ezra had anything to do with the canonization or editing of the Torah, we do not know. Among the Qumran scrolls are several manuscripts of the Torah from the Hellenistic period, some of them in paleo-Hebrew script. These manuscripts, coupled with the variant readings provided by the Greek and the Samaritan versions, show that the Torah text with which we are now familiar was not firmly established until the second century B.C.E. Before that point, and to some extent even afterward the Torah circulated in at least three recensions.

Similarly, the status of the Torah as the sole literary expression of the revelation of God to Moses was still subject to challenge as late as the second century B.C.E. Some Jews believed that they still had the option of reformulating the narratives and laws attributed to Moses. These Jews wrote the *Temple Scroll* and the book of *Jubilees*. The former, discovered among the Dead Sea Scrolls, is either a very early work of the Essenes, perhaps of their founder (mid-second century B.C.E.?), or is a work inherited by the Essenes from some earlier group or school (perhaps third century B.C.E.). The *Temple Scroll* rewrites the laws of the Torah, rearranges them, reformulates them, expands upon them, and even adds new laws not found in the original. But the *Temple Scroll* is no mere paraphrase of the Torah. It presents itself as *the* Torah. In the Torah some anonymous narrator tells us that God spoke to Moses or the children of Israel, but in the *Temple Scroll* God speaks to Moses directly. Laws that refer to God in the third person in the Torah refer to God in the first person in the *Temple Scroll.* The alleged author of the work is God.

The book of *Jubilees,* which was written in the 160s B.C.E., rewrites the narrative portion of the Torah, from Genesis through Exodus 12 (precisely the point at which the *Temple Scroll* begins). The work greatly expands upon the Torah, and tries to prove the authenticity of the solar calendar and the pre-Sinaitic origin of the commandments. The alleged author of the work is an angel who reveals to Moses the content of various heavenly tablets.

Do the *Temple Scroll* and *Jubilees* accept the canonicity of the Torah? I shall argue below that, in paradoxical fashion, the canonization of scripture allowed the Jews both more and less freedom than they had enjoyed previously in treating their sacred tradition. The fantastic retellings of scripture, especially the Torah, which became popular in the second century B.C.E. in both Israel and the diaspora, testify to the newly gained freedom. But the *Temple Scroll* and *Jubilees,* especially the former, seem not to have been written from this perspective. Their goal is not to *supplement* scripture but to *supplant* it. If this interpretation is correct, the Torah did not enjoy unchallenged authority in the land of Israel even in the middle of the second century B.C.E.

In the diaspora, however, the authority of the Torah was secure. In the third century B.C.E. the Jews of Alexandria translated the

Torah into Greek, obviously because they regarded it as their sacred constitution. The *Letter of Aristeas,* a fictional story about the translation (written by an Egyptian Jew around the year 100 B.C.E.), contains the earliest extant references to the Torah as "the Book" (the *Bible*) and "scripture" (*Letter of Aristeas* 155, 316). Diaspora Jews soon applied these terms to the Greek translation of the Torah as well, and had no doubt that the translation allowed them to read the very words written by Moses. (By the first century C.E., in both Israel and the diaspora, the terms "scripture" and "the Book" came to include all the sacred writings, not merely the Torah.)

The Prophets

Around the year 200 B.C.E., Ben Sira writes about the scribe that "he who devotes himself to the study of the law of the Most High will seek out the wisdom of all the ancients, and will be concerned with prophecies" (Ben Sira 39:1). Ezra had been a skilled scribe in the Torah of Moses, but two hundred and fifty years later a scribe had to know "wisdom" and "prophecies" too. Ben Sira himself was such a man, as his grandson testifies in the prologue to the Greek translation of his book: "My grandfather Jesus, after devoting himself especially to the reading of the law and the prophets and the other books of our fathers, and after acquiring considerable proficiency in them, was himself also led to write something pertaining to instruction and wisdom." In his praise of famous men, a historical survey of the heroes of Israel, Ben Sira includes Isaiah, Jeremiah, Ezekiel, and "the twelve prophets" (Ben Sira 49:10). It is difficult to say whether Ben Sira is referring merely to important figures of the past or to canonical books. He gives no indication that he believes that their prophecies either are eternally valid or address the needs of any time other than the one for which they were first enunciated. Ben Sira thinks it important for a scribe and a learned Jew to know prophecies and wisdom, but this hardly means that the books are "canonical."

In the height of the religious crisis of the middle of the second century B.C.E., the author of Daniel sought to unlock the secret to the events that were taking place. The answer was to be found in the book of Jeremiah (Dan. 9:2): "I, Daniel, perceived in the books the number of years which, according to the word of the Lord to Jeremiah the prophet, must pass before the end of the desolations of Jerusalem, namely, seventy years." Jeremiah's promise of restoration, prophesied to the Babylonian exiles several hundred years earlier, was understood by the author of Daniel to promise the restoration of Israel after the depredations of Antiochus Epiphanes. Thus did the words of Jeremiah's prophecy live on, their potency and veracity undiminished long after their own time. The same attitude toward the prophets is well attested in the *pesharim* from Qumran (see below), in the New Testament, and in rabbinic literature. Once the prophets are read from this perspective, they are "canonical." It seems, then, that the prophetic books (the three major and the twelve minor) were edited before the time of Ben Sira and became canonical during the second and first centuries B.C.E. The Samaritans, who separated themselves from the Judean community at the end of the second century B.C.E., did not take the prophets with them.

The Writings

For some Jews, especially in the land of Israel, the second part of the Bible was now closed. It consisted of the historical books Joshua–Kings, which were a preface to the prophetic books (or an epilogue to the Torah), and the prophetic books themselves. Additions to the canon were incorporated in a third section that ultimately became known simply as "the Writings." When the book of Daniel, which was written in the 160s B.C.E., came to be canonized it was included not in the Prophets, which was already complete, but in the Writings. Until recently, scholars used to state that the rabbinic "synod" at Yavneh (or Jamnia) finalized the canonization of the Hebrew Bible about 100 C.E., but this view has lost favor, primarily because of lack of evidence. These scholars also assumed that the Yavnean rabbis were motivated by a desire to exclude Christianity from the fold and to exclude Christian and apocalyptic books from the canon. This interpretation too has lost favor in recent years, as I shall discuss more fully in the next chapter. In any case, no additions to the biblical canon were made after the first century C.E. The rabbis in the third and fourth centuries were still debating the sanctity of various books. Esther in particular had to fight for its place in the canon. The Jews of Qumran did not read Esther (not a single fragment of the book has been found there); Esther is missing from the earliest extant patristic list of biblical books, written in the second half of the second century C.E.; and the rabbis still were not entirely sure about the book a century or two later. But in the end Esther triumphed. The Writings are a motley assortment of works. Most of them are books of wisdom, the third item on the curriculum of the scribe according to Ben Sira, but others are hymns, histories, and novellas. Its strangest book is the Song of

Songs, which seems to be a collection of secular love songs. By the first century C.E. these works had been collected and regarded as the inspired word of God; presumably they were also regarded as eternally valid and existentially meaningful. By rabbinic times at the latest, all of the Writings were regarded in this light, but such an attitude is attested in the first century C.E. only toward the Psalms (see next section). Whoever included the Song of Songs within the canon probably interpreted it, as the rabbis of the second century did, as a sacred love song between God and Israel.

Thus the tripartite canon was born: Torah, Prophets, and Writings. This canon was accepted by many Jews in both the land of Israel and the diaspora. Some Jews, however, like those of Qumran, preferred not to define a canon at all; some, like the author of 4 Ezra, had a canon of twenty-four books, but an additional collection of apocalyptic works besides; others, especially some Jews of the diaspora, clearly defined the Torah, but otherwise were content to preserve a collection of authoritative literature that did not distinguish between Prophets and Writings, between the divinely inspired and the uninspired, and between the eternally valid and the transient.

The Tripartite Canon

Ben Sira divided the curriculum of the scribe into law, wisdom, and prophecies. This classification reflects the ancient distinction between priest, sage, and prophet. Four hundred years before Ben Sira, the Israelites rejected Jeremiah's prophecies of doom and insisted that life would proceed normally: "For instruction *(Torah)* shall not perish from the priest, nor counsel from the wise, nor the word from the prophet" (Jer. 18:18). In Jeremiah's time Torah, counsel, and the word of God were sought from living people; in Ben Sira's time they were sought through the study of books, and the master student was the scribe. Ben Sira's grandson slightly revises his grandfather's classification, changing the designation of the third category from "wisdom" to "the other books," and departing from the order of Jeremiah. The grandson speaks of "the law and the prophets and the other books of our fathers." Neither Ben Sira nor his grandson is familiar with a tripartite "canon," but the foundations were laid, and the tripartite canon clearly emerged in the first century C.E.

Three passages of the first century C.E. describe a tripartite classification of the literature of the ancients, and two of these texts clearly refer to a canon. In all three, the Psalms (or "hymns") accompany the wisdom books as the most prominent component of the third category. Philo writes of the Therapeutae (*On the Contemplative Life* 3, §25) that they study "laws and oracles delivered through the mouths of prophets, and psalms and anything else which fosters and perfects [or: and psalms and other books which foster and perfect] knowledge and piety." Whether this is a "canon" is hard to tell. Philo himself regards the Torah as the inspired word of Moses (or the revealed word of God) and devotes enormous energy to its interpretation (see below); he practically ignores the rest of the Bible, canonical or not. The second passage is Luke 24:44, in which the risen Jesus tells his disciples "that everything written about me in the law of Moses and the prophets and the psalms must be fulfilled." The Psalms too are now regarded as the work of prophecy, whose statements must be "fulfilled." The New Testament often regards the Psalms in this light; Psalms and Isaiah are the two biblical books most frequently cited in the New Testament. The Jews of Qumran wrote a commentary on the Psalms just as they did on Habakkuk and other prophets.

The third passage is the most important, because it is the earliest explicit evidence that the Jews of antiquity had a clearly articulated theory of "canonical" and "noncanonical." The passage is from the *Against Apion* of Josephus (1.8, §38–41):

> We [Jews] do not possess myriads of inconsistent books, conflicting with each other. Our books, those which are justly accredited [or: those which are rightly believed to be divine], are but two and twenty, and contain the record of all time. Of these, five are the books of Moses, which comprise the laws and the tradition from the creation of man to the death of Moses. This period is slightly less than three thousand years. From the death of Moses until Artaxerxes, who succeeded Xerxes as king of Persia, the prophets subsequent to Moses wrote the history of the events of their own times in thirteen books. The remaining four books contain hymns to God and precepts for the conduct of human life. From Artaxerxes to our own time the complete history has been written, but has not been deemed worthy of equal credit with the earlier records, because of the failure of the exact succession of the prophets.

Although Josephus does not use the word "canon," he clearly is describing a collection of books that we (and the church fathers of the fourth century) would call "canonical." The context of this passage, an attack on Greek historiography, explains its peculiar emphasis on "the Bible as history." The Greek histories are filled with errors and contradictions, because they were written by men who have no regard for either truth or accuracy. The Jewish histories, by contrast, are truthful and free of contradictions.

According to Josephus, all twenty-two books of the canon were inspired by God (and therefore are authoritative and free of contradictions); written by prophets (men who learned about previous times from God and about their own times from personal experience), all of whom lived before the reign of Artaxerxes (465–425 B.C.E., the period of Ezra); and transmitted accurately by the priests. The canon is divided in three parts: the five books of Moses, the thirteen prophetic writings, and four books of hymns and precepts.

This passage implies that *all* Jews had a biblical canon of twenty-two books arranged in the configuration 5-13-4, but Josephus is either poorly informed or deliberately misleading (after all, he is trying to emphasize Jewish unanimity!). The rabbinic canon, as described in a passage of the Babylonian Talmud (*Baba Batra* 14b–15a), consists of twenty-four books instead of the Josephan twenty-two, but this disagreement probably reflects not two different canons but two different ways of counting the canonical books (the lower numeration counts Ruth as part of Judges, and Lamentations as part of Jeremiah). Similarly, 4 Ezra knows a canon of twenty-four books. More significant is the fact that the rabbinic division of the canon has a very different tripartite configuration: five in the Torah, eight in the Prophets, and eleven in the Writings, or 5-8-11.

The most striking evidence, however, is provided by the manuscripts of the Greek translation of the Bible and by the patristic lists of the canonical books. Although both of these sources are of Christian origin, many scholars argue that they reflect, at least to some degree, the biblical canons used by the Jews of the Greek diaspora. Some of the canons attested in these sources are tripartite, but none of them is identical with the canon of either Josephus or the rabbis (for example, one father has twelve books of history, five books of poetry, and five prophetic books, or 12-5-5). Many of the canons are not tripartite at all (for example, one father describes a canon of four Pentateuchs: the five books of the laws, of poetry, of the writings, of the prophets, with the addition of Ezra and Esther at the end, for a total of twenty-two, configured 5-5-5-5-2), and some have no discernible pattern of arrangement. Another set of these canons (virtually all the manuscripts and some of the patristic lists) includes the "apocryphal" works, which neither Josephus nor the rabbis nor anyone else in the land of Israel, as far as is known, saw fit to include.[4] If the Christian evidence reflects the practices of the Greek diaspora, Josephus errs when he implies that all Jews everywhere had a tripartite canon of twenty-two books. All Jews agreed that the first five books of the canon were the Torah; most Jews agreed that these were followed by the historical books Joshua–Kings; after that the near-unanimity breaks down completely. (And, of course, some Jews, like the men of Qumran, may not have had a clear notion of canon at all.)

Why These and Not Those?

In another important respect Josephus' description of the canon is wrong. Josephus states, and his view is supported by 4 Ezra and rabbinic tradition, that all the books in the biblical canon were written before the time of Artaxerxes. It is easy to see how the Jews came to this view, because none of the books in the Hebrew canon explicitly refers to the period after Ezra and Nehemiah. But in fact, many books in the Bible were written long after that period. The late books certainly include Chronicles, Ruth, Ecclesiastes, Esther, and, of course, Daniel which was written (utilizing older material in the first part) only in the 160s B.C.E. Several others may be late as well: Job, Song of Songs, Jonah, Joel, sections of Proverbs, the second half of Zechariah, and many of the psalms. The date of all these works must have been forgotten by the first century C.E., so that Josephus could claim that the entire Bible predates the reign of Artaxerxes. The Jews represented by the Christian canons of the Bible did not agree with Josephus and rabbinic tradition. These Jews included in their Bible books that were written even later than Daniel (1 Maccabees, 2 Maccabees, Wisdom of Solomon), and works that did not even pretend, as Daniel did, to be the product of the Persian period (Ben Sira, 1 Maccabees, 2 Maccabees). Furthermore, these Jews obviously did not believe that a book had to be divinely inspired (or eternally valid) in order to be included in the Bible.

The entire process of the canonization of the Tanak raises the question, Why were these books included but not those? Why Ecclesiastes but not Ben Sira? Why Ruth but not Tobit? Why Esther but not Judith? Why Daniel but not *Enoch*? Why Chronicles (a rewrite of Samuel–Kings) but not the *Temple Scroll* (a rewrite of the laws of Exodus–Deuteronomy)? There are no objective and absolute criteria that will distinguish the works which were included from those which were not. The biblical books were not the only ones that claimed divine inspiration. Some nonbiblical books were written in Persian or early Hellenistic times (Tobit, *1 Enoch*, Ben Sira), and thus are virtually contemporary with many of the works that were included in the Writings. The latest book in the Bible, Daniel, is contemporary with *Jubilees*, Judith, and a host of other works. Why these but not those?

Part of the answer is provided by the social setting of the literature. Fourth Ezra remarks that the twenty-four books (of the Tanak) are to be read by "the worthy and the unworthy" alike, while the seventy other works which Ezra re-created through divine inspiration were to be read only by "the wise among your people" (4 Ezra 14:45–46). In other words, the books of the Bible are not esoteric. Even if Isaiah 65, Nehemiah 10, and Daniel 11–12 were originally the products of small and distinct groups, by the time the books entered the biblical canon they were the proud possession not of an elite few but of the entire people. Works that remained the esoteric possessions of sects and other such groups were never canonized. Many cultures in antiquity (especially in the East) venerated "sacred writings," and these works usually were esoteric or under the exclusive domain of the priests (as in Egypt). In Judaism, however, the "sacred writings" were the possession of the entire community, not the jealously guarded preserve of any one group. Hence *Jubilees*, the *Temple Scroll*, the Essene writings known from Qumran, and the "apocalyptic" literature (except Daniel) were not incorporated into the Bible. Why exoteric works like Ben Sira and Judith were excluded is not as clear. Of course, even in the pre-exilic period certain works were excluded from the emerging biblical tradition. The Tanak itself refers to several works that are now lost. These include, for example, the Book of Yashar (Josh. 10:13 and 2 Sam. 1:18); the Book of the Wars of the Lord (Num. 21:14); the Chronicle of the Kings of Judah (1 Kings 14:29, etc.); the Chronicle of the Kings of Israel (1 Kings 14:19, etc.). Why did no one care to preserve them? Why weren't these books "canonized"? Centuries later, why weren't Tobit, Ben Sira, and Judith canonized? We do not know.

Conclusion

The definition of "biblical canon" in antiquity is elusive. For Josephus, the rabbis, and those modern scholars willing to follow them, the definition is easy and straightforward: the canon contains books that were inspired or revealed by God. But not all Jews accepted this theological definition which, in any case, is not attested before the first century C.E. I have offered instead the "existential" definition of canonicity, but I fully concede that it too was not necessarily accepted by all the Jews of antiquity. In fact, the definition of canon was not a subject that interested the Jews of antiquity. They managed to get along without any word for "canon" and without any discussion of the history of the canonization of the Bible.

In spite of the elusiveness of the topic, certain important points are clear. Canonization is a process, not an event. In the final analysis it is the Jewish community, not some elite, which determines canonicity, since for a book to become canonical it must be accepted by the community as authoritative. Different communities had different canons, and viewed their canons differently. The Tanak of Josephus (in his *Against Apion*) and the rabbis represents one of the shortest biblical canons (except for its inclusion of Esther, it is the shortest), while the Bibles of the Jews of Qumran, the apocalyptic seers (if indeed these two groups viewed their own literatures as part of the Bible), and the Jews of the diaspora (if indeed the Christian canons derive from Jewish sources) were much longer.

The Implications of Canonization

The Jews of the second temple period saw themselves as living in a postclassical age. They collected and treasured the works of the ancients because they knew that God spoke more directly and more clearly to their ancestors than to themselves. They no longer tried to write a Torah, or a work of classical prophecy, or (with one or two exceptions) a history in the style of Judges or Kings; these were genres that belonged to a bygone age. And even in the works that they did write, they did not assert their identities. The last Judean author known by name is Ben Sira, who lived about 200 B.C.E. Otherwise, all the literature produced in the the land of Israel during the last part of the second temple period is either anonymous or pseudonymous.

The canonization of the Tanak was accompanied by the growth of the ideal of scriptural study (see chapter 3) and the emergence of people who claimed political and religious authority on the basis of their scriptural expertise (see chapter 5). The study of scripture led to the creation of three new literary genres: scriptural translation, paraphrase, and commentary. The very existence of these genres shows that the Bible was regarded as an authoritative book, and their content often shows that the Bible was regarded as a "canonical" text. Its laws were explicated and made relevant, its prophecies were applied to the events of the day or the very recent past, and its narratives were quarried for model lessons in piety (and impiety!) and paradigms of God's management of human affairs.

However, in paradoxical fashion, even as the Jews declared their loyalty to scripture they liberated themselves from it. Many of the extant scriptural translations, paraphrases, and commentaries, from both second temple and rabbinic times, are remarkably fanciful and capricious, and even those that claim to be accurate interpretations of the original, as often as not, do not live up to their claims. The emergence of canonized texts allowed the Jews great freedom in interpreting their sacred traditions, a freedom that had earlier been denied them when the traditions circulated in fluid form. When the original was still susceptible to change, the distinction between text and interpretation was not clear, and the custodians of the sacred originals would be wary of capricious modifications. They did incorporate comments and interpolations that had a variety of exegetical purposes, but they resisted all major expansions and all comments that could not be intimately attached to their source texts. However, once the traditions were established in fixed and unchanging form, that is, once written texts were edited, venerated, and canonized, the imagination was allowed to soar. A free or adventurous interpretation no longer did any harm, since the sacred original was left untouched. The folk imagination provided many episodes and sagas completely unknown to scripture, and the scholarly imagination was permitted to exercise itself in interpretations that, sometimes at least, completely ignored or destroyed the intent of the original.

Further license to creative interpretation was the belief that the canonical texts were multivalent, that is, that they convey numerous different meanings. Since no single interpretation could accurately reflect all the meanings imparted by the text (an attitude common both to modern literary critics and to ancient Jewish exegetes), all interpretations were permitted as long as they could somehow be tied to the text. Only sects argued that they alone understood the true import of the Tanak, and even they, for the most part, insisted on their exclusive possession of the truth only in legal matters. Other passages could be variously interpreted. The creation of a canon allowed the Jews great freedom in the interpretation of their sacred traditions.

Thus the canonization of the Tanak did not stifle the creative spirit as much as it redirected it. All of the Jewish literature written in the Hellenistic and Roman periods draws on the Tanak for imagery and ideas—ancient Judaism has left us few works that are "secular" or nonreligious. In some cases the influence of the biblical models is so strong that the later work is but an imitation of the earlier: First Maccabees imitates Judges and Kings, and the numerous prayers and hymns of the period (for example, the Qumran Hymns) echo the Psalms and other liturgical passages of the Tanak (although often with new content).

Far more common than the imitation of biblical models was the production of works in styles and genres unknown to the Tanak. Hellenistic novellas and romances were immensely popular, and influenced the literature written in Greek (for example, Third Maccabees), Hebrew (for example, Judith), and Aramaic (for example, the *Genesis Apocryphon*). The book of Judith, in spite of its nationalist message and its Maccabean origin (it was almost certainly written by a supporter of the Maccabees in order to extol battle on behalf of the Torah and the Lord), is a perfect specimen of a Hellenistic romance, with a beautiful and virtuous heroine, a wicked villain, and a seduction scene. (The only element missing is a handsome groom for the heroine.) Greek-speaking Jews wrote wisdom books that owe more to Greek diatribes, dialogues, and gnomic poetry than to Proverbs or Job (for example, Wisdom of Solomon, Pseudo-Phocylides); poetry that owed more to Homer and Euripides than to Isaiah and Amos (for example, Philo the Poet, Ezekiel the Tragedian); history that owes more to Herodotus, Thucydides, and Hellenistic historiography than to Kings and Chronicles (for example, Second Maccabees, Josephus); and oracles that owe more to Greek precedents than to biblical prophecy (the *Sibylline Oracles*). Hebrew-speaking Jews no longer wrote prophecies but apocalypses (see below), and they developed a genre of testaments (for example, *Testament of Moses, Testament of Levi*).

The literature of the latter part of the second temple period is a product of two contradictory tendencies. First and foremost was a feeling of inferiority and subordination to the past. The Jews sensed that they were living in a postclassical or "silver" age, and that they lacked the religious authority, perhaps authenticity, of their forebears. For the most part they no longer wrote works in biblical style and (at least the writers in Hebrew) seldom put their own names on their work. Instead of (or in addition to) seeking God through living prophets, they sought God through the study of the words of the prophets of old. But, as often occurs in such cases, the inferiority complex served as a goad to be creative in new areas. The canonization of the Tanak was both a restraint and a stimulant. It freed the imagination, since the word of God was now safely enshrined, and it compelled the Jews to develop new literary genres. Through creative exegesis the Jews could claim fidelity and subservience to the sacred texts and simultaneously free themselves from their tyrannical grip. When approaching the legacy of their ancestors, the Jews of the latter part of the second temple period (and of rabbinic times as well, as I shall discuss in the next chapter) saw themselves as both subservient and free, both inferior and autonomous.

Since this is not the place for a full discussion of these complex issues, I shall treat briefly only two of the major implications of canonization: the transformation of prophecy to apocalypse and the growth of scriptural interpretation.

The Transformation of Prophecy

Prophecy and Apocalypse: A Comparison

Prophecy did not cease so much as it was transformed. In classical prophecy from the eighth to the sixth centuries B.C.E. the prophet receives a direct revelation from God, and in turn transmits that revelation to the people. His favorite phrases are "Thus says the Lord" and "The Word of God." Occasionally the divine message is represented by means of an image or a symbol. For the most part these images are of normal objects and phenomena, and it is the divine voice which informs the prophet of their meaning (for example, Amos 8:1–3 and Jer. 1:11–15). The prophet speaks publicly and clearly; he has been uniquely privileged to receive an oracle from God, and his function is not to keep the information secret but to broadcast it to all who will listen. By announcing God's plans he hopes to goad the people to repentance. Some prophecies emphasize, instead, the inevitability of the divine decree, minimizing the possibility or efficacy of repentance (for example, Jer. 27), but the dominant function of classical prophecy, according to its own self-conception (see especially Ezek. 33), was not to predict some inescapable fate, but to stimulate piety and righteous conduct (see chapter 3). Another function of the prophet, therefore, is to beseech God to forgive his people and not to punish them as he had threatened (the classic model of this behavior is Moses; see Ex. 32 and Num. 14).

Since the prophet was such an important intermediary between God and humanity, his identity was important. All the prophetic books in the biblical canon are ascribed to named individuals. Even if modern scholarship has demonstrated that certain sections are really anonymous interpolations or additions that were incorrectly attributed to some of the named prophets (like Isa. 40–66), the fact remains that classical prophecy is for the most part the work of named individuals whose identities were preserved as well as their words.

By the second century B.C.E. classical prophecy had evolved into *apocalypse*. Scholars have long debated whether the term "apocalypse" designates a genre, a motif, or a mode of thought. The term is most useful if it is used to designate a genre: an *apocalypse* is a literary work that has an angel or some inspired worthy revealing a secret or unraveling a mystery (the Greek verb *apocalyptein* means "to reveal, to uncover"). The secret that is being revealed can be of various types. The Book of the Giants, one of the constituent parts of the book of *Enoch*, written apparently in the third century B.C.E., is an apocalypse in which an angel reveals to Enoch astronomical and cosmological lore. In the book of *Jubilees*, written in the 160s B.C.E., an angel reveals to Moses the content of some heavenly tablets. As I discussed briefly above, *Jubilees* is basically a rewrite of the first part of the Torah, but one of its goals, if not its major goal, is to legitimate the solar calendar. In pre-Maccabean times, then, the content of apocalypses was mysteries of nature. This fact implies a connection between early apocalypse and wisdom (compare Job 28). Apocalyptic literature never lost its interest in cosmology, but in response to the profanation of the temple and the persecution of Judaism by Epiphanes, it shifted its attention to the secrets of history and eschatology. This type of apocalypse, whose best-known representative is the book of Daniel, marks the final evolution of classical prophecy.

Like classical prophecy, apocalypses are revelations from God that address some of the fundamental concerns of the human condition: life, death, fate, sin, and theodicy. Like the prophet, the visionary seeks to explain God's ways, or laments his inability to do so. Many of the phrases, motifs, and ideas of the apocalypses derive from the classical prophets, so that even though the apocalyptic seers did not explicitly refer to their prophetic predecessors, they certainly looked upon themselves as their continuators. But if the eighth to sixth centuries B.C.E. were the golden age of prophecy, the second and first centuries B.C.E. were an age of silver, or perhaps bronze. Unlike prophets, apocalyptic seers are not direct intermediaries between humanity and God, because they do not receive a direct revelation from God. They do not proclaim, "Thus says the Lord." Rather, they are reporting what was revealed to them by an angel, and it is the angel who now functions as an intermediary. Often the divine message is represented by means of an image or symbol. For the most part these images are fantastic or extraterrestrial, and it is an angel who reveals their meaning (for example,

Dan. 7). Unlike the prophet, the apocalyptic seer speaks neither publicly nor clearly. Even after the angel has spoken to the seer and explained the meaning of his vision, the message remains obscure; only the wise will understand it (Dan. 12). What was mysterious before the revelation is only slightly less mysterious after it.

Apocalypse is an esoteric literature; as Fourth Ezra says, it is intended only for the wise (although Daniel 12:3 implies that the wise are supposed to communicate the revealed secrets to the people). Whether it is a sectarian literature is not clear, because the social setting of the apocalyptic seers is unknown. The Jews of Qumran, at least, believed that they were living near the end time and had a vivid interest in eschatological speculations, but they did not have much interest in apocalypses. They expressed their eschatological dreams in nonapocalyptic works like the *War of the Sons of Light Against the Sons of Darkness* and especially in their scriptural commentaries (*pesharim;* see below). In contrast, the early Christians were very interested in apocalypses; they preserved many Jewish apocalypses of the second temple period and wrote new apocalypses themselves. The prophets had the masses for their audience, but the apocalyptic seers had only the wise.

The implicit message of the apocalypses is that events on the cosmic or national scale have been predetermined by God, but that individuals, forewarned by the vision, can ally themselves with the forces of God through repentance and righteousness. God's plan for world events was set centuries or millennia before the current time, and there is nothing that humans can do now to affect its course. In particular, one view that became widespread was the theory of four empires, which postulated that either Israel or the world would come under the dominion of four successive empires, each worse than the next. The last would launch a great persecution against God's elect, and in the midst of that crisis the series of empires would come to an end as God and his hosts would restore justice in the world. The theory was first enunciated by Daniel (chapters 2 and 7) and exerted enormous influence on the Jews and Christians of antiquity and the Middle Ages. In this scheme sin and righteousness, punishment and reward, obduracy and repentance, are irrelevant because the series of empires was decreed by God to be part of the unchangeable cosmic order. Thus do the apocalyptic seers explain the nature of the crisis that currently besets "the righteous" and "the elect." Let them remain faithful to God and they will prosper. This tension between fate or predetermination (for the nation or the world) and free will or repentance (for the individual) appears frequently in second temple and rabbinic Judaism (see chapter 3). The prophets had not been concerned with the life and death of the individual, but the apocalyptic seers were.

Unlike the prophetic books, which almost always are credited to their real authors, apocalyptic works *never* are. The works are either anonymous or, what is more often the case, *pseudepigraphic*, that is, falsely attributed to someone other than their real authors (from the Greek *pseudo*, false, and *epigraphos*, ascription). This pseudepigraphy is not the result of the accidental and incorrect attribution of an anonymous work but is the result of deliberate misattribution by the author. Rather than admit their own identities the authors of these works hid behind the masks of figures who lived at the very beginning of the world. Adam, Seth, Enoch, and Noah were special favorites, although later figures were sometimes used as well (for example, Abraham, Moses, Isaiah, and Baruch).

(The term *pseudepigrapha*, like the term *apocrypha*, has been much abused. A few church fathers refer to "pseudepigraphic" works, that is, works that bear false ascriptions, and this is the meaning I accept. Modern scholars often use the phrase *"The* Pseudepigrapha" as a designation for those Jewish books which are found neither in the Tanak nor in "the Apocrypha"—except for Philo, Josephus, the Qumran scrolls, and the rabbinic works. Some of the works included in "the Pseudepigrapha" are in fact pseudepigraphic, but many are not. The result is confusion and the loss of the term "pseudepigraphic" as an accurate description for a specific literary phenomenon. The modern usage gained currency only in the twentieth century and is best avoided.)

Anonymity and pseudepigraphy are not restricted to apocalypses alone. Testaments, romances, commentaries, wisdom works, hymns, laws—all these were written anonymously or pseudonymously in late second temple times. The last Judean author known by name is Ben Sira. Greek-speaking Jews were more willing than their Hebrew-speaking co-religionists to put their names on their works. This phenomenon can be explained in various ways; it can even be dismissed as inconsequential. Nevertheless, modern literary criticism suggests an attractive explanation. Every act of writing, and all the more so the arrogation of credit for what one has written, is a sign of hybris. A writer claims to have accomplished something in his work and challenges the reader to compare his work with that of his predecessors and competitors. Clement of Alexandria, a church father of the late second century c.e., opens his most important work (the *Stromata*, or "Miscellanies") with a long apology for daring to put his thoughts in writing. After all, the only book a Christian needs is the New Testament! But the heretics have already written their gospels, and why should Christians be able to read heretical gospels but not the Christian truth which Clement wishes to teach? In other words, Clement's hesitation to write is caused (in part) by his fear of competing with the Gospels. Perhaps Jews who wrote in the language of Moses and Isaiah felt the same way. How could they compete with the written Torah, with "scripture"? In the third and fourth centuries C.E. the rabbis stated that "the Oral Law," the body of rabbinic laws and scriptural interpretations, was not to be written (or at least was not to be used in written form in the sessions of the rabbinic schools), because to do so would challenge the authority of the written Torah. The apocalyptic seers, the epigones of the classical prophets, had enough courage to write their thoughts, but not enough courage to assert their own identity.

But the apocalyptic seers were usually not content with mere anonymity; they generally practiced pseudepigraphy. The Greek-speaking Jews of the diaspora attributed some of their literary products to distinguished pagans of the past, presumably because they wished to show that Judaism was a respected religion in the eyes of the greats. But the meaning of the pseudepigraphy practiced by the apocalyptic seers of the land of Israel is not as clear. It is unlikely that the authors were attempting to deceive their readers or, in fact, that their readers really were deceived. The predilection for antediluvian figures like Adam and Enoch suggests that the pseudepigraphy was intended to highlight the correspondence between the beginning and the end of time. Many eschatological schemes present the end of time as a new creation, and the pseudepigraphy allows the witnesses to the first creation to describe the second as well. It also emphasizes the idea that God has predetermined the course of human history and that all events are part of the cosmic order which was in place at the creation of the world. But whatever its explanation, pseudepigraphy shows that the true identity of the apocalyptic seer was not important. A prophet had authority as an intermediary between humanity and God, but an apocalyptic seer did not.

From Prophecy to Apocalypse, from Prophets to "Holy Men"

The transition from prophecy to apocalypse was already underway in the Persian period, as the prophecies of Zechariah demonstrate. Zechariah refers three times (1:4, 7; 7:12) to "the former prophets," thus indicating an awareness that one era has passed and that another is about to begin. Zechariah's contemporary Haggai still writes in classical style, declaiming, "Thus says the Lord of hosts," but Zechariah does not; it is the angel, not the prophet, who says "Thus says the Lord" (for example, Zech. 1:16). The prophet is being replaced by an angel as the intermediary figure who transmits and interprets God's message. Similarly, when the prophet beholds an image or symbol, it is an angel, not God, who presents it and interprets it (for example, Zech. 1:7–15). Some of the symbolic visions seen by Zechariah were fantastic and unreal, like those of the later apocalypses (for example, Zech. 6). Later Jews believed that prophecy ceased in the Persian period, and in large measure they were correct (although we would say "transformed" rather than "ceased"). Josephus, Fourth Ezra, and the rabbis defined the biblical canon on the basis of their belief that "the accurate succession of the prophets" ceased around the time of Ezra. Even those Jews who had a broader or more fluid notion of canon (for example, the Jews of Qumran and the Greek Jews who bequeathed their canon to the early church) did not preserve the words of any named prophet who lived after the reign of Artaxerxes.

The transformation was complete by the middle of the second century B.C.E. This period witnessed the shift in the focus of apocalypse from cosmology to theodicy and eschatology (see above), and the canonization of the prophetic books. The same period also provides the first explicit testimony that many Jews believed that classical prophecy had ceased. In two passages First Maccabees records that the Jews took a certain course of action that would remain valid "until a true prophet should appear" and instruct them otherwise (1 Macc. 4:46; 14:41). True prophets were a phenomenon of the past and the future, not the present.

Prophecy became apocalypse, and prophets became apocalyptic seers. Other heirs of the prophetic tradition were "holy men," miracle workers, "charismatic" healers, foretellers of the future, and mystics. From the second century B.C.E. until the end of antiquity figures of these types flourished. Prophets had always been regarded as "men of God," people endowed with unusual powers who were not to be molested in any way (Jer. 26). The performance of miracles and healings characterized prophecy's "preliterary" phase, exemplified by Elijah and Elisha, but even the classical prophets performed healings on occasion (Isa. 38:21). Both Isaiah and Ezekiel, when being commissioned by God to assume their prophetic roles, beheld God sitting on his throne surrounded by fiery angels singing (according to Isaiah), "Holy, holy, holy is the Lord of Hosts." These visions certainly can be called "mystical" (Isa. 6 and Ezek. 1). Foretelling the future was always one of the most striking aspects of prophecy, so much so that in the popular imagination even in antiquity the two are virtually identical. The successors of the prophets continued these traditions.

The Jews had a well-deserved reputation among the Greeks and Romans as practitioners of magic and miracles, especially healings. Judean society in the first century B.C.E. and the first century C.E. was marked by the presence of numerous predictors of the future, holy men, and healers. Many rabbis of the third and fourth centuries in both Israel and Babylonia were believed to be endowed with extraordinary powers. In some cases these figures are said to be "prophets" or to possess the gift of prophecy. Admirers of John Hyrcanus credited him with the gift of prophecy because in two wondrous incidents he correctly foretold the future. The Jews of Galilee who beheld Jesus thought that he was "one of the prophets," probably because he performed many miracles (Matt. 16:14 and parallels). Although some of these people were called prophets, their authority and prestige, unless augmented from some other source (for example, the position of high priest or judge) was much less than that enjoyed by the classical prophets. The image of Jesus in the Gospels and in later Christian tradition has been shaped by the belief that classical prophecy had returned and that Jesus was a prophet like Moses, but it is difficult to know to what extent these ideas derive from Jesus' contemporaries. (And, of course, Jesus was also viewed by his followers as king, high priest, messiah, and "son of God.")

Scriptural Interpretation

The canonization of the Tanak meant the creation of a scripturally oriented society. People studied scripture, memorized it, and tried to live by it. In order to understand God's ways, they meditated upon it. When praying they quoted from it liberally, and in their public liturgies they read it and studied it. They sought the meaning of current events not through the writing of histories but through the study of scripture. (Only Greek-speaking Jews like Josephus wrote histories; one thousand years would elapse after the composition of First Maccabees before a Jew wrote another history in Hebrew.) Law, theology, eschatology—everything could be found within the pages of scripture.

The role of the Tanak, and especially the Torah, within Judaism bears a superficial analogy to the role of Homer within Greco-Roman culture. All Greeks and Romans knew at least something of the *Iliad* and the *Odyssey*. The educated knew the poems by heart, studied them closely, cited them liberally in their conversations, drew inspiration from them in their writings, and labored long and hard to establish their correct texts and to clarify their numerous obscurities. Greek literature begins with Homer; Roman literature begins with the translation of Homer into Latin in the third century B.C.E. The similarities between all this and the place of the Tanak within Judaism are numerous and striking. All Jews knew at least something of the Tanak, especially the Torah. The educated knew it by heart, studied it closely, cited it liberally in their conversations, drew inspiration from it in their writings, and labored long and hard to establish its correct text and to clarify its numerous obscurities. Jewish literature begins with the Tanak; the literature of Greek-speaking Jews begins with the translation of the Torah into Greek in the third century B.C.E.

But here the similarities end, because, except for a few philosophers, the Greeks and Romans did not look upon Homer as a guide to life, a source of law and custom, a "constitution," or a text to be absorbed and "internalized." They did not see it as eternally valid and existentially meaningful. For the Jews, the Tanak was all these and more; it was the word of God, whose study brought one closer to God and the observance of whose dictates brought immeasurable rewards. As Josephus remarks (*Against Apion* 1.8, §44–45), Jews were prepared to die for their Torah, but what Greek was prepared to die for the classics of Greek literature?

When the Jews studied and interpreted the Bible, they were not reading a uniform document. Not all books of the Bible were created equal. The Torah clearly ranked (and ranks) the highest. It was canonized first and placed at the head. It provided the texts for the weekly lections. It was written by Moses, the servant of God and the greatest of the prophets. Philo is interested only in the Torah, and seldom quotes any other biblical book. Perhaps he regarded the prophets as divinely inspired, but he paid them almost no heed. Similarly, the rabbis of the third and fourth centuries state that law can be derived only from the Torah, not the Prophets or the Writings, although the rabbis certainly believed that all three parts of the Bible were divinely inspired. The early Christians probably accepted the primacy of the Torah, but accorded the Prophets and the Writings a much higher place than the rabbis did, not only in matters of theology and eschatology but also legal practice (for example, Matt. 12:3–4, contrasted with 12:5–6).

But the primacy of the Torah did not mean that there was no ambiguity about its status. In the first part of this chapter I routinely used the phrase "divinely inspired or revealed" when describing the books of the Bible, especially the Torah. There is a substantial difference between these ideas. The first emphasizes the importance of Moses in the writing of the Torah. Greek Jews regularly referred to Moses as their "lawgiver" and to the Torah as their "constitution" *(politeia),* just as rabbinic Jews called Moses "our master" or "our teacher" *(rabbenu).* Moses wrote the Torah but did so while inspired by God, just as the other prophets are responsible for their own words. This conception allows human agency a substantial role in the creation and transmission of the divine message. The second idea emphasizes the status of the Torah as the revealed word of God, and many works of the second temple and rabbinic periods cite the Torah, and indeed other books of the Tanak, as the word of God. "Scripture says" and "God says" are synonymous expressions. It is not the human agent who is speaking in these pages but God. This conception allows human agency a relatively small role in the creation and transmission of the divine message.

I do not know of any text of the second temple period that addresses this question explicitly, but some texts address it implicitly. In certain passages Philo, for example, argues that the Torah must be divine because it is perfect; elsewhere he argues that the Torah must be perfect because it is divine. The first perspective sees the divinity of the Torah as a consequence of its perfection. Moses, the great lawgiver and philosopher, wrote a perfect law; the essay that develops this point of view, the *Life of Moses,* omits the epiphany at Mount Sinai, because the divinity of the Torah does not depend on it. The second perspective sees the divinity of the Torah as the source of its perfection; the Torah was not merely divinely inspired but revealed. This perspective appears frequently in Philo's commentaries on the Torah.

But whether inspired or revealed, the text of scripture had to be interpreted. Does the act of interpretation uncover meanings that were present all along, or does it add new meanings to the text? Were Moses and the prophets merely the vehicles for a message they may not have fully understood? On these weighty matters too there were contrasting opinions. Philo assumes throughout his essays that Moses was aware of the full range of meanings of the words of the Torah, both the literal and the philosophical, both the exoteric and the esoteric. The rabbis in the Palestinian Talmud state *(Peah* 2:6, 17a) that "any novelty which a student might advance while studying with his master was already dictated (by God) to Moses at Mount Sinai." In contrast, when interpreting Habakkuk 2:1–2 the Jews of Qumran noted that "God told Habakkuk to write down things that are going to come upon the last generation, but the fulfillment of the end time he did not make known to him." In other words, Habakkuk did not fully understand his own prophecies! According to a rabbinic story (Babylonian Talmud *Menahot* 29b), one day Moses returned from the next world in order to sit in the academy of Rabbi Aqiba. Although he was unable to understand the lecture, he was relieved to hear the rabbi conclude with the remark that the entire contents of the lecture derived from the Sinaitic revelation to Moses. In the perspective of this story, Moses himself did not appreciate the full import of the words he wrote. Similarly the rabbis never precisely defined the relationship of the "Oral Torah" to the written; does the oral derive from the written, supplement it, or interpret it? The answer is all three.

Perhaps as a result of this debate among ancient Jewish thinkers, some literary works are completely autonomous of the Tanak, seldom quoting it or referring to it, while other works are completely dependent on it. Contrast, for example, the apocalypses, which (unlike Dan. 9) do not present themselves as the "fulfillments" of biblical prophecies, with the Qumran *pesharim,* which describe the eschatological hopes of the Qumran group through scriptural exegesis. Contrast the Mishnah, which presents its laws with only few references to the Torah, with various other rabbinic works, which have as their goal the demonstration that the laws of the Mishnah can be derived exegetically from the Torah. The same contrast can sometimes be observed in Greek-Jewish literature as well. In most of his essays Philo connects his theological and moral teachings with scriptural verses and episodes, but in several essays he does not, although he certainly could have done so had he wished.

These questions are important for an understanding of the self-definition of ancient Judaism, but they cannot be pursued here. Even if the Jews of antiquity believed that God authorized humans to add to the revelation contained in scripture or to ferret out meanings that were unknown to the original authors, this belief did not detract from the unique status of scripture, especially the Torah. Jews could not hope to write new works that would equal those of scripture, but they could gain mastery over scripture by interpreting it.

Modes of Scriptural Interpretation

The Hebrew word *midrash* literally means "research" or "investigation," but through rabbinic usage the term has come to mean the investigation of scripture. A commentary on scripture, a piece of scriptural exegesis, a veiled allusion to a scriptural passage, a retelling of scriptural material—all these are called *midrash* (in plural, *midrashim*). The term has become so popular in recent years that in modern parlance it is virtually synonymous with "exegesis," and any textual interpretation that is not absolutely true to its source is dubbed "midrash." (And since—according to modern literary critics—*no* textual interpretation can be absolutely true to its source, therefore all textual interpretation is midrash.)

Since the term "midrash" is so slippery and vague, I shall avoid it here, preferring instead to use more specific English terms like commentary, allusion, exegesis, and allegory. However, the history of the term is significant. The noun *midrash* appears only twice in the Tanak, in each case as the title of a (lost) work cited by the Chronicler: "the *midrash* of Iddo the prophet" (2 Chron. 13:22) and "the *midrash* of the book of the kings" (2 Chron. 24:27). The term probably should be translated here "story" or "history." The Greek word *historia* has the same literal meaning as the Hebrew *midrash*, "research" or "investigation," but while the Greek word came to mean "an investigation into the past," hence "a work that presents the results of research into the past," the Hebrew term came to mean "investigation into scripture," hence "a work that presents the results of research into scripture." In Chronicles the term seems to have a meaning akin to that which would become normal in Greek but which fell from Hebrew usage.

The verb *darash*, from which the noun *midrash* derives, also undergoes an important shift. Biblical Hebrew often refers to people "seeking" God, or "inquiring" of God, or "searching" for God. Sometimes the phrase clearly means "to seek an oracle from God" (for example, Gen. 25:22; Ex. 18:15; 1 Sam. 9:9). The verb used is *darash*. But in two texts of the Persian (or early Hellenistic) period, the object of the verb no longer is God. "For Ezra had set his heart to study *(lidrosh)* the instruction (Torah) of the Lord" (Ezra 7:10). "Salvation is far from the wicked, for they do not seek your statutes" (Ps. 119:155). Ezra seeks not God but the Torah of God. The wicked are accused not of failing to seek God (Isa. 9:12; Jer. 10:21), but of failing to seek his statutes. With the canonization of the Torah, Jews no longer seek God directly. They seek God through the Torah. That process is midrash.

The essence of exegesis is the notion "X = Y." When scripture says X, it really means Y. In some instances, the formula can be represented as "X + Y," where the exegesis adds Y to the X of scripture. What distinguishes one mode of exegesis from another is the nature of the "X's" (that is, what sorts of passages and difficulties prompt exegesis?); the method by which the X is demonstrated to be equivalent to the Y; and the nature of the "Y's" (that is, what is the exegesis supposed to accomplish?). Usually exegesis is prompted by some sort of difficulty: two laws or narratives seem to contradict each other; the heroes of scripture act in a manner unbecoming their piety and grandeur; the scriptural account seems dull, trivial, obscure, pointless, or absurd, and so on.

Problems of this sort proved equally bothersome to the Greek-speaking Jews of the diaspora and to the Hebrew-speaking Jews of the land of Israel. The earliest known exegete from the diaspora, a Jew named Demetrius who lived in Egypt in the second half of the third century B.C.E., is disturbed by the apparent inconsistency in biblical chronology and does his best to prove that Jacob was able to sire all his children in the time allotted him by Genesis, and that Zipporah, the descendant of Abraham through Keturah, really was of the same generation as her husband Moses. Demetrius' concern for exactitude in biblical chronology and genealogy also appears in various works of the land of Israel (notably *Jubilees* and some rabbinic works). In another passage Demetrius asks how the Israelites, who fled Egypt unarmed, managed to obtain weapons for their various battles. His answer (they obtained arms by stripping them from the Egyptian corpses at the Red Sea) is a good illustration of the X + Y method, in which the exegete adds important information omitted by scripture. The same technique is frequently found throughout the exegetical works of the land of Israel as well. Greek, Hebrew, and Aramaic works add details to scripture in order to make it more colorful, dramatic, and exciting (see, for example, the *Jewish Antiquities* of Josephus, the *Testament of Levi,* and the *Genesis Apocryphon* from Qumran).

Perhaps the most radical function of scriptural exegesis was that it allowed the Jews to affirm undying loyalty to a text written centuries earlier for a very different society living under very different conditions. They could claim loyalty to the sacred text even as they freed themselves from it by interpreting it. A living culture cannot live in accordance with the dictates of an immovable text. Either a way must be found to introduce flexibility into the text, or the text sooner or later will have to be rejected. In the United States the interpretations of the Supreme Court allow the government to function in accordance with a document written by a group of eighteenth-century politicians. The Supreme Court pretends to "interpret" the Constitution, but, of course, routinely interprets it in a manner that would have amazed the Founding Fathers. No matter. Historians must try to determine what the Constitution meant in its eighteenth-century context, but the Supreme Court must determine what it means for contemporary society. Rather than write a new constitution every few generations (as France does), the United States authorizes the Supreme Court to misinterpret the Constitution for the common good. Similarly, the Jews of antiquity routinely misinterpreted (the usual euphemism is reinterpreted) scripture in order to remove laws and ideas they found objectionable, and in order to introduce laws and ideas that answered their own needs. The Jews of the Greek diaspora had different needs from those of the land of Israel, and so their scriptural interpretations often seem very different, but they both are following the same process.

Characteristic of the diaspora Jews is their desire to make the Torah appear philosophically respectable and reasonable. Aristobulus, a Greek Jew of the second century B.C.E., is bothered by the Torah's anthropomorphic, and decidedly unphilosophical, conception of God. Philo finds it impossible to believe that Moses spent forty days and nights with God only to return with a book filled with unedifying stories about the domestic troubles of one ancient clan; obviously the stories of Genesis about the patriarchs must be trying to reveal something significant. For Philo, the stories are really about the ascent of the soul from the world of visible forms to the world of the archetypes and the Monad. The episodes in the lives of the patriarchs are really way stations in the journey of the soul. The laws too, which at first glance seem strange and unreasonable, can be made to yield their inner meaning. Thus, already in the *Letter of Aristeas* there is the explanation that the prohibited foods represent vices which Jews must avoid, just as the permitted foods represent virtues which Jews must pursue. For Philo, the laws not only represent moral qualities to be avoided or pursued; they also teach philosophical principles about God and his creation: the laws of the Torah are consonant with the laws of nature as established by God at the creation of the world.

The identification of biblical laws and heroes with philosophical principles and moral qualities is known as *allegory*. This type of exegesis found a secure home in Christianity, and became one of the favored ways for explaining why Christians do not obey the laws of the "Old Testament." Since Christians obey the allegorical meaning of the laws (the "Y"), they need not obey the literal meaning (the "X"). In fact, some Christian polemicists in the second century C.E. argued that the laws were never even intended to be followed literally![5] Philo knew allegorists who advanced the same argument, and against them he insisted that allegorical meaning does not negate literal meaning (*On the Migration of Abraham* 16, §89–93). The commandment of circumcision represents the excision of lustful inclinations, but even if you excise your lustful tendencies, you must still circumcise your eight-day-old son. For Philo, scripture has various levels of meaning, both external (the literal) and internal (the allegorical), which are not mutually exclusive. The rabbis agreed with Philo that scripture has levels of meaning, but they, like their compatriots in the second temple period, did not as a rule engage in allegorical exegesis. The unphilosophical image of God and the unreasonableness of the scriptural laws did not bother the Jews of the land of Israel, and so they had little need for allegory.

The Jews of the land of Israel, much more than the Jews of the diaspora, devoted their exegetical energies to the details of the laws of the Torah. This activity is well represented at Qumran, in the book of *Jubilees*, in some of the dispute stories in the Gospel tradition, and of course throughout rabbinic literature. In numerous matters, the laws outlined by the Torah either were impractical or inadequate or problematic, because customs and society had changed radically. New institutions and rituals existed that were not even mentioned by the Torah. One of the tasks of exegesis was to set these matters right: to reconcile Torah law with the legal, social, and institutional reality of the second temple period (and, later, of the rabbinic period as well).

Also characteristic of Palestinian exegesis is the effort to affirm the continuing validity of the biblical prophecies and narratives by discovering contemporary situations through which they were fulfilled. The biblical texts contain *types* or *paradigms*. The exodus from Egypt is a type for all future redemptions, just as the destruction of Jerusalem by Nebuchadnezzar is a type for all future destructions. These events are not unique occurrences, but recur in different ways throughout later history. For example, the desecration of Jerusalem by Epiphanes, the conquest of the city by the Romans in 63 B.C.E., and its destruction in 70 C.E., were seen by many Jews as "replays" of the events of 587 B.C.E. Antiochus and Vespasian were the new Nebuchadnezzars, the Syrians and the Romans were the new Babylonians, and so on. Typological exegesis plays an important role in the New Testament and in rabbinic Judaism.

By the same logic, the prophecies were believed to refer not to a single set of events but to future times as well. The only trick was to figure out which prophecies were valid for the contemporary situation. Sometimes it was easy; Josephus remarks that Jeremiah predicted the destruction of Jerusalem that took place "in our day" (*Jewish Antiquities* 10.5.1, §79). Usually, however, it was much more difficult. The early Christians believed that the messianic prophecies of Isaiah were "fulfilled" through Jesus, but most other Jews did not agree. The Jews of Qumran, in a series of commentaries known as *pesharim* ("interpretations"), argued that the prophecies of Habakkuk and Nahum, as well as the "prophecies" of the Psalms, were fulfilled by events in the sect's history, and would be further fulfilled by the sect's imminent rise to glory and destruction of its enemies. Jews outside of Qumran rejected this exegesis. All Jews agreed that the words of the prophets contained eternal verities— this belief is one of the hallmarks of canonization—but which verity referred to the events of the day was a question that aroused some dispute.

Many of these exegetical techniques and concerns are to be found in scripture itself. Scriptural authors borrow motifs and ideas from each other, and in the process reinterpret them. Throughout the Tanak interpolators and redactors have tried to minimize contradictions, clarify obscurities, and remove theological difficulties. Those people who preserved the constituent documents of the Torah and the words of the prophets must have had means for interpreting them. In other words, biblical interpretation has a long history in ancient Israel even before the final canonization, but canonization made interpretation inevitable and distinct. Inevitable, because how can one accept the unity of a book that abounds in apparent contradictions and obscurities unless one engages in exegesis? How can one accept the authority of a book that abounds in laws and ideas that seem offensive and unedifying unless one engages in exegesis? Distinct, because the canonization of scripture no longer permitted the incorporation of interpolations and glosses into scripture. Interpretation, now a distinct enterprise, adopted a character of its own, sometimes amazingly free, almost frivolous, at other times very earnest, almost pedantic. All Jews who affirmed the validity of scripture had to engage in exegesis. They did not always agree—the Sadducees rejected the traditions of the Pharisees—but all were involved in the same activity.

Scriptural exegesis is scattered throughout all the literary remains of ancient Judaism. I conclude this chapter with a brief survey of the three literary genres that are the most direct consequence of scriptural interpretation: translation, paraphrase, and commentary.

Translation

The earliest translation of the Bible was the *Septuagint.* According to the story that was in circulation by the end of the second century B.C.E., king Ptolemy Philadelphus (285–246 B.C.E.), who wished the royal library to have a copy of the sacred law of the Jews, invited seventy-two scholars (hence the name *Septuagint*, Latin for seventy) to travel from Jerusalem to Alexandria and translate the Torah into Greek. This the scholars did, and the resulting work found favor not only with the king but also with the Jews of Alexandria. Most scholars regard this legend as Jewish propaganda and assume that the Jews of Alexandria needed the translation for themselves, because so many of them no longer knew enough Hebrew to read and study the Torah in the original. In the course of the following centuries the other books of the Tanak were translated as well, and the whole work, with the inclusion of some books whose Hebrew originals have not been preserved or which were written originally in Greek, is popularly, if inaccurately, known as the Septuagint (frequently abbreviated LXX).

The very existence of this translation is significant, because it implies that Judaism was a "book" religion. Few other ancient peoples translated their sacred literatures into Greek or Latin, apparently because they did not feel the need to do so. Judaism was becoming a religion based on scripture, and the Greek-speaking Jews of Alexandria made a great concession to modernity and necessity when they translated the Torah into a language that all could understand. The purpose of the translation, then, was not to make Judaism accessible to non-Jews but to make it accessible to Jews, and in all likelihood this same purpose governed the production of most of the Greco-Jewish literature that followed the Septuagint. Josephus, perhaps, in his paraphrase of scripture in the *Jewish Antiquities*, was trying to make Judaism attractive to gentiles, just as the representatives of various other ethnic groups had been trying to do for centuries for their own native cultures (Persians, Egyptians, Babylonians, Lydians), but none of these accounts was a translation. The Septuagint was virtually unique.

The Jews of the Eastern diaspora and, to some extent, of the land of Israel as well, needed a translation too, not a translation into Greek but into Aramaic. These translations are known as *targumim* (singular, *targum*). Rabbinic tradition (Babylonian Talmud *Megillah* 3a), based on Nehemiah 8:7–8, attributes the genesis of these translations to Ezra, but whether this is correct we have no way of knowing. The earliest extant *targum* is the translation of Job found among the Qumran scrolls. Jewish manuscript tradition preserves several different *targumim* of the Torah, one complete *targum* for the Prophets and Writings, and fragments of various others. Like the Septuagint, the *targumim* apparently originated in a liturgical setting. Instead of, or in addition to, the reading of the Torah in

Hebrew, the lection was read in translation, in order to make the word of God accessible to all. In recent years many scholars have used these *targumim* as a window into Jewish piety of the first century of our era, but none of the extant *targumim* (except for the one from Qumran) reached its current form before the early Middle Ages, and there is no reason to assume that every exegetical twist and turn is the residue of ancient tradition. Like the rest of rabbinic literature, the *targumim* are collective works, written over a long span of time.

The Septuagint and some of the *targumim* (notably *Targum Onqelos*) are "word for word" translations. The translators seldom paraphrase or expand the text; obscurities are left obscure, and tantalizing references are left to tantalize. In the first century C.E., after the emergence in the land of Israel of a new standard text of the Tanak, some Jews felt that the Septuagint was no longer accurate enough, and they began to revise it in order to make it conform more closely to the text as it had developed. This activity continued in the second century, with the result that by the time of the church father Origen (first half of the third century), several different Greek translations of the Tanak were extant, and Origen, for the sake of the church, edited them and tried to clarify their differences. Hebrew- and Aramaic-speaking Jews had no use for any of these translations and abandoned them to the Christians. For the Christians, who knew little Hebrew, the Septuagint became the "Old Testament." Some Jews in the sixth century were still using Aquila, one of the second-century revisions of the Septuagint, but how numerous these Jews were is a very difficult question.

Some of the Aramaic translations (notably *Targum Jonathan*), however, are very free. They may translate one verse rather closely, only to expand radically in the next (additions are much more characteristic than omissions). There is absolutely no reason to think that these "free" *targumim* are later than those which are consistently faithful to the text. The two different types of *targumim* are the products of different theories of translation. At a certain point, free translations are indistinguishable from paraphrases.

Paraphrase

The social setting for translations is the liturgy; in synagogues and other places of public worship, scripture was read and studied in the original and in translation. Paraphrases, by contrast, seem to have folk piety as their original setting. Schoolteachers and tellers of tales would rewrite the stories and laws of scripture, embroidering and elaborating as they went. From folk piety it entered the literary genres of the elite.

Unlike translations, paraphrases do not follow the original word for word. Some paraphrases preserve the words of the original, but overlay them with so many additions and expansions that they are no longer easily recognizable. Numerous works of the second temple period, whether written in Hebrew (for example, *Jubilees*, the *Temple Scroll*, Pseudo-Philo's *Biblical Antiquities*), Aramaic (the *Genesis Apocryphon*), or Greek (for example, Artapanus, the *Jewish Antiquities* of Josephus, Philo's *Life of Moses*), are paraphrases of scripture. Even more numerous are those works which, among other things, include paraphrases of scripture (for example, the *Testaments of the Twelve Patriarchs*). A reader of a paraphrase has no way of knowing when the paraphrase is following its original with reasonable fidelity, and when it is not. Pseudo-Philo, for example, adds to the book of Judges a saga featuring the heroism of Kenaz. Artapanus adds to the Torah an involved story about Moses' invasion of Ethiopia; Josephus has a somewhat different version of the same tale, with the notable addition of a beautiful princess who marries the hero (is this the origin of the story? see Num. 12:1). The *Genesis Apocryphon* adds numerous wonderful episodes to the lives of Noah and Abraham. Some of the *Testaments of the Twelve Patriarchs* invent great military exploits for the sons of Jacob. Aside from major expansions of scripture, these paraphrases also introduce numerous minor changes (additions, omissions, modifications). A paraphrase need not be a free retelling of its source, but most of the extant paraphrases take great liberties with sacred writ. The canonization of scripture set free the wellsprings of the imagination.

The rabbis of antiquity avoided scriptural paraphrase. They wrote and preserved *targumim* and commentaries, but not paraphrases. Not until the Middle Ages did the paraphrase style begin to make an impact on rabbinic literature. Why this is so is not entirely clear.

Commentary

A commentary is characterized by the fact that it stands outside its source text and is subordinate to it. A commentary quotes its source text (the quotation or heading is called a *lemma*, Greek for "something that is taken"), discusses it, and then proceeds to the next text. The lemma might be long or short, a whole paragraph or a single word. The demarcation between text and commentary is clear. In contrast, a translation and a paraphrase do not relate explicitly to the source text; they are independent works that, from a literary point of view, replace their source text. A commentary has a different atmosphere about it altogether. Translations derive from a liturgical setting; paraphrases derive (apparently) from folk piety, from tellers of tales; commentaries derive from schools, the learned elite.

Jews probably learned to write commentaries from the Greeks. Commentaries on Homer and other "canonical" authors were staples of Hellenistic scholarship, and the first Greek Jewish exegete, the Demetrius mentioned above (who is more an "essayist" than a "commentator"), shows the influence of the Hellenistic literary form. The earliest extant commentaries are the *pesharim* from Qumran, which comment not on the Torah but on some of the prophets and the psalms. Many of Philo's essays are written in commentary form, all of them treating the Torah exclusively. The rabbis too at first wrote commentaries only on the Torah. The earliest rabbinic commentaries are on Exodus–Deuteronomy. Later they added Genesis (the initial omission of Genesis would have astonished Philo) and some of the other biblical books (mostly those that were used in the liturgy). The earliest commentary on the entire Hebrew Bible was written by a Babylonian rabbi in the tenth century.

Conclusion

Jewish literature of the second temple period was the product of two contradictory tendencies. On the one hand, the Jews sensed that they were living in a postclassical age, and that it was their duty to collect, venerate, and study the works of their great ancestors. This tendency ultimately yielded the Bible and the idea that classical prophecy is no longer alive. On the other hand, the sense that they could not compete with their past, because their ancestors were giants but they themselves were but dwarfs, impelled them to express their literary creativity in new forms: apocalypses, testaments, romances, histories, poems, hymns, oracles, translations, paraphrases, commentaries, and others. Social and religious change accompanied literary change. Prophets were replaced by apocalyptic seers, healers, and magic men; priests were replaced by scribes and lay scholars; the temple was replaced by sects; and sacrifices were replaced by prayer and Torah study. Theology and eschatology also underwent revolutionary change. All of this religious and social ferment is the result of a quest for new ways to find God. The Jews were living in an age of silver but were seeking gold.

7

The Emergence of Rabbinic Judaism

As I explained in chapter 1, for the purposes of this book the "rabbinic period" begins in 70 C.E. and ends in the sixth century C.E. Historians of the ancient world usually refer to these centuries as "late antiquity," because they mark the end of the classical world. During this period the Roman empire declined and fell, paganism was replaced by Christianity as the official religion of the state, and the institutions and social patterns that characterized the world of antiquity were replaced by those that would characterize the medieval world. For historians of Judaism these centuries also mark the end of one world and the beginning of another. The shift from second temple Judaism to rabbinic Judaism is not a mere chronological transition but a substantive change. In this chapter I shall briefly assess the nature of this change.

"The Rabbis" and "The Rabbinic Period"

The term "rabbi" designates a member of that select society which, between the second and the sixth centuries C.E., produced the Mishnah and numerous other works, notably the Palestinian Talmud and the Babylonian Talmud (plural, Talmudim). Linked by their common education, vocabulary, values, and "culture," the rabbis clearly constitute a unified group. Rabbinic literature is a remarkably homogeneous corpus. If by some magic we could take a second-century Palestinian rabbi and deposit him in a fifth-century Babylonian academy, he certainly would need to make several adjustments (not least because Babylonian Aramaic and Palestinian Aramaic are different dialects), but would soon feel at home. Because of these facts rabbinic texts have usually been studied as if they constitute one seamless whole, as if all the works together constitute "the" Oral Torah. Because of these facts, throughout this book I have referred to "the rabbis" and "the rabbinic period."

But these facts do not mean that rabbinic literature really is seamless or that all rabbis of antiquity thought and behaved in identical fashion. The homogeneity of the rabbinic corpus is offset to some extent by geographical, chronological, and literary diversity. Works of Palestinian provenance have certain distinctive characteristics missing from works of Babylonian provenance, and vice versa. Every generation of rabbis had its own interests. In particular the rabbis of the second century, known as *tannaim* (literally "repeaters," or "teachers"), who produced the Mishnah and other tannaitic works, must be distinguished from the rabbis of the third to fifth centuries, known as *amoraim* (literally, "speakers"), who produced the two Talmudim and other amoraic works. Each document within the rabbinic "canon" has its own characteristic methods, themes, and message.

An accurate interpretation of rabbinic Judaism requires an assessment of both sets of facts, both the unity and the diversity. Much of this scholarly work remains to be done, and obviously this is not the place to do it. In the following discussion I shall continue to refer to "the rabbis," "the rabbinic period," and "rabbinic literature," but I shall also try to identify some of the distinctive characteristics of the rabbinic Judaism of the second century, and of the major literary monument of that Judaism, the Mishnah. (For the sake of brevity I treat only Palestinian Judaism and its history.)

From Second Temple Judaism to Rabbinic Judaism

Within a span of seventy years the Jews of Palestine suffered two major disasters. As a result of the war of 66–70 C.E. the temple was destroyed, Jerusalem was devastated, hundreds of thousands of people were killed or enslaved, and, throughout the country, land and property were confiscated by the Romans. The effects of the Bar Kokhba war were equally serious. Judea was ruined, thousands of people were killed or enslaved, Jerusalem was rebuilt as a pagan city, and the country was renamed Palestine ("land of the Philistines") instead of Judea ("land of the Jews"). In many respects second temple Judaism had already laid the foundations for a Judaism without a temple, a priesthood, and a sacrificial cult, but in others it had not, and adjustments now were required. Following the order of chapters 2 to 6 of this book, I shall briefly compare the dominant patterns of rabbinic Judaism with those of the second temple period.

Relations with Gentiles

Rabbinic attitudes toward political, cultural, and social relations with gentiles were substantially identical with those established by second temple Judaism. The two disasters confirmed the political wisdom of Jeremiah. Armed rebellion would not free the Jews from the grip of their gentile rulers. Instead they were to pray for the peace of the state in which they lived and await the deliverance that would come from God at the appointed time. Perhaps a few rabbis supported Bar Kokhba, but most did not. The rabbinic stories about the wars of 66–70 and 132–135 depict the revolutionaries as misguided fools or wicked sinners. The righteous Rabban Yohanan ben Zakkai fled the city of Jerusalem during the siege and hailed Vespasian as the emperor and conqueror. Collaboration with the enemy was no sin, if the enemy was granted dominion by God and if the enemy's Jewish opponents were themselves sinners. (The rabbis debated to what extent they could or should collaborate with the Romans, but the principle of collaborating was clearly established.) The Jews had no choice but to accept the divine decree.

Many scholars have suggested that as a result of the disasters of 70 and 135 C.E. the rabbis turned their backs on the outside world and isolated themselves from gentiles and gentile culture. The matter is not so simple, however. The beauty of Japheth (Hellenism) dwelt in the tents of Shem (rabbinic Judaism), as the Talmud says (see chapter 2). The Mishnah contains hundreds of Greek and Latin words, and the Talmudim and other works add hundreds more. The rabbinic modes of argumentation and scholarly analysis are those of Hellenistic rhetoricians. One of the major forms of rabbinic literary expression, the commentary, is of Greek origin. Rabbinic ethics closely resemble those of the Stoics. Even the "chain of tradition," by which the rabbis traced their spiritual ancestry back to Moses, is modeled on the chains of tradition that the Greek philosophical schools constructed in order to demonstrate their descent from their founding sages (Plato, Aristotle, etc.). These parallels and many others like them prove that the rabbis were not isolated from the cultural currents of their society and that in their own way they were a typical group of scholars and philosophers doing what scholars and philosophers were supposed to do. Thus the rabbis certainly were "Hellenized" to some extent.

But just as much evidence can be marshaled on the other side of the argument. It is unlikely that any rabbi in antiquity ever read Plato or Aristotle (who are never mentioned anywhere in rabbinic literature); some rabbis clearly never even heard of them. No rabbi evinces any knowledge of any of the technical jargon of Greek philosophy. Perhaps some rabbis knew enough Greek in order to communicate with Roman officials and with Greek-speaking Jews, but only a very few seem to have acquired any real facility with the language. And, most important, the content of the Mishnah and the Talmudim is so unlike anything in classical literature that it is difficult to imagine that their authors were active participants in classical culture.

The degree of rabbinic isolation from gentiles also is not easy to determine. The rabbis freely accepted converts to Judaism even if they no longer sought them actively. Some rabbis had negative attitudes toward converts, but the dominant view was positive. Rabbinic literature is filled with disparaging remarks about pagans and paganism. The Mishnah devotes an entire tractate *(Abodah Zarah)* to the rules that Jews must observe in order not to derive benefit from any object which might have been used for idolatrous purposes (compare Paul's ruling about meat sacrificed to idols). These rules are part of a larger effort to inhibit social (and sexual) intercourse between Jews and gentiles. Whether all this represents a distinct turning inward in the wake of the destruction of the temple is not so clear. Many Palestinian Jews, and even some diaspora Jews, of the second temple period would have agreed with the rabbinic disparagement of paganism and the effort to erect social barriers between Jews and gentiles.

An indication of a more ecumenical attitude toward gentiles and paganism is the notion of "Noahide laws" which was elaborated by the rabbis of the second century. Righteous gentiles need not convert to Judaism in order to have a share in the world to come. They need obey only a certain basic minimum which God revealed to Noah and which was to be observed by all of Noah's descendants, that is, the gentiles. The rabbis debated among themselves the number and identity of these laws (the usual number was seven). According to the dominant view, one of these laws was the prohibition of idolatry, which meant that a pagan had to deny paganism in order to attain salvation in the hereafter. Nevertheless, the very idea of "Noahide laws" shows a remarkable tendency toward recognizing the validity of cultures other than one's own, and of affirming the common bond of all civilized peoples. The Noahide laws, which perhaps are lurking in some form in the background to Acts 15, had a profound influence on the development of the concepts of international law and natural law in the sixteenth and seventeenth centuries.

Rabbinic Religion

For some Jews the destruction of the temple posed a theological crisis no less severe than that which had been felt in the wake of the destruction of the first temple in 587 B.C.E. and the profanation of the second in the 160s B.C.E. Why did God abandon the Jews and allow the enemy to triumph? Why does the world appear to be dominated by evil? Is God still loyal to his people? These questions are addressed by Fourth Ezra and the *Syriac Apocalypse of Baruch,* both written shortly after 70 C.E. (A very different sort of response was written by Josephus in his *Jewish War.*) In contrast, the Mishnah and, generally, the rabbis of the second century seem thoroughly unconcerned with these questions. They certainly did react to the absence of the temple, but the sense of crisis and urgency that pervades Fourth Ezra and the *Syriac Apocalypse of Baruch* is absent. And when the rabbis did turn to these questions in the fourth, fifth, and sixth centuries, they did not write apocalypses, engage in detailed eschatological speculations, or attribute the dominion of this world to the forces of Satan. Instead they told stories about the horrors of the wars and marveled, in the manner of the psalmist, at God's forbearance.

Why was the rabbinic response so moderate, so restrained? Why so little so late? Apparently because the piety of second temple Judaism had prepared the rabbis for a temple-less world. If the ancestors of the rabbis were the Pharisees, and if the Pharisees were a sect, then the rabbis certainly would have been prepared to live without a temple, because even when the temple was standing, sects had a very ambivalent attitude toward it. But the sects were merely the extreme representatives of the democratization of Judaism, which affected sectarians and nonsectarians alike. The regimen of daily prayer, Torah study, participation in synagogue services, and observance of the commandments sanctified life outside the temple and, in effect, competed with the temple cult, just as the new lay scholar class, the scribes and others, in effect competed with the priests. After the destruction of the temple, which must have been felt keenly in all reaches of the population, what could have been more natural than to take the extra-temple piety that had developed in the preceding centuries and view it as the equivalent or replacement for the temple cult? This perspective is advanced explicitly in the two Talmudim and various other works. For example, a tannaitic commentary on Deuteronomy remarks that the phrase "love God and serve him" includes Torah study and prayer, as well as the sacrificial cult.[1]

The response of the Mishnah is much more subtle. More than half of the Mishnah is devoted to one aspect or another of the temple and its cult, either because the Mishnah is confidently awaiting the time of their restoration, or because the temple cult had been ordained by God and the study of its regulations was now the equivalent of their implementation, or because the rabbis were attempting to create in their minds an ideal and perfect world to which they could escape from the imperfect world around them (compare the apocalypses, which in a very different way are doing the same thing). What the Mishnah is saying by its very existence is that God can be found through the study of his laws, even those laws which cannot be observed in daily life. The Mishnah has very little to say about prayer, and almost nothing to say about synagogues, because initially the rabbis believed that Torah study was more important than prayer. Only later, when they began to extend their power into the synagogues, did they see prayer as an equally important means of communing with God.

There is much scholarly debate and little certainty about the origins and intent of the Mishnah's laws. All scholars, I think, would agree that some of the laws derive from second temple times, while others are the innovations of the rabbis of the second century C.E.; that some of the laws are of "sectarian" provenance or are quintessentially rabbinic, while others are part of the Judaism of all Jews; that some of the laws were meant to be applied in daily practice in contemporary society, either by the masses or by the rabbinic elite, while others were entirely speculative and utopian. The problem is to figure out which law belongs in which category, not an easy task. Aside from the laws that are attributed to the houses of Hillel and Shammai, which are concerned for the most part with purity, Sabbath and festivals, and meals (see chapter 5), few laws are attributed to figures of second temple times. As a result, in order to reconstruct the history and social setting of the Mishnah's laws, scholars have to rely on whatever clues the Mishnah itself provides (as I have done in my discussion of the *Shema*), or on parallels from other Jewish sources (for example, *Jubilees,* the *Temple Scroll,* Philo), or on parallels from other cultures (for example, the ancient law codes of the Semitic East, which illuminate much of the Mishnah's civil legislation), or on conjectural analysis of the logic and intent of the laws. Needless to say, there is much scholarly disagreement on both method and conclusions, and I shall not even attempt to treat these questions here.

I turn now from law to theology. As I discussed in chapter 3, Judaism is not a creedal religion. Not a single tractate of the

Mishnah is devoted to a theological topic. We may be sure that the rabbis of the second century believed in a world to come, resurrection of the dead, messianic deliverance, corporate and individual reward and punishment, the efficacy of repentance, and an eternal covenant between God and Israel, but except for one chapter and an occasional paragraph the Mishnah is not interested in these topics. The Talmudim show a markedly greater interest in theology, but no rabbinic work sets forth the dogmas or essential beliefs of Judaism. The lone chapter of the Mishnah that treats theological topics begins as follows (*Sanhedrin* 10:1):

> All Israel has a share in the world to come. . . But these have no share in the world to come: he who says that there is no resurrection of the dead [or: he who says that the doctrine of the resurrection of the dead cannot be derived from the Torah]; [he who says that] Torah is not from heaven; and the Epicurean.

This Mishnah refers to three core doctrines of rabbinic Judaism: resurrection of the dead, the divine origin of the (written and the oral) Torah, and divine supervision of human affairs (which the Epicureans deny). But the Mishnah does not elevate these beliefs to the status of dogmas, and does not compose any creeds that would demonstrate how essential these beliefs are to the self-definition of Judaism. Nor does this Mishnah attempt to be complete; it omits, for example, the belief in the messiah (an omission that was sensed by the Talmudim). Those who deny these rabbinic doctrines are not excluded from synagogues or cursed, but are excluded from the world to come. This is a punishment that is administered by God, not humans. Denial of these beliefs carries no social penalty.

One of the major distinctions between the theology of the rabbis and the theology of the second temple period is the rabbis' complete lack of interest in either apocalyptic literature or eschatological speculations. Instead of writing apocalypses, those rabbis who saw visions and heard heavenly voices wrote mystical works that described journeys to the seventh heaven in order to see God sitting on his throne and hear the angels singing the Qedushah. These works, known as *hekhalot* (the "chambers" of the heavenly palace) or *merkabah* (the "throne" or "chariot" of God) literature, have much in common with the "angelic liturgy" of Qumran and with the apocalypses, but also differ markedly from them. The Qumran "angelic liturgy" was recited by the Jews of the Qumran community, since the goal of the sectarians was to join their prayers to those of their heavenly counterparts, but the rabbinic mystical literature did not, as far as is known, have either a communal setting or a liturgical function. Some apocalypses (notably *1 Enoch* 14) contain descriptions of the seer's ascension to heaven and tour of its wonders. These descriptions closely resemble the rabbinic *hekhalot* literature. But, as a rule, in the apocalypses the direction of movement is from heaven to earth: the heavenly forces descend to earth and involve themselves in the affairs of humanity. An angel reveals heavenly secrets to a visionary; history comes to an end when God creates the world anew, fights a cosmic battle against the forces of evil, or causes the heavenly Jerusalem to descend to earth. In the rabbinic mystical literature, however, the direction of movement is exclusively from earth to heaven; the mystic ascends to the seventh heaven and enjoys his proximity to God. How many rabbis in Israel and Babylonia sought to commune with God in this fashion, and how they relate to the rabbis who produced the Mishnah and related works, are questions that still have not been answered.

Society and Institutions

In 70 C.E. the temple was destroyed, the high priesthood and the sanhedrin ceased to exist, and the priests lost not only their jobs but also the institutional base of their power. The Jewish community of the land of Israel no longer had a recognized social elite or "establishment," and the Jews of the diaspora no longer had a center that bound them together. This was the vacuum the rabbis tried to fill. Ultimately they succeeded, but victory was gained only after a struggle. The rabbis were opposed by various segments among the wealthy and the priesthood, and by the bulk of the masses in both Palestine and the diaspora. The local aristocracies, especially in the cities, were not going to subject themselves voluntarily to the hegemony of a new power group; the priests still thought of themselves as the leaders of the people; and the masses were indifferent to many aspects of rabbinic piety. The rabbis triumphed over their opponents among the aristocracy and the priesthood by absorbing them into their midst, or at least coming to terms with them. The rabbis triumphed over the indifference of the masses by gradually gaining control of the schools and the synagogues. The exact date of the triumph is hard to determine, but it was not earlier than the seventh century C.E.

The central political office of Palestinian Jewry after the destruction was the *nasi* (Hebrew) or *patriarch* (Greek and Latin). The powers claimed and exercised by the patriarch rose substantially from the second century, when the office first appears, to the end of the fourth century. At the beginning of the second century the patriarch was the head of the central rabbinic academy (other rabbis led disciple circles); the chair of the rabbinic sanhedrin (an assembly of rabbis that intended to replace the sanhedrin of the second temple period, which had been chaired by the high priest); and the officer in charge of regulating the calendar (a function formerly exercised by the priests of the temple). By the end of the second century, the patriarch was recognized by the Roman government as the de facto, if not de jure, leader of the Jews of Palestine; was collecting taxes from the Jews of Palestine for the support of his administration; was appointing judges to the internal court system of the Jewish community of Palestine; and, as befitted a man of his importance, was claiming descent from King David. In the third century C.E. the patriarch was appointing school instructors and communal functionaries in some of the Jewish communities of Syria and Palestine, and was described by the church father Origen as a veritable "king of the Jews."[2] In the course of the fourth century the patriarch was authorized by the Christian Roman emperors to claim jurisdiction over all the Jews of the empire, including their synagogues and synagogue officials; was granted senatorial rank by the emperors; and collected taxes not only from the Jews of Palestine but from all the Jews of the empire. In approximately 425 C.E. everything came crashing down when in unclear circumstances the office was abolished.

The patriarchate began as a rabbinic office. Its most enduring product is the very first rabbinic document, the Mishnah, which was edited in about 200 C.E. by Rabbi Judah the Patriarch, often called simply "Rabbi." However, as the office expanded its power and prestige, it became less rabbinic. The goals of the patriarch were no longer identical with those of the rabbis. Most of the rabbis of the second century, if we may trust the evidence of the Mishnah and other tannaitic corpora, were well-to-do landowners who lived in villages and small towns. The civil legislation of the Mishnah (and some of its religious legislation as well) treats questions that interested this economic class. In the third century, however, the rabbinic estate came to include the poor, who depended on charity or public employment for their survival, and became increasingly urban, with centers in Caesarea, Tiberias, and Sepphoris. In other words, the patriarchate was becoming the leader not just of the rabbis but of Palestinian Jewry as a whole, and the office of rabbi was becoming a profession as much as the affectation of a social elite. This transition was largely the work of Judah the Patriarch and his immediate successors. The urban elites who originally opposed rabbinic hegemony were gradually brought into the patriarchal government. Many rabbis resisted these changes, and the two Talmudim preserve many stories of great tension between the rabbis and the patriarch in the third century. But these changes were essential to the ultimate triumph of rabbinic Judaism, because they broadened the rabbis' reach and placed them at the center of communal life.

It took much longer for the rabbis to establish control over synagogues. As I explained in chapter 3, synagogues were neither a rabbinic invention nor a uniquely rabbinic institution. The patriarch in the fourth century was granted jurisdiction over synagogue officials throughout the Roman empire, but it is unclear to what extent he actually exercised this authority and to what extent he would have been interested in promoting the interests of the rabbis abroad. In any case, the Mishnah and the two Talmudim have little legislation concerning the synagogue, and few narratives which imply that the rabbis were authority figures in the synagogue. The synagogue was the home of popular piety, and as a result many rabbis in both the second century and later recommended prayer in the *bet midrash,* the safe confines of the rabbinic school, rather than the synagogue. Some said outright that study was more important than prayer.

Archaeologists have discovered the remains of dozens of Palestinian synagogues of the late third to seventh centuries. These synagogues were built in a wide variety of styles, sizes, and shapes. Many of them were decorated with mosaics or carvings, whether of geometric patterns, animals, fruits, birds, zodiacs, Jewish cult objects (like the menorah), or biblical scenes. Most striking are those synagogues, predominantly in Galilee in the late fourth to sixth centuries, that have on the floor at the center of the main hall a mosaic of the twelve signs of the zodiac revolving around the sun chariot. The diaspora has provided one remarkable example of a decorated synagogue; this is the third-century synagogue of Dura Europos on the Euphrates (in modern-day Syria), whose four walls were covered with paintings of biblical scenes. Before these discoveries were made, it was widely believed that the second of the Ten Commandments, the prohibition of graven images, effectively precluded the existence of "Jewish art." After the discoveries were made, scholars restudied the rabbinic interpretation of the prohibition and concluded that some rabbis, at least, would not have objected to these synagogue decorations. But even if some rabbis in antiquity would have *tolerated* this art, would they have wanted it in the first place? If the synagogues had been bastions of rabbinic Judaism, would they have been decorated in this fashion? The answer to this question is still being debated as more archaeological evidence is being assembled, but the answer seems to be no.

Furthermore, many of the synagogues contain inscriptions that record donations or name the officers of the congregation. Rabbis seldom figure in these inscriptions, and when they do they invariably are donors, not officers. Therefore, it is most unlikely that the rabbis were in control of the synagogues of Palestine in the second to sixth centuries. Some synagogues undoubtedly were under their sway—archaeologists have recently unearthed the remains of a seventh-century synagogue from Beisan (in the valley south of the Sea of Galilee) whose central mosaic was an excerpt from the Palestinian Talmud concerning tithes—but many, if not most, were not. And if this was true of Palestine in the sixth century, it most certainly was true of Palestine in the second century and the diaspora throughout antiquity. Rabbinic domination of the synagogue was the result of a long and gradual process.

The End of Sectarianism

In the first century C.E. Judaism was marked by numerous sects and groups: Pharisees, Sadducees, Essenes, the Jews of Qumran, Zealots, Sicarii, "the Fourth Philosophy," Christians, Samaritans, Therapeutae, and others. Judaism after 70 C.E., in contrast, was not marked by sectarianism. Samaritans persisted as a marginal group in Jewish society (even if they were numerous and active in their own right); Christians became predominantly gentile and ultimately a separate religion; but all the other groups virtually disappeared from the historical record, except for occasional rabbinic and patristic references to the second temple period. In their stead the rabbis emerged as virtually the only group about which any information is extant. How can these facts be explained? There are two basic possibilities: either the shift in the nature of the available evidence gives the erroneous impression that sectarianism ceased, or the cessation of sectarianism was somehow caused by the war of 66–70 and the destruction of the temple. Scholars agree that the latter is far more likely than the former, but the subject is complex and both possibilities require discussion.

The Nature of the Available Documentation

Our knowledge of the history of Judaism in the post-70 period derives almost exclusively from rabbinic texts. Pagan, Christian, and archaeological sources contribute isolated details, nothing more.

The expression "rabbinic period" reflects the fact that we are well informed about the rabbis and about no one else. One of the remarkable characteristics of the Mishnah is how little information the text reveals about itself, its origins, authors, history, sources, and social setting. The two Talmudim and the rest of rabbinic literature are more forthcoming with such information (whether the information is reliable is another matter entirely), but at no point do the rabbis feel constrained to identify their opponents precisely or to describe competing groups in Jewish society. The rabbis often refer to gentiles, heretics, and irreligious or nonobservant Jews, but had no interest in describing the manifold varieties of each of these categories. Rabbinic literature is an "internal" literature, written by, about, and for the rabbis.

Perhaps, then, we could argue that sects and groups did continue a vigorous existence after 70 C.E., and that it is an accident of literary history that we are poorly informed about this fact. Aside from the Qumran scrolls, most of the documentation illustrating the varieties of Judaism in the second temple period (Josephus, Philo, apocalypses, pseudepigraphic literature of whatever genre, etc.) was preserved by Christianity, but the increasing distance between Judaism and Christianity at the beginning of the second century meant that very few Jewish works written after 100 C.E. were incorporated in the literary heritage of the new religion. The fact that so little Jewish nonrabbinic literature exists from the rabbinic period proves that neither the rabbis nor the Christians desired to preserve this material; it does not necessarily prove that such literature never existed. Perhaps the demise of sectarianism really took place long after 70 C.E., and some future discovery, like that of the Dead Sea Scrolls, will prove how variegated Judaism was even after the destruction of the second temple.

What future discoveries may bring is, of course, unknown. No one could have predicted the treasures revealed at Qumran, and no one can predict what discoveries await the historian of the rabbinic period. But the evidence now available is consistent. Except for Samaritans and Jewish Christians, sects disappeared after 70 C.E. Many Jews, perhaps most Jews, did not yet regard the rabbis as their leaders, and did not regard rabbinic Judaism as the standard of behavior and belief. The rabbis themselves refer to *amme haares*, literally "peoples of the land," Jews who observe the Sabbath and various other commandments but who slight or ignore the rules of purity and tithing, or who simply do not affect a rabbinic way of life.[3] These are the Jews, we may presume, who built and frequented those synagogues in which the rabbis did not feel at home. The church fathers refer to Jews who deny the resurrection of the dead, pray to angels, and do various other things of which the rabbis would have disapproved.[4] And outside the rabbinic pale altogether were the Greek-speaking Jews of the diaspora who had minimal contacts with the rabbis of Palestine and were well established in their own communities with their own religious traditions.

The absence of sectarianism therefore does not mean the absence of diversity. But no source connects this diversity to sects, or even hints that sects and other organized groups continued to exist. One Christian writer of the third century remarks that after the destruction of the temple and the rejection of the Jews by God, Satan no longer bothers to tempt the Jews to sin. Instead Satan directs his attentions to the Christians. Therefore, Christianity is beset with heresy and discord, while Judaism is not.[5] After 70 c.e. Jewish society was not marked by sects.

The Destruction of the Temple and the Disappearance of Sectarianism

During the war of 66–70 c.e. the Romans exterminated or at least greatly weakened many of the sects. The revolutionary groups (Zealots, Sicarii, Fourth Philosophy) were destroyed. Groups of Sicarii held out at Masada and other places for a few years, but their numbers were few and their actions (even if spectacular) were inconsequential. The Qumran community was destroyed in 68 c.e. Insofar as the Sadducees consisted of temple priests and high priests, their numbers were severely reduced by the military actions of both the Romans and the revolutionaries. Aside from removing various sects, the war also removed the focal point of sectarianism. Sectarianism requires an evil reality against which to rail and protest, something that can serve as the focal point of its separatist energies. The chief focal point of ancient Jewish sectarianism was the temple (see chapter 5), and with its destruction and the humbling of the high priesthood the sects lost much of their reason for existing. Thus the war prepared the way for a society without sects.

The Pharisees disappeared too, but transformed themselves into rabbis. As I discussed in chapter 5, the rabbis see themselves not as "Pharisees" but as "the sages of Israel." Neither the Mishnah nor any other rabbinic work betrays a Pharisaic self-consciousness. When the rabbis told stories about the second temple period, they were sure that their opponents were Sadducees (and Boethusians, a group mentioned only in rabbinic literature), but they were not as insistent that their ancestors were Pharisees. We might be tempted to conclude that the rabbis really have little connection with the

Pharisees, a thesis that has been defended by several scholars in recent years, but the links between the two groups are numerous and strong.

The rabbis were latter-day Pharisees who had no interest in publicizing the connection, not only because sectarian groups seldom see themselves as sects, but also because the rabbis had no desire to exclude anyone. There is no evidence either that *all* the members of the new rabbinic movement were Pharisees or the descendants of Pharisees, or that the rabbis wished to exclude non-Pharisees. Until recently scholars argued that the final separation between Judaism and Christianity was caused by the rabbis of Yavneh (in Greek: Jamnia), the first generation of rabbis after the destruction who assembled at this town west-northwest of Jerusalem. (According to legend, Yavneh was the place to which Rabban Yohanan ben Zakkai went after fleeing Jerusalem during the siege.) There, according to both Talmudim, the rabbis instituted the "benediction against the heretics" *(birkat ha minim)*, a prayer to God to destroy "heretics" or "sectarians" and to frustrate their plans. Who were these "heretics"? Scholars argued that the intended victims were the Christians. Since the Christians could not recite this benediction, and presumably would have been uncomfortable in the presence of those who did, the effect of the institution of this benediction was to expel Christians from the synagogues. Scholars found confirmation for this interpretation in John's references to the expulsion of Christians from synagogues (John 9:22; 12:42; 16:2), and in the assertions of various church fathers that the Jews curse Christ and/or Christians in their daily prayers. If this reconstruction is correct, the rabbis were triumphalist Pharisees who eagerly excluded their rivals.

But this reconstruction no longer commands universal assent. Obviously the Christians of John's community were expelled from their local synagogues, but this hardly means that all Jews everywhere expelled Christians. Synagogues were not beholden to any central body; every community ran its synagogue in its own way. Even if the rabbis wished to expel Christians from all the synagogues of the empire, they lacked the power and the authority to do so. Furthermore, although by the fourth century the "benediction against heretics" was directed against Christians or some Jewish-Christian sects, its original version was a generic denunciation of all heretics. The intent was not to single out Christians or any other specific group, but to proclaim the end of sectarianism.

One of the peculiar characteristics of the Mishnah is the prevalence of legal disputes. The very first paragraph of the Mishnah opens with a question that receives three different answers, and virtually every page of rabbinic literature repeats this pattern with numerous variations. This characteristic of the Mishnah is new in two respects. First, for the most part second-temple literature attributes legal disputes to sects, not individuals. Even in rabbinic literature the vast majority of legal disputes ascribed to pre-70 figures involve the houses of Hillel and Shammai, not individuals. After 70 C.E., the disputes between the houses, no less than the disputes between sects, cease, to be replaced by disputes between individual rabbinic masters. Second, sectarian dispute was the consequence of exclusivity and social division, but rabbinic dispute was not. The rabbis of the Yavnean period, who were able to maintain normal social intercourse among themselves in spite of their legal disputes, imagined that the houses of Hillel and Shammai had been able to do the same (see chapter 5).

It is unlikely, therefore, that the rabbis felt a need to exclude anyone from their number; on the contrary, their ultimate success derived from the fact that they were prepared to absorb even those elements which originally opposed them. The real concession that the rabbis demanded of all comers was that they forgo any sectarian affiliation. Legal disputes would be tolerated, even fostered, but sectarian disputes must cease. This was the message of the benediction against heretics. The rabbis prayed that God destroy all those who persisted in maintaining a separatist identity in a world without a temple and in a society that was prepared to tolerate disputes.

If this reconstruction is correct, the institution of the benediction against heretics was an important milestone in the self-definition of rabbinic Judaism, but not a crucial moment in the birth of Christianity. The separation of Christianity from Judaism was a process, not an event. The essential part of the process was that the church was becoming more and more gentile, and less and less Jewish, but the separation manifested itself in different ways in each local community where Jews and Christians dwelt together. In some places, the Jews expelled the Christians; in others, the Christians left of their own accord. The benediction against heretics perhaps shows why the Christians would have felt unwelcome in the rabbinic community of Palestine, but it has only minimal relevance to the process as a whole.

Canon and Literature

The canonization of the Tanak is another action that, until recently, was widely credited by scholars to the Yavnean rabbis. According to this view, as part of their program to define "orthodoxy" and expel unwanted elements, the Yavnean rabbis eliminated all the apocalypses (except Daniel) from the canon, and ignored, if not suppressed, all the literature written in Greek. This reconstruction has few adherents today, not only because the evidence for this Yavnean program is tenuous, as I have just discussed, but also because the formation of the canon is too complex a process (again, a process, not an event) to be attributed to a single generation of scholars whose authority over the people was dubious. The rabbis debated the canonical status of various books, but for the most part they were not creating a canon but confronted by a canon that had already been determined. The rabbis did, to be sure, ignore apocalypses and Greek Jewish literature, but these facts can be explained in various ways and need not be attributed to anti-Christian animus. Apocalypses in general were esoteric, not popular, works, and if the majority of the framers of the Mishnah were country squires, as I suggested above, their ignorance of Greek literature, both Jewish and pagan, is scarcely surprising.

The rabbis preserved and developed the Targums and prayers, but ignored the histories, apocalypses, testaments, romances, wisdom books, hymns, and biblical paraphrases that had been written in such abundance in second temple times. They wrote a series of commentaries on the Torah (and, at the end of the rabbinic period, on several other biblical books as well) that far exceed in length and detail anything written before 70 C.E. Mystical circles took many motifs and ideas from the apocalypses and developed the *hekhalot* literature (see above). But the most distinctive and most important rabbinic works, namely the Mishnah and the two Talmudim, were written in new genres.

The Mishnah is a digest or anthology; indeed, it resembles the *Digest* of Roman law published by the emperor Justinian in 533 C.E. Both works are topical collections of legal dicta ascribed to various authorities who lived for the most part in the second and early third centuries C.E. Neither work is a law code, since each contains historical reminiscences and narratives, quotations from Homer (in the *Digest*) or the Torah (in the Mishnah), polemics, and, of course, divergent opinions. But each work is a source of law; each work contains material from which laws can be derived.

Whatever may have been the Mishnah's original intent (see above), the Talmudim assume that the Mishnah's main purpose was legislative, and therefore concentrate on those sections which deal with practicable laws. The Talmudim reduce the ambiguity of the Mishnah's legal disputes by determining which of its divergent opinions on any given subject is correct. The Talmudim also clarify the Mishnah's obscurities, reconcile its contradictions, and expand its rulings into areas that the Mishnah did not consider. In sum: the Talmudim comment on the Mishnah and treat it as a canonical work of law, but because the Talmudim are so discursive, so elaborate, so prone to expansion, and so ready to follow their own agenda, they are not really "commentaries" at all.

One item on the agenda of both Talmudim is to connect the laws of the Mishnah to the Torah. Only on rare occasions does the Mishnah show how its laws can be derived exegetically from the words of the Torah; even rarer are those occasions when the Mishnah claims that a certain law was received from ancient tradition or was innovated by a specific rabbi at a specific time. In sum: the Mishnah does not reveal the origin either of itself as a whole or of its constituent laws. The only passage that does is the chain of tradition which opens the *Chapters of the Fathers:* "Moses received Torah [or: the Torah] from Sinai and transmitted it to Joshua, and Joshua [transmitted it] to the elders," etc. The chain of masters and disciples ends with the patriarchal house and the sages of the Mishnah. This passage claims that the Mishnah is part of the Torah which Moses received at Mount Sinai, but the precise nature of the claim is ambiguous. It might mean that all of the Mishnah's laws, perhaps even its very words, were revealed by God to Moses; throughout the generations Jews have only been preserving and rediscovering that which Moses already knew. Or it might mean that the kernel of the Mishnah, its basic principles and ideas—in other words, the distinctive characteristics of rabbinic Judaism—were revealed by God to Moses; throughout the generations Jews have been building and expanding upon this foundation.

Of these two possibilities, the Talmudim opted for the former. They routinely attempt to show that the laws of the Mishnah can be derived from scripture, because humans do not have the authority to innovate religious law. Just as the Jews gained mastery over the Torah through interpretation, the rabbis of the Talmud gained mastery over the Mishnah through interpretation. They subordinated it to an earlier canonical text of higher authority. In practice, of course, the rabbis of both the Mishnah and the Talmudim were innovators as well as conservators, but whereas the Mishnah admitted this implicitly, the Talmudim felt constrained to deny it. The tension between these rival perspectives continued in medieval Judaism; and in the ongoing debates between fundamentalist and liberal Judaism it continues to this day.

Conclusion

From the Maccabees to the Mishnah is a span of about three hundred and fifty years. During this period Judaism gradually assumed the shape that it would maintain until the rise of modernity. It became a "book" religion, which sought God not only through prayer and liturgy but also through the study of, and total immersion in, the written word of God. Study was for its own sake, as well as for the sake of learning the requirements of the religion. In the Torah, Moses detailed the rules and regulations that the Israelites had to obey if they were to remain loyal to the covenant. The rabbis, following the precedent that had been established in second temple times, took the scriptural regulations and expanded them, added to them, and changed them. They accepted many of the theological, legal, and institutional innovations of the second temple period. But like their ancestors and their descendants, the rabbis saw themselves not as the creators of something new, but as the bearers of something old. They were Israel, heirs to the eternal promise that God had sworn to Abraham, Isaac, and Jacob.

Notes

Chapter 1. Ancient Judaism: Chronology and Definitions

1. J. Liver, "The Half-Shekel Offering in Biblical and Post-Biblical Literature," *Harvard Theological Review* 56 (1963), 173–198.

2. Philo, *Against Flaccus* 7, §46, and *Embassy to Gaius* 36, §281 (mother city); *On Providence* 2, §64 (pilgrimage).

3. Dio Cassius 66.4.3, in M. Stern, *Greek and Latin Authors on Jews and Judaism* II, no. 430, p. 373.

Chapter 2. Jews and Gentiles

1. The four versions of the story are conveniently available in Jacob Neusner, *Development of a Legend* (Leiden: E. J. Brill, 1970).

2. Dio Cassius 66.12–15, in Stern, *Greek and Latin Authors* II, no. 440, pp. 392–393, and *Historia Augusta, Life of Hadrian* 14.2, in Stern, *Greek and Latin Authors* II, no. 511, p. 619.

3. Jerome, *Epistle* 22, available in the Loeb edition of *Select Letters of St. Jerome.*

4. Babylonian Talmud *Megillah* 9b.

5. Shaye J. D. Cohen, "Sosates the Jewish Homer," *Harvard Theological Review* 74 (1981), 391–396.

6. Tacitus, *Histories* 5.5.2, in Stern, *Greek and Latin Authors* II, no. 281, p. 26.

7. Epictetus in Stern, *Greek and Latin Authors* I, no. 254, p. 543.

8. Numenius in Stern, *Greek and Latin Authors* II, no. 363, pp. 209–211.

Chapter 3. The Jewish "Religion": Practices and Beliefs

1. Josephus, *Jewish War* 7.3.3, §50, and *Jewish Antiquities* 20.5.2, §100 (apostasy); 20.2.1, §17, and 20.2.4, §41 (conversion); Philo, *On the Virtues* §102–108 (in vol. 8 of the Loeb edition).

2. J. N. D. Kelly, *Early Christian Creeds* (3rd ed., New York: Longman, 1972; repr. 1983), pp. 215–216.

3. *Sifre Deuteronomy* §41, pp. 87–88 in the edition of Louis Finkelstein (*Sifre on Deuteronomy;* New York: Jewish Theological Seminary, 1969).

4. *Daily Prayer Book: Ha-Siddur Ha-Shalem*, ed. by Philip Birnbaum (New York: Hebrew Publishing Co., 1949; frequently reprinted), p. 86.

5. P. W. van der Horst, *The Sentences of Pseudo-Phocylides* (Leiden: E. J. Brill, 1978). A translation is also available in James H. Charlesworth, *The Old Testament Pseudepigrapha*, vol. 2 (Garden City: Doubleday & Co., 1985).

6. Duris of Samos as quoted by Athenaeus 6.63, p. 253 D–F (translation available in the Loeb Classical Library). For the Greek text see Felix Jacoby, *Die Fragmente der griechischen Historiker*, no. 76 F 13.

7. R. Pinhas in the name of R. Judah b. Simon in Palestinian Talmud *Berakhot* 9:1, 62b–63a in the Vilna edition, 12a in the Venice edition.

8. John Cassian, *Conferences* 10.3, in *Western Asceticism*, ed. by Owen Chadwick (Philadelphia: Westminster Press, 1958, frequently reprinted), p. 235.

Chapter 4. The Community and Its Institutions

1. J. and G. Roux, *Revue des Etudes Grecques* 62 (1949), 281–296. See too B. Lifshitz, *Donateurs et fondateurs dans les synagogues juives* (Paris: Gabalda, 1967), pp. 81–83, no. 100. The discussion in Shimon Applebaum, *Jews and Greeks in Ancient Cyrene* (Leiden: E. J. Brill, 1979), pp. 160–167, is very inaccurate.

2. D. M. Lewis, "The Jewish Inscriptions of Egypt," nos. 1440 (p. 141) and 1532 (p. 164), in *Corpus Papyrorum Judaicarum* III, ed. by Victor Tcherikover et al. (Cambridge, Mass.: Harvard University Press, 1964).

3. Lifshitz, *Donateurs*, pp. 70–71, no. 79.

4. *Corpus Inscriptionum Judaicarum* II, ed. by J. B. Frey (Rome: Pontifico Istituto di Archeologia Cristiana, 1952), pp. 142–143, no. 945.

5. Palestinian Talmud *Ketubot* 8:11, 32c, and Babylonian Talmud *Baba Batra* 21a.

6. D. Urman, *Israel Exploration Journal* 22 (1972), 21–23; Joseph Naveh, *On Stone and Mosaic: The Aramaic and Hebrew Inscriptions from Ancient Synagogues* (in Hebrew) (Israel: Israel Exploration Society, 1978), p. 25, no. 6.

7. Tosefta *Erubin* 6.4, p. 119 in the edition of Saul Lieberman (see the manuscript variants); Tosefta *Pesahim* 3.11, p. 154 in Lieberman's edition (*The Tosefta;* 5 vols.; New York: Jewish Theological Seminary, 1955–73).

Chapter 5. Sectarian and Normative

1. Irenaeus, *Refutation of All the Heresies* 3.

2. Origen, *Against Celsus* 3.12, p. 135 in the translation of H. Chadwick (Cambridge: University Press, 1953).

3. The phrase is from the Vincentian Canon (Vincent of Lérins, *Commonitorium* 2.3).

4. Pliny, *Natural History* 5.73, in Stern, *Greek and Latin Authors* I, no. 204, p. 472; and Dio Chrysostom, in Stern, *Greek and Latin Authors* I, no. 251, p. 539.

5. Tosefta *Berakhot* 3:25, p. 18 in the edition of Saul Lieberman.

6. *Fathers According to Rabbi Nathan*, version A ch. 5 (see Judah Goldin, *The Fathers According to Rabbi Nathan;* New Haven: Yale University Press, 1955, p. 39), or version B ch. 10 (see Anthony Saldarini, *The Fathers According to Rabbi Nathan*; Leiden: E. J. Brill, 1975, pp. 85–86).

7. Tosefta *Yoma* (or *Kippurim*) 1:8, p. 222 in the edition of Saul Lieberman; Tosefta *Sukah* 3:16, p. 270; and Tosefta *Parah* 3:8, p. 632 in the edition of M. S. Zuckermandel.

8. Jerome, *Epistle* 112, in A. F. J. Klijn and G. J. Reinink, *Patristic Evidence for Jewish-Christian Sects* (Leiden: E. J. Brill, 1973), p. 201.

Chapter 6. Canonization and Its Implications

1. Rudolf Pfeiffer, *History of Classical Scholarship from the Beginnings to the End of the Hellenistic Age* (Oxford: Clarendon Press, 1968), pp. 203–208.

2. Diodorus of Sicily 1.94.1–2 (from Posidonius?) in Stern, *Greek and Latin Authors* I, no. 58, pp. 171–172.

3. Josephus, *Jewish Antiquities* 16.6.2, §164; *Jewish War* 2.12.2, §228–231; and *Jewish Antiquities* 20.5.4, §113–117.

4. For these canon lists see H. B. Swete, *An Introduction to the Old Testament in Greek*, rev. by R. R. Otley (Cambridge: University Press, 1902; repr. New York: Ktav Publishing House, 1968), pp. 201–214.

5. See especially the *Epistle of Barnabas*.

Chapter 7. The Emergence of Rabbinic Judaism

1. *Sifre Deuteronomy* §41, pp. 87–88 in the edition of Louis Finkelstein.

2. Origen, *Epistle to Africanus on the Story of Susanna*, in J. P. Migne, *Patrologia Graeca* 11.81, 84.

3. See especially Babylonian Talmud *Berakhot* 47b and *Pesahim* 49a–b.

4. For example, Origen, *Against Celsus* 1.26, p. 26, and 5.14, p. 274, in the translation of Henry Chadwick.

5. *Didascalia Apostolorum* 23, p. 211 in the translation of Arthur Vööbus (Corpus Scriptorum Christianorum Orientalium; Louvain: CSCO, 1979).

Suggestions
for Further Reading

Note: This book covers a wide variety of topics, and the number of possible suggested readings is enormous. Here is a brief selection of books and articles written in English. Advanced students will want to track down additional bibliography not only in English but also in French, German, Hebrew, and other languages.

Sources

Throughout this book I frequently cite or allude to the following works (listed more or less chronologically). I list the editions which provide the translations cited in this book (except that occasionally I have introduced modifications or alternative versions).

The "Old Testament," the "New Testament," and the Apocrypha (which includes Ben Sira [=Sirach or Ecclesiasticus], 1 Maccabees, 2 Maccabees, 4 Ezra [=2 Esdras]) are cited from the Revised Standard Version as published in *The New Oxford Annotated Bible with the Apocrypha*, ed. by H. G. May and B. M. Metzger (expanded edition; New York: Oxford University Press, 1977).

The Dead Sea Scrolls are available in two fine English translations, one literal and dry, the other free and poetic. The first is *The Dead Sea Scrolls in English*, tr. by Geza Vermes (2nd ed.; Harmondsworth: Penguin Books, 1975); the second is *The Dead Sea Scriptures*, tr. by Theodore H. Gaster (3rd ed.; Garden City: Doubleday & Co., 1976). Three recent and useful translations of specific documents are: Maurya P. Horgan, *Pesharim: Qumran Interpretations of Biblical Books* (Washington, D.C.: Catholic Biblical Association of America, 1979); Bonnie P. Kittel, *The Hymns of Qumran: Translation and Commentary* (Chico, Calif.: Scholars Press, 1981); and Johann Maier, *The Temple Scroll* (Sheffield: JSOT Press, 1985).

Works of "the Pseudepigrapha" (which include *Enoch* [=*1 Enoch*], *Jubilees*, *Prayer of Manasseh*, *Letter of Aristeas*, and the *Syriac Apocalypse of Baruch*) are cited from *The Old Testament Pseudepigrapha*, ed. by James H. Charlesworth (2 vols.; Garden City: Doubleday & Co., 1983–85). Another useful recent selection is *The Apocryphal Old Testament,* ed. by H. F. D. Sparks (Oxford: Clarendon Press, 1984).

The works of Philo and Josephus are cited from the bilingual editions of the Loeb Classical Library: *The Complete Works of Philo,* ed. by F. H. Colson and G. H. Whitaker (10 vols. and 2 suppl. vols.; London: William Heinemann; and Cambridge, Mass.: Harvard University Press, 1929–62; frequently reprinted), and *The Complete Works of Flavius Josephus,* ed. by H. St. J. Thackeray, R. Marcus, A. Wikgren, and L. H. Feldman (9 vols.; London: William Heinemann; and Cambridge, Mass.: Harvard University Press, 1926–65; frequently reprinted).

The Mishnah is cited from the translation of Herbert Danby (London: Oxford University Press, 1933; frequently reprinted).

The Tosefta has been translated by Jacob Neusner (6 vols.; New York: Ktav Publishing House, 1977). The standard English translation of the Babylonian Talmud is that edited by Isadore Epstein (London: Soncino Press, frequently reprinted).

References to Jews and Judaism in classical literature have been collected and translated by Menahem Stern, *Greek and Latin Authors on Jews and Judaism* (3 vols.; Jerusalem: Israel Academy of Arts and Sciences, 1974–84).

Chapter 1: Ancient Judaism: Chronology and Definitions

For a detailed survey of the history of the latter part of the second temple period, consult any of the following standard works: Emil Schürer, *The History of the Jewish People in the Age of Jesus Christ,* vol. 1, rev. and ed. by Geza Vermes, Fergus Millar, et al. (Edinburgh: T. & T. Clark, 1973); *Compendia Rerum Iudaicarum ad Novum Testamentum,* section I: *The Jewish People in the First Century,* ed. by S. Safrai and M. Stern (2 vols.; Philadelphia: Fortress Press, 1974–76); *The World History of the Jewish People,* vol. 6: *The Hellenistic Age,* ed. by A. Schalit (1972), and vol. 7: *The Herodian Period,* ed. by M. Avi-Yonah and Zvi Baras (1975; New Brunswick: Rutgers University Press); and E. Mary Smallwood, *The Jews Under Roman Rule* (Leiden: E. J. Brill, 1976, repr. 1981).

For ongoing bibliographical surveys of works on ancient Judaism, see the following journals: *New Testament Abstracts; Elenchus Bibliographicus Biblicus* (a supplement to *Biblica*); *Journal for the Study of Judaism in the Persian, Hellenistic, and Roman Periods;* and *Revue de Qumran.* Two recent book-length bibliographies are very useful: Menahem Mor and Uriel Rappaport, *Bibliography of Works on Jewish History in the Hellenistic and Roman Periods 1976–1980* (Jerusalem: Zalman Shazar Center, 1982; further installments are expected), and Louis H. Feldman, *Josephus and Modern Scholarship 1937–1980* (Berlin and New York: Walter de Gruyter, 1984). Because of the centrality of Josephus, Feldman's bibliography covers virtually all aspects of Jewish history of the later second temple period.

Chapter 2: Jews and Gentiles

On the entire complex of themes see the two standard works of Martin Hengel: *Judaism and Hellenism* (2 vols.; Philadelphia: Fortress Press, 1974), and *Jews, Greeks, and Barbarians* (Philadelphia: Fortress Press, 1980).

Political: On the Maccabean rebellion see Jonathan Goldstein's brilliant but idiosyncratic commentaries on 1 and 2 Maccabees in the Anchor Bible series. Otherwise the best studies in English are Victor Tcherikover, *Hellenistic Civilization and the Jews* (Philadelphia: Jewish Publication Society, 1966), and Elias Bickerman, *The God of the Maccabees* (Leiden: E. J. Brill, 1979). See also Elias Bickerman, "The Maccabean Uprising: An Interpretation," in *The Jewish Expression*, ed. by Judah Goldin (New York: Bantam Books, 1970; repr. New Haven: Yale University Press, 1976), pp. 66–86. On the wars of 66–74, 115–117, and 132–135 c.e., see the full discussion in Schürer-Vermes (listed above). On the war of 115–117 see Stern's commentary on fragments 348 and 437 in his *Greek and Latin Authors* II. On the war of 132–135 c.e., see Glen Bowersock, "A Roman Perspective on the Bar Kochba War," in *Approaches to Ancient Judaism*, vol. 2, ed. by William Scott Green (Chico, Calif.: Scholars Press, 1980), pp. 131–142, and Benjamin Isaac and Aharon Oppenheimer, "The Revolt of Bar Kokhba: Ideology and Modern Scholarship," *Journal of Jewish Studies* 36 (1985), 33–60.

Cultural: Moses Hadas, *Hellenistic Culture: Fusion and Diffusion* (New York: Columbia University Press, 1959); Morton Smith, *Palestinian Parties and Politics That Shaped the Old Testament* (New York: Columbia University Press, 1971), especially pp. 57–81; Elias Bickerman, *Studies in Jewish and Christian History* (3 vols.; Leiden, E. J. Brill, 1976–86); J. N. Sevenster, *Do You Know Greek?* (Leiden: E. J. Brill, 1968); John J. Collins, *Between Athens and Jerusalem: Jewish Identity in the Hellenistic Diaspora* (New York: Crossroad Publishing Co., 1983).

Social: On conversion to Judaism see Bernard J. Bamberger, *Proselytism in the Talmudic Period* (Cincinnati: Hebrew Union College, 1939; repr. New York: Ktav Publishing House, 1968). On attitudes toward converts, see Joseph Baumgarten, "Exclusions from the Temple: Proselytes and Agrippa I," *Journal of Jewish Studies* 33 (1982), 215–225. The evidence for my discussion of intermarriage and conversion is provided in "From the Bible to the Talmud: The Prohibition of Intermarriage," *Hebrew Annual Review* 7 (1983), 23–39, and "The Origins of the Matrilineal Principle in Rabbinic Law," *Association for Jewish Studies Review* 10 (1985), 19–53. On immersion/baptism, see H. H. Rowley, "Jewish Proselyte Baptism and the Baptism of John," in his *From Moses to Qumran: Studies in the Old Testament* (New York: Association Press, 1963), pp. 211–235. A. Thomas Kraabel argues that the "God-fearers" never existed, but this position is untenable; see his "The Disappearance of the 'God-Fearers,' " *Numen* 28 (1981), 113–126. On "anti-Semitism" see J. N. Sevenster, *The Roots of Pagan Anti-Semitism in the Ancient World* (Leiden: E. J. Brill, 1975), and John G. Gager, *The Origins of Anti-Semitism* (New York: Oxford University Press, 1983).

Chapter 3: The Jewish "Religion": Practices and Beliefs

The classic study of ancient Judaism is George Foot Moore, *Judaism in the First Centuries of the Christian Era* (3 vols.; Cambridge, Mass.: Harvard University Press, 1927–30, frequently reprinted). More recent works include Ephraim Urbach, *The Sages: Their Concepts and Beliefs* (2 vols.; 2nd ed., Jerusalem: Magnes Press, 1979); E. P. Sanders, *Paul and Palestinian Judaism* (Philadelphia: Fortress Press, 1977); and Emil Schürer, *The History of the Jewish People in the Age of Jesus Christ*, vol. 2, rev. and ed. by Geza Vermes, Fergus Millar, et al. (Edinburgh: T. & T. Clark, 1979). Each of these books treats in some detail the topics discussed in this chapter. I list a few additional specialized studies below.

On the cult of the temple, see Menahem Haran, *Temples and Temple Service in Ancient Israel* (Oxford: Clarendon Press, 1978). On prayer, see Joseph Heinemann, *Prayer in the Talmud: Forms and Patterns* (Berlin: Walter de Gruyter, 1977) and Jakob Petuchowski, "The Liturgy of the Synagogue: History, Structure, and Contents," in *Approaches to Ancient Judaism*, vol. 4, ed. by William Scott Green (Chico, Calif.: Scholars Press, 1983), pp. 1–64. On "The Civic Prayer of Jerusalem," see the article by Elias Bickerman in *Harvard Theological Review* 55 (1962), 163–185.

On the santification of life through the study and observance of the Torah, the classic work of Solomon Schechter, *Aspects of Rabbinic Theology: Major Concepts of the Talmud* (New York: Macmillan Co., 1909; repr. New York: Schocken Books, 1961), still is valuable. See too Jacob Neusner, *The Way of Torah* (3rd ed.; N. Scituate, Mass.: Duxbury Press, 1979).

On magicians and miracle workers, see Morton Smith, *Jesus the Magician* (San Francisco: Harper & Row, 1978).

On monotheism vs. polytheism, see Robert M. Grant, *Gods and the One God*, in this series (Philadelphia: Westminster Press, 1986). On angels and other supernatural beings who complement or compete with God, see Alan F. Segal, *Two Powers in Heaven* (Leiden: E. J. Brill, 1977), and J. E. Fossum, *The Name of God and the Angel of the Lord: Samaritan and Jewish Concepts of Intermediation and the Origin of Gnosticism* (Tübingen: J. C. B. Mohr [Paul Siebeck], 1985). On the God of the philosophers vs. the God of the Bible, see the classic study of Philo by Harry Wolfson (*Philo: Foundations of Religious Philosophy in Judaism, Christianity, and Islam;* Cambridge, Mass.: Harvard University Press, 1947; frequently reprinted), and David Winston's introduction and commentary to the Wisdom of Solomon in the Anchor Bible edition (*The Wisdom of Solomon;* Garden City: Doubleday & Co., 1979).

On resurrection and life after death, see George Nickelsburg, *Resurrection, Immortality, and Eternal Life in Intertestamental Judaism* (Cambridge, Mass.: Harvard University Press, 1972), and Hans C. C. Cavallin, *Life After Death: Paul's Argument for the Resurrection* (Lund: Gleerup, 1974). The burial practices of second temple times confirm that the belief in resurrection and life after death was widespread; see Eric M. Meyers, *Jewish Ossuaries: Reburial and Rebirth* (Rome: Biblical Institute Press, 1971) and Pau Figueras, *Decorated Jewish Ossuaries* (Leiden: E. J. Brill, 1983).

On apocalyptic literature and eschatology, see D. S. Russell, *The Method and Message of Jewish Apocalyptic* (Philadelphia: Westminster Press, 1964); Paul D. Hanson, *The Dawn of Apocalyptic* (rev. ed.; Philadelphia: Fortress Press, 1979); John J. Collins, ed., *Apocalypse: The Morphology of a Genre* (*Semeia* 14; Missoula, Mont.: Scholars Press, 1979); David Hellholm, ed., *Apocalypticism in the Mediterranean World and the Near East* (Tübingen: J. C. B. Mohr [Paul Siebeck], 1983); John J. Collins, *The Apocalyptic Imagination: An Introduction to the Jewish Matrix of Christianity* (New York: Crossroad Publishing Co., 1984).

Chapter 4: The Community and Its Institutions

The classic modern discussion of the social institutions of ancient Judaism (the temple, the sanhedrin, the priesthood, guilds, sects) remains Joachim Jeremias, *Jerusalem in the Time of Jesus* (Philadelphia: Fortress Press, 1975). See too *The World History of the Jewish People*, vol. 8: *Society and Religion in the Second Temple Period*, ed. by Michael Avi-Yonah and Zvi Baras (New Brunswick: Rutgers University Press, 1977), and John G. Stambaugh and David L. Balch, *The New Testament in Its Social Environment*, in this series (Philadelphia: Westminster Press, 1986). On the sanhedrin see Hugo Mantel, *Studies in the History of the Sanhedrin* (Cambridge, Mass.: Harvard University Press, 1965). On the *politeumata* of the diaspora see Aryeh Kasher, *The Jews in Hellenistic and Roman Egypt* (Tübingen: J. C. B. Mohr [Paul Siebeck], 1985).

On the history of the synagogue see Joseph Gutmann, ed., *The Synagogue: Studies in Origins, Archaeology, and Architecture* (New York: Ktav Publishing House, 1975), and idem, ed., *Ancient Synagogues. The State of Research* (Chico, Calif.: Scholars Press, 1981); Lee Levine, ed., *Ancient Synagogues Revealed* (Jerusalem: Israel Exploration Society, 1981; Detroit: Wayne State University Press, 1982). On the *haburah*, see Saul Lieberman, "The Discipline in the So-Called Dead Sea Manual of Discipline," *Journal of Biblical Literature* 71 (1952), 199–206, and C. Rabin, *Qumran Studies* (Oxford: Clarendon Press, 1957; repr. New York: Schocken Books, 1975). On schools see R. A. Culpepper, *The Johannine School* (Missoula, Mont.: Scholars Press, 1975), and David Goodblatt, *Rabbinic Instruction in Sasanian Babylonia* (Leiden: E. J. Brill, 1975) (with a discussion of earlier material as well).

Chapter 5: Sectarian and Normative

There is no recent accessible survey in English. Marcel Simon, *Jewish Sects at the Time of Jesus* (Philadelphia: Fortress Press, 1967), is out-of-date. See the discussions in the books listed for chapter 3.

On the definition of sects, see Bryan Wilson, ed., *Patterns of Sectarianism* (London: William Heinemann, 1967). On the rules of purity and the temple as focal point, see Jacob Neusner, *The Idea of Purity in Ancient Judaism* (Leiden: E. J. Brill, 1973). On the proto-sectarianism of the Persian period, see Morton Smith, "The Dead Sea Sect in Relation to Ancient Judaism,"

New Testament Studies 7 (1961), 347–360; Hanson, *The Dawn of Apocalyptic* (listed above for chapter 3); and Joseph Blenkinsopp, "Interpretation and the Tendency to Sectarianism," in *Jewish and Christian Self-Definition*, vol. II: *Aspects of Judaism in the Graeco-Roman Period*, ed. by E. P. Sanders et al. (Philadelphia: Fortress Press, 1981), pp. 1–26.

On Pharisees and Sadducees, see Jacob Neusner, *Rabbinic Traditions About the Pharisees Before 70* (Leiden: E. J. Brill, 1971), and *From Politics to Piety* (Englewood Cliffs, N.J.: Prentice-Hall, 1973); and Ellis Rivkin, *A Hidden Revolution* (Nashville: Abingdon Press, 1978). See further the bibliography for chapter 7.

On the Essenes, the Qumran sect, and the Therapeutae, see the detailed discussion in Schürer-Vermes, vol. 2 (listed above for chapter 3), and J. Murphy-O'Connor, "The Essenes and Their History," *Revue Biblique* 81 (1974), 215–244. On the archaeology of the settlement and the scrolls, see Roland de Vaux, *Archaeology and the Dead Sea Scrolls* (London: Oxford University Press for the British Academy, 1973).

On the Fourth Philosophy, Sicarii, and Zealots, see Morton Smith, "Zealots and Sicarii: Their Origins and Relations," *Harvard Theological Review* 64 (1971), 1–19; David Rhoads, *Israel in Revolution* (Philadelphia: Fortress Press, 1976); John S. Hanson and Richard A. Horsley, *Bandits, Prophets, and Messiahs: Popular Movements at the Time of Jesus* (Minneapolis/Chicago/New York: Winston-Seabury, 1985).

On the Samaritans, see R. J. Coggins, *Samaritans and Jews* (Atlanta: John Knox, 1975).

Chapter 6: Canonization and Its Implications

On the social setting of canon, see James Sanders, *Torah and Canon* (Philadelphia: Fortress Press, 1972), and *Canon and Community: A Guide to Canonical Criticism* (Philadelphia: Fortress Press, 1984), and the relevant sections of Brevard S. Childs, *Introduction to the Old Testament as Scripture* (Philadelphia: Fortress Press, 1979), and *The New Testament as Canon* (Philadelphia: Fortress Press, 1985). For a full discussion see now Roger Beckwith, *The Old Testament Canon of the New Testament Church* (Grand Rapids: Wm. B. Eerdmans Publishing Co., 1986).

On prophecy and its transformation see Joseph Blenkinsopp, *Prophecy and Canon* (Notre Dame: University of Notre Dame Press, 1977), and *A History of Prophecy in Israel from the Settlement in the Land to the Hellenistic Period* (Philadelphia: Westminster Press, 1983), and David E. Aune, *Prophecy in Early Christianity and the Ancient Mediterranean World* (Grand Rapids: Wm. B. Eerdmans Publishing Co., 1983).

On apocalyptic literature see the works listed for chapter 3.

For surveys of the literature of the latter part of the second temple period, see George Nickelsburg, *Jewish Literature Between the Bible and the Mishnah* (Philadelphia: Fortress Press, 1981); Michael Stone, ed., *Compendia*

Rerum Iudaicarum ad Novum Testamentum, section II, vol. 2: *Jewish Writings of the Second Temple Period* (Philadelphia: Fortress Press, 1984); and J. J. Collins, *Between Athens and Jerusalem* (listed in the bibliography for chapter 2).

On biblical interpretation see James Kugel and Rowan Greer, *Early Biblical Interpretation*, in this series (Philadelphia: Westminster Press, 1986), and Michael Fishbane, *Biblical Interpretation in Ancient Israel* (Oxford: Clarendon Press, 1985).

Chapter 7: The Emergence of Rabbinic Judaism

On the political history of the rabbinic period, see Michael Avi-Yonah, *The Jews of Palestine: A Political History from the Bar Kokhba War to the Arab Conquest* (Oxford: Basil Blackwell, 1976), and G. Alon, *The Jews in Their Land in the Talmudic Age* (2 vols.; Jerusalem: Magnes Press, 1980–84). On the rabbis' cooperation with the Romans, see David Daube, *Collaboration with Tyranny in Rabbinic Law* (London: Oxford University Press, 1965).

On rabbinic "Hellenism" see the two classic but difficult volumes of Saul Lieberman, *Greek in Jewish Palestine* (New York: Jewish Theological Seminary of America, 1942; repr. New York: Feldheim, 1965), and *Hellenism in Jewish Palestine* (New York: Jewish Theological Seminary, 1962). More accessible is his article "How Much Greek in Jewish Palestine?" reprinted in the useful anthology of Henry Fischel, *Essays in Greco-Roman and Related Talmudic Literature* (New York: Ktav Publishing House, 1977), pp. 325–343. For a philosophical and nonhistorical study of the Noahide laws, see David Novak, *The Image of the Non-Jew in Judaism* (Lewiston, N.Y.: Edwin Mellen Press, 1983).

On rabbinic Judaism see the readings suggested for chapter 3. For an anthology of rabbinic statements about various theological topics, see Claude G Montefiore and Herbert Loewe, eds., *A Rabbinic Anthology* (London: Macmillan & Co., 1938; frequently reprinted). On rabbinic mysticism and mystical literature, see David Halperin, *The Merkabah in Rabbinic Literature* (New Haven: American Oriental Society, 1980).

On the patriarch see Lee Levine, "The Jewish Patriarch (Nasi) in Third Century Palestine," in *Aufstieg und Niedergang der römischen Welt*, part II, vol. 19.2, ed. by Wolfgang Haase and Hildegard Temporini (Berlin and New York: Walter de Gruyter, 1979), pp. 649–688; Marvin Goodman, *State and Society in Roman Galilee, A.D. 132–212* (Totowa, N.J.: Rowman & Allanheld, 1983); and Shaye J. D. Cohen, "Pagan and Christian Evidence on the Ancient Synagogue," in *The Synagogue in Late Antiquity*, ed. by Lee Levine (Durham: American Schools of Oriental Research, forthcoming).

The pioneering and still classic presentation of the archaeological evidence is Erwin R. Goodenough, *Jewish Symbols in the Greco-Roman Period* (13 vols.; Princeton: Princeton University Press for the Bollingen Foundation, 1953–1968). The best place to begin is Morton Smith, "Goodenough's *Jewish Symbols* in Retrospect," *Journal of Biblical Literature* 86 (1967), 53–68.

On Yavneh see Shaye J. D. Cohen, "The Significance of Yavneh: Pharisees, Rabbis, and the End of Jewish Sectarianism," *Hebrew Union College Annual* 55 (1984), 27–53. John Bowker denies any connection between the rabbis and the Pharisees; see his *Jesus and the Pharisees* (Cambridge: University Press, 1973). On "the benediction against heretics," see Reuven Kimelman, *"Birkat Ha-Minim* and the Lack of Evidence for an Anti-Christian Jewish Prayer in Late Antiquity," *Jewish and Christian Self-Definition,* vol. 2: *Aspects of Judaism in the Graeco-Roman Period,* ed. by E. P. Sanders et al. (Philadelphia: Fortress Press, 1981), pp. 226–244; Asher Finkel, "Yavneh's Liturgy and Early Christianity," *Journal of Ecumenical Studies* 18 (1981), 231–250; and W. Horbury, "The Benediction of the *Minim* and Early Jewish-Christian Controversy," *Journal of Theological Studies* 33 (1982), 19–61.

On the interpretation of the Mishnah, see Jacob Neusner, *The Modern Study of the Mishnah* (Leiden: E. J. Brill, 1973). Neusner argues that each document within the rabbinic canon must be interpreted as an independent work, and that the Mishnah is a philosophical response to the destruction of the temple; see his *Judaism: The Evidence of the Mishnah* (Chicago: University of Chicago Press, 1981). On the interpretation of the Mishnah by the Talmudim, see Jacob Neusner, *Midrash in Context* (Philadelphia: Fortress Press, 1983).

Glossary
of Technical Terms

amoraim: Literally "speakers," the rabbis of the third to fifth centuries C.E. in Israel and Babylonia who composed the two Talmudim.

Apocrypha: Literally "things hidden away," Apocryphal books are books of uncertain or disputed canonicity; they are to be "hidden away," that is, not read in public. The Apocrypha is the collection of Jewish books that are included in the Greek or Latin Old Testament of the church but not in the Hebrew Tanak of the Jews.

apocalypse: Literally "revelation," a work that reveals, usually through the intermediation of an angel, some secret of nature or history. Most apocalypses of the second temple period treat eschatological themes, and probably were written in the expectation that the end time was imminent.

Aristeas, Letter of: A pseudepigraphic treatise or epistle, attributed to a gentile courtier of Ptolemy Philadelphus, but written by a Jew probably in the last part of the second century B.C.E. Its story is the translation of the Hebrew Bible into Greek, but its theme is the easy coexistence of Judaism with Hellenism.

Ben Sira: A teacher in Jerusalem who, in about 200 B.C.E., wrote a wisdom book now contained in the Apocrypha. (The book is sometimes called Sirach or Ecclesiasticus.)

bet midrash: Literally "house of study," a school or academy.

Chapters of the Fathers: A tractate of the Mishnah which, because of its exclusive focus on ethical and moral exhortations and its complete neglect of legal matters, is unlike any other tractate. Its opening two chapters are a chain of tradition depicting the transmission of the Torah from God to Moses, and from Moses ultimately to the rabbis of the Mishnah.

cult: System of worship.

diaspora: The "scattering" of the Jews throughout the world outside the land of Israel.

Enoch, book of: A collection of pseudepigraphic works attributed to the antediluvian figure of Genesis 5. The earliest of these works is the product of the third century B.C.E.

eschatology: Doctrine of the end (or end times). Eschatology includes the notions of life after death, resurrection, the final judgment, national restoration, messianic deliverance, etc.

Fourth Ezra: Also called Second Esdras, an apocalypse now in the Apocrypha written shortly after the destruction of the temple in 70 C.E.

haburah: Literally "fellowship" or "association," a group of pietists whose regulations are detailed in rabbinic literature. The members of the group punctiliously observed the laws of purity and tithes, and may have had a connection with the Pharisees.

Hellenistic period: The period from 334 B.C.E., the conquest of Persia by Alexander the Great, to the rise of the Maccabees in the 160s B.C.E.

Josephus: A Jewish historian of the first century C.E., whose works are our major sources for the history of the latter part of the second temple period. The *Jewish War,* completed in the early 80s C.E., treats Jewish history from the rise of the Maccabees to the fall of Masada in 73/4 C.E. The *Jewish Antiquities* was completed in 93/4 C.E.; its first part paraphrases the Bible, its second surveys the second temple period from Hellenistic times to the eve of the revolt of 66 C.E. The *Against Apion,* completed around 100 C.E., is an apology for Judaism and an attack on anti-Judaism.

Maccabees: The dynasty founded by Mattathias the Hasmonean and his son Judah the Maccabee, which ruled the Jews from the 160s B.C.E. to 63 B.C.E., when the Romans entered Jerusalem.

Mishnah: Literally "repetition," a book of legal statements on various topics produced by the rabbis of the second century C.E. and edited by Judah the Patriarch. The book is arranged in six divisions; each division contains tractates. Any individual paragraph of the Mishnah is also called Mishnah.

Palestine: Literally, "the land of the Philistines," the name given by the Romans to the land of Judea after the defeat of Bar Kokhba in 135 C.E. In this book, "Palestine" and "the land of Israel" are synonymous.

Persian period: From 539 B.C.E., the conquest of Babylonia by Cyrus the Great, king of Persia, until 334 B.C.E., the conquest of Persia by Alexander the Great.

Philo: An Alexandrian Jew of the first half of the first century C.E., best known for his numerous and lengthy commentaries and essays on the Torah, especially Genesis.

politeuma: An autonomous ethnic community within a Greek city.

purity or ritual purity: The avoidance of sources of pollution: corpses, impure animals, sexual discharges, etc. The regulations are contained primarily in Leviticus, but are greatly elaborated in many of the works from Qumran and in rabbinic literature.

Pentateuch: See Torah.

Pseudepigrapha: Works that bear "false ascriptions," i.e., works that claim to have been written by someone other than their true author. Modern scholars speak of "the Pseudepigrapha" as if there were a single corpus of such works, but such a corpus did not exist until modern scholars created it. Many works included by modern scholars in "the Pseudepigrapha" are not pseudepigraphic.

Ptolemies: The Macedonian (or Greek) rulers of Egypt, from the end of the fourth century B.C.E. to the end of the first century B.C.E.

Qedushah: The prayer that features the recitation of the *Sanctus* ("Holy, holy, holy, is the Lord of Hosts," from Isaiah 6:3).

rabbi: A title of respect (literally "my master"), originally used only in the second person but later used in the third person as well. The noun "rabbi" and the adjective "rabbinic" are usually used as technical terms for the persons and culture of the society that produced the Mishnah and related works.

Roman period: From 63 B.C.E., the entrance of the Romans into Jerusalem, until the early seventh century, when the East was conquered by the Persians and, later, the Arabs. (Most scholars use the term "Byzantine" to refer to the Roman empire after the fourth century.)

sect: A small organized group which separates itself from a larger religious body and asserts that it alone embodies the ideals of the larger group because it alone understands God's will.

Seleucids: The Macedonian (or Greek) rulers of Syria and Asia, from the end of the fourth century B.C.E. to the early first century B.C.E.

Shema: The paragraph beginning "Hear, O Israel" from Deuteronomy 6:4–9. According to the Mishnah this paragraph is combined with Deuteronomy 11:13–21 and Numbers 15:37–41 to form a single prayer.

statutory prayer: A prayer that is recited to fulfill an obligation to pray. The prayer is not occasioned by any special need or event, but is seen as a religious obligation in itself.

Talmud (plur. Talmudim): Literally "study," the commentary on the Mishnah, which because of its size and discursive character, is not really a commentary but an independent work. The rabbis of Israel in the third to fourth centuries C.E. produced the Palestinian Talmud, or Jerusalem Talmud, while the rabbis of Babylonia in the third to sixth centuries produced the Babylonian Talmud. Sometimes the word is used to designate rabbinic literature as a whole (which includes more than just the Mishnah and the Talmudim).

Tanak: An acronym for Torah, Nebiim (Prophets), and Ketubim (Writings). The Hebrew Bible or Old Testament.

tannaim: Literally "teachers" (or "repeaters"), the rabbis of Palestine in the second century C.E. whose statements are contained primarily in the Mishnah but also in other rabbinic works.

Targum (plur. Targumim): A translation of scripture into Aramaic.

theodicy: Literally "divine justice," the doctrines that seek to explain why a good and powerful God allows evil to exist in the world.

Torah: Literally "instruction," the first five books of the Bible. In second temple times, Greek-speaking Jews referred to it as "the Law." The church fathers coined the name Pentateuch, literally "the five rolls." In rabbinic texts Torah is often a synonym for Judaism.

Yavneh (or Jamnia): The town west-northwest of Jerusalem where the rabbis first gathered after the destruction of the temple.

Index